INTELLIGENCE

INTELLIGENCE

Measurement, Theory, and Public Policy

*Proceedings of a Symposium
in Honor of
Lloyd G. Humphreys*

Edited by
ROBERT L. LINN

UNIVERSITY OF ILLINOIS PRESS
Urbana and Chicago

© 1989 by the Board of Trustees of the University of Illinois
Manufactured in the United States of America
C 5 4 3 2 1

This book is printed on acid-free paper.

Library of Congress Cataloging-in-Publication Data

Intelligence: measurement, theory, and public policy: proceedings of
 a symposium in honor of Lloyd G. Humphreys/edited by Robert L.
 Linn.
     p. cm.
     Held at the University of Illinois at Urbana-Champaign, Apr.
 30-May 2, 1985 and sponsored by the Dept. of Psychology . . . [et
 al.].
     Bibliography: p.
     "Publications of Lloyd G. Humphreys"—P.
     Contents: Introduction/Robert L. Linn—The early years of
 intelligence measurement/Ernest R. Hilgard—Models of
 intelligence/John Horn—Intelligence, wisdom, and creativity/
 Robert J. Sternberg—Protecting general intelligence/Sandra
 Scarr—Construct validation after thirty years/Lee J. Cronbach—
 Intelligence and law/Barbara Lerner—Intelligence: three
 kinds of instability and their consequences for policy/Lloyd G.
 Humphreys.
     ISBN 0-252-01535-5 (alk. paper)
     1. Intellect—Congresses.   2. Intelligence tests—Congresses.
 3. Intellect—Government policy—Congresses.   4. Humphreys, Lloyd G.
 I. Humphreys, Lloyd G.   II. Linn, Robert L.   III. University of
 Illinois at Urbana-Champaign. Dept. of Psychology.
 BF431.I54 1989
 153.9—dc19   87-35989
                                                            CIP

Contents

Preface

The chapters in this book are based on the papers that were presented at a symposium held at the University of Illinois at Urbana-Champaign on April 30 through May 2, 1985, in honor of Professor Lloyd G. Humphreys on the occasion of his retirement from the Departments of Psychology and of Educational Psychology. Although Professor Humphreys's doctoral studies and early publications focused on human conditioning, and his work on partial reinforcement first published in 1939 is still considered a classic, he is best known for his contributions to the study of human abilities and individual differences. This work began during World War II with the Army Air Force's Aviation Psychology Program and has continued for more than 40 years.

Humphreys's long-standing interest in the measurement and theory of intelligence and their implications for public policy provided a natural focus for the symposium in his honor. The three themes of the symposium—the measurement of intelligence, the theory of intelligence, and intelligence and public policy—represent his fundamental and continuing contributions to the science of psychology and to society.

The symposium was made possible by the efforts and support of many individuals and groups. Financial support for the symposium was provided by the Department of Psychology, the Department of Educational Psychology, the College of Liberal Arts and Sciences, the College of Education, the Graduate College, the Center for Advanced Studies, the Miller Committee, the Division of Conferences and Institutes in the Office of Continuing Education and Public Services, the Office of the Vice-Chancellor for Academic Affairs, and the Office of the Chancellor of the University of Illinois at Urbana-Champaign. The enthusiastic support that was provided by such a broad array of groups attests not only to the importance of Professor Humphreys's scientific contributions but to those that he has made to the University of Illinois during his 28-year tenure.

Many individuals deserve thanks for their efforts to make the symposium a success. Emanuel Donchin provided leadership and initial support for the idea. Larry Jones chaired a committee that originally proposed the idea for the symposium. The detailed plan and its implementation were the responsibility of the program committee that was ably chaired by Patrick Laughlin. Other members of the program committee were Delwyn Harnisch, Robert Linn, Alfreda Mitchell, and Harry Triandis. Arrangements were handled by Anne Colgan and Kris Eaton of the Division of Conferences and Institutes and Janet Taylor of the Krannert Center for the Performing Arts. Finally, thanks are due to the speakers whose papers are contained in this volume and, most of all, to the person in whose honor it is dedicated, Lloyd G. Humphreys.

ROBERT L. LINN

Introduction

Intelligence is both a scientific and a folk concept. This fact is often the source of confusion and can disrupt communication. Popular definitions of intelligence refer to the *capacity* of an individual and carry the surplus meaning that intelligence is an inherited, unchangeable characteristic. Lerner refers in her chapter to the two popular ideas that intelligence is "fixed at birth" and is passed on in "mirror-image" fashion from one generation to the next as part of the "straw-bogy" definition of intelligence. These ideas lead to the expectation that a test of "real intelligence" should measure this unalterable capacity and to the rejection of all tests because none of them lives up to this expectation.

It is, of course, unfair to blame the public for the confusion about the meaning of intelligence and what can and cannot be measured by intelligence tests. Psychologists have contributed to the confusion by their hereditarian emphasis and overinterpretation of data showing differences in average scores for racial and ethnic groups (e.g., Brigham, 1923; Jensen, 1969). The recurring nature-nurture controversy (see Hilgard, this volume) has centered on intelligence. For someone who conceives of intelligence as a fixed capacity, it is natural to consider a test to be unfair if it is affected by differences in environmental opportunities.

As Humphreys has shown on several occasions (1971, 1979, this volume), however, *real* intelligence in the sense used above is a will-of-the-wisp. It is neither genotype nor phenotype, but an imaginary entity. On this much there is a broad consensus among psychologists. However, the consensus begins to break down when we attempt to move beyond this to define intelligence, to identify acceptable measures of intelligence, and to consider the questions of intelligence and public policy. Nonetheless, there is, as Carroll and Horn (1981) have noted,

1

more "agreement than disagreement about the fundamentals of ability measurement" (p. 1013). This agreement provides the basis for productive scientific debate leading to the improved understanding and measurement of human abilities. The chapters in this volume should contribute to that improvement.

To understand the current issues in the theory and measurement of intelligence, it is helpful to have some historical context. In his chapter "The Early Years of Intelligence Measurement," *Ernest R. Hilgard* traces the history of intelligence measurement from the mid-nineteenth century to the mid-twentieth century. The evolving scientific notions of intelligence are clearly depicted in his dispassionate analysis. So, too, are the seeds of controversy about the appropriate interpretations, uses, and public policy implications of this emerging science and technology.

Contrasting views about the scientific value of a concept of general intelligence are provided in the chapters by *John Horn* and *Sandra Scarr.* Horn, in his chapter "Models of Intelligence," describes three different approaches: A compound model, most closely associated with the work of Spearman and more recently with the writings of Jensen (e.g., 1984); an essence model, in which one basic process, efficient neural transmission, is thought to underlie all intellectual abilities (e.g., Eysenck, 1982); and a mixture model, which is most clearly articulated by Humphreys (1962, 1979, this volume). Although Horn sees the latter model as the most consistent with the current practice in measuring intelligence, he finds all three models wanting for purposes of guiding future research and advancing the science of human abilities. He proposes, instead, a differentiated model with several distinct intelligences and presents evidence showing that these distinct intelligences have different developmental patterns and different implications for the understanding of human abilities.

As is evident from the title of her chapter, "Protecting General Intelligence: Constructs and Consequences of Interventions," *Sandra Scarr* finds the concept of general intelligence that combines a variety of human abilities to have considerable utility. She focuses on the practical importance of the generalized concept of intelligence and on possible interventions affecting its development. Although it is clear that it is easier to change a more limited ability domain, it is more important to change general ability. Her results suggest that those wishing to intervene to improve intelligence have too often focused on approaches that have little chance of having a major impact because they emphasize between-family environmental variation, whereas the primary variation occurs within families. She also sketches a theory predicting ways in which genotype can affect environmental experiences and the implications of this theory for intervention.

Robert J. Sternberg, in "Intelligence, Wisdom, and Creativity: Their Natures and Interrelationships," reviews the substantial progress that has been made in our efforts to understand intelligence. He identifies three broad approaches that have influenced the current understanding of intelligence: (a) the psychometric approach, which has relied on factor analytic methods, (b) information-processing approaches that have sought to understand intelligence through correlations with lower level cognitive processes and by top-down analyses of the cognitive components involved in solving test items, and (c) diversified-ability approaches, typified by Gardner's (1983) theory of multiple intelligences and his own recent work (Sternberg, 1985) on a triarchic theory of intelligence. He suggests that conceptions of intelligence need to be broadened beyond the relatively limited range of abilities that are currently assessed by conventional intelligence tests. He also suggests that there are two other important aspects of mental functioning—wisdom and creativity—that can be distinguished from intelligence and that deserve greater attention in both measurement and theory.

It has long been recognized that the central issue in the measurement of intelligence, wisdom, creativity, or any other human ability is validity. The conception of test validation was fundamentally altered some 30 years ago by the publication of the "Technical Recommendations for Psychological Tests and Diagnostic Techniques" (American Psychological Association, 1954) and Cronbach and Meehl's (1955) landmark paper on construct validity. The chapter by *Lee J. Cronbach,* "Construct Validation After Thirty Years," provides a review of the development of this idea and an analysis of its evolution and application. In bringing his ideas about construct validation up-to-date, Cronbach notes that although progress is evident, the "construct validity" sections of most test manuals fail to give sufficient attention to serious alternative interpretations or to the integrative logical arguments that are fundamental to construct validation. Using program evaluation as a model, he suggests that there is a potentially important role to be served by independent evaluators of tests, who, unlike the traditional test reviewer, would conduct research designed to evaluate key rival hypotheses about the interpretation of the tests.

The final two chapters move from issues of theory and measurement into the realm of public policy. In "Intelligence and Law," *Barbara Lerner* contrasts Humphreys's broad definition of intelligence with the counterfactual interpretations that intelligence is unalterable and the basis for locking future generations into inherited castes. She argues that social scientists have contributed to these erroneous interpretations of intelligence and that these and other false doctrines have had an undesirable impact on judicial decisions and on the educational progress of black students, the intended beneficiaries of the decisions. She concludes by suggesting that a return to more stringent academic and disciplinary standards for all students would provide a surer road to accomplishing the goals that social scientists, educators, and federal judges have sought by other means for the last 30 years.

In the concluding chapter, "Intelligence: Three Kinds of Instability and Their Consequences for Policy," *Lloyd G. Humphreys* elaborates on his earlier (1971) definition of intelligence as "the acquired repertoire of intellectual (or cognitive) skills available to the person at a particular point in time." So defined, intelligence is a phenotypic trait and no assumptions are required about the relative effects of genetic or environmental influences. Using this definition, he presents data showing that intelligence is relatively unstable (a) for a given individual over an interval of several years, particularly for young children, (b) from parent to child, and (c) for whole populations. While recognizing that social policy is, and sometimes should be, influenced more by values than by scientific evidence, he emphasizes the importance of using solid evidence to inform policy decisions.

The seven chapters that follow bring to bear a variety of perspectives on intelligence. Differences in perspective are seen in the various models of intelligence that are discussed by Horn, Humphreys, Scarr, and Sternberg. Distinctions among intelligence, wisdom, and creativity are presented, and their interrelationships are explored.Influences of genetics and environmental factors on intelligence are not merely described, but are evaluated in terms of their implications for enhancing intelligence through interventions and social policies.

As is clear in the three chapters by Scarr, Lerner, and Humphreys that delve into the policy implications of the scientific evidence relating to intelligence, wishful thinking and reliance on what Humphreys refers to as "mythical or completely inadequate data" lead to the acceptance of seemingly desirable and popular approaches to problems, but not to solutions. The implications based on the hardheaded analyses of evidence provided by these three authors may lack popularity, but they provide a much better basis for informing policy decisions.

REFERENCES

American Psychological Association. (1954). *Technical recommendations for psychological tests and diagnostic techniques.* Washington, DC: Author.

Brigham, C. C. (1923). *A study of American intelligence.* Princeton, NJ: Princeton University Press.

Carroll, J. B., & Horn, J. L. (1981). On the scientific basis of ability testing. *American Psychologist, 36,* 1012–1020.

Cronbach, L. J., & Meehl, P. E. (1955). Construct validity in psychological tests. *Psychological Bulletin, 52,* 281–302.

Eysenck, H. J. (Ed.). (1982). *A model for intelligence.* New York: Springer-Verlag.

Gardner, M. (1983). *Frames of mind: The theory of multiple intelligences.* New York: Basic Books.

Humphreys, L. G. (1962). The organization of human abilities. *American Psychologist, 17,* 475–483.

Humphreys, L. G. (1971). Theory of intelligence. In R. Cancro (Ed.), *Intelligence: Genetic and environmental influences* (pp. 31–42). New York: Grune & Stratton.

Humphreys, L. G. (1979). The construct of general intelligence. *Intelligence, 3,* 105–120.

Jensen, A. R. (1969). How much can we boost IQ and scholastic achievement? *Harvard Educational Review, 39,* 1–23.

Jensen, A. R. (1984). Test validity: g versus the specificity doctrine. *Journal of Social and Biological Sciences, 7,* 93–118.

Sternberg, R. J. (1985). *Beyond IQ: A triarchic theory of human intelligence.* New York: Cambridge University Press.

1

The Early Years
of Intelligence Measurement

ERNEST R. HILGARD

Preamble: The Early Career of Lloyd G. Humphreys

Because this volume honors Lloyd Humphreys on the occasion of his retirement, before entering upon my discussion of the early years of intelligence measurement I wish to reminisce about the beginning of my acquaintance with Lloyd in 1936 during the early stage of his career. When I came to know him, he and his wife to-be, Dorothy Jane Windes, were both students at Stanford enrolled in psychology, and they met for the first time in a class I taught. They were married the following year, before he had earned his doctorate.

Lloyd soon became involved with me preparatory to doing his dissertation on various aspects of conditioned responses, particularly the conditioning of the human eyeblink response. Lloyd was overheard telling another student that he was not particularly interested in conditioning, but it was congenial to gain this added experience in experimental psychology, and he was willing to work under my supervision as a couple of his friends had done before him. He completed his dissertation, published a half-dozen articles on his own, and two others on which we collaborated. In 1938–1939 he spent a postdoctoral year with Clark Hull at Yale and that was essentially the end of his career as a conditioned response psychologist; he returned to the study of individual differences and the use of factor analysis that he had already learned at Indiana University.

He had, however, made a lasting contribution to our knowledge of conditioned responses by his work on what was called the partial

Much of the material presented here is reproduced from a chapter in my book in preparation at the time of the symposium on the history of twentieth-century psychology in America, now published as Hilgard (1987).

reinforcement effect, or sometimes simply "Humphreys' effect" or "Humphreys' paradox" (Kimble, 1961, p. 287). He showed that if a conditioned response was reinforced on only a fraction of the trials during acquisition, the response was more resistant to subsequent extinction. This finding appeared to threaten two beliefs associated with conditioning: the uniform operation of the law of effect, and the inhibitory explanation of extinction. His own explanation was in terms of expectancy, foreshadowing later developments in cognitive psychology (Humphreys, 1939a, 1939b).

Of course he did not spend all of his time in the laboratory, but improved his statistical skills, building upon his earlier work in factor analysis, in preparation for his later work in measurement, begun particularly with the U.S. Army Air Force where he reached the rank of captain during World War II. After other academic posts, it was a pleasure to have Lloyd and Dorothy back at Stanford during the years 1948 to 1951, when he succeeded me in the teaching of educational psychology to graduate education students. I felt that I wanted to take this opportunity to express the satisfaction that every professor feels in a student who turns out so well.

Now to turn to my topic.

The Early Years of Intelligence Measurement

It is always possible to find some anticipations of modern events in the writings of the Greeks, but I have chosen to begin arbitrarily with the mid-nineteenth century, and to stop with another arbitrary choice in the mid-twentieth century.

Before the "new" nineteenth-century psychologists expressed much interest in individual differences, the German anatomist Franz Joseph Gall (1758–1828) did much to call attention to physical differences as correlates of differences in the psychological faculties assumed to compose the mind. Gall's phrenology became a practical matter in America during the nineteenth century in the hands of the Fowler family over several generations. They promoted the use of cranial measurements in predicting vocational fitness, thus stirring up some interest in what would later become modern aptitude testing. All this, however, went on largely outside the academic community (Davies, 1955).

The Mid-Nineteenth Century

By the mid-nineteenth century, Alexander Bain (1818–1903), the British psychologist and writer of widely used textbooks, a man who greatly influenced William James, was clearly mindful of individual differences in the ability to learn. He discussed the problem 35 years before James's *Principles* (Bain, 1855). Without any measurements, he had noted that the differences might be in single abilities, such as mechanical skills, art, or language. In that case, they would be referred to special or local endowments. However, some individuals seemed to be superior in all aspects of learning, a form he regarded as due to a general power of retentiveness. This is one of the first recognitions by a psychologist of a general intellectual ability, accompanied by special abilities. Bain, however, did no experimental work.

Only a year later, in 1856, Edouard Seguin (1812–1880), a French physician who later moved to America, invented his form board, later incorporated into performance scales. He sought to improve the training of mentally deficient children so that they might become better able to live more satisfying lives (Seguin, 1856).

Darwinian thinking soon became pervasive in both England and America. In the hierarchy that was established between lower animals and man, intellectual differences took first place. Although lower animals were more skilled than human beings at many activities for which they were specially adapted, man was seen as superior in thinking and reasoning. The theory of evolution called attention to differences within a species so that in the evolutionary process the more competent would survive. If the human species was to maintain its status, many felt that uncontrolled breeding must not be allowed to lower competence; instead, the principles of eugenics began to be espoused. Here the problems of heredity versus environment that were to haunt the study of individual differences were raised, with competence as represented by intelligence often the primary focus. The one who brought the problems to the fore and initiated methods to deal with them was the Englishman Sir Francis Galton (1822–1911), a cousin of Charles Darwin.

Galton and Individual Differences

Galton's major books were *Hereditary Genius* (1869/1952) and *Inquiries Into Human Faculty* (1883). The dates show that the new lines that he was opening up were coming at about the same time as Wundt's new laboratory was getting underway in Leipzig. We shall see how both trends were to come together through James McKeen Cattell (1860–1944), the brash young American who studied with Wundt but was perhaps more influenced by Galton.

In his studies of hereditary genius, Galton revealed that eminence followed a few family lines in particular (including the family to which he belonged), hence he stressed the importance of biological heredity.

Later critics found these views of hereditary influence extreme and uncritical, for so many of these distinguished people had wealth, leisure, excellent educations, and the stimulation and examples of their forebears to set their goals. With the early evolutionist Erasmus Darwin as his grandfather, why should not Charles Darwin be motivated to pursue the study of natural science? Was not Galton himself encouraged to do the work he did because of Charles Darwin and his own sense that he, too, was destined for distinction?

Galton was too wise to be entirely one-sided in his interpretations, and it was he who assigned to the heredity-environment problem the useful cliché of *nature versus nurture*. Still, his emphasis on the hereditary basis of genius had an elitist flavor about it that was continued in later intelligence testing by others.

In his continuing studies of human differences, Galton turned to physical and psychological measurements in a laboratory that he established in the South Kensington Museum in London in 1884. Although he called his tests anthropometric (a term now usually restricted to physical measurements, such as cranial size), the tests included psychological functions such as keenness of vision and hearing, dynometric pressure, and reaction time. Galton invented instruments of measurement, and he appears to have been the first to use correlation to represent the degree of agreement between pairs of measurements on the same individual. He presented correlation graphically as early as 1877, but relied on his student, Karl Pearson (1857–1936), to develop the mathematical method of correlation in 1884, still known as the Pearson product-moment correlation and designated by the coefficient r. It is to Galton's credit that he measured carefully what he set out to measure, although the interpretations of what he found were biased by some of the stereotypes characteristic of the culture in which he was immersed. As Pearson, his most distinguished associate and immediate successor lamented, about all that people came to know about Galton as a psychologist was that he initiated the use of correlation. There were those who knew better. Cattell, after his studies with Wundt, spent 2 years with Galton and was willing to say that Galton was the greatest man he had ever met (Cattell, 1929). Joseph Jastrow (1864–1955), who along with Cattell had earlier studied with G. Stanley Hall at Johns Hopkins University and who went on to a distinguished career at the University of Wisconsin, had corresponded with Galton as early as 1887 and had early published a proposal for testing college students reflecting Galton's influence (Jastrow, 1892). Further, he arranged an exhibit at the Chicago World's Fair in 1893 in which much of Galton's equipment was not only on exhibit but also in use. For a small fee visitors could be "tested" and receive a card with a record of their scores, similar to Galton's earlier practice. Cattell's personal score card as tested in Galton's laboratory has been recently republished (Sokal, 1981, p. 328).

When Galton turned to the study of individual differences, he developed a number of methods, some already used by others, some original with him, such as test batteries (i.e., a series of special tests designed to be given together), the method of word association, and the twin-method in inheritance studies. In statistics, in addition to the concept of regression and correlation, he familiarized psychologists with the normal curve and centile ranks. At the practical level, he invented a simple card sorter that anticipated later developments of mechanical and electronic devices for retrieving stored information (Diamond, 1980).

Early Developments of Mental Testing

The initial tests of individuality, such as those of Galton, tended to rely on quite specific functions. These methods were picked up in America by Cattell, after he returned from his studies with Wundt and Galton, and Cattell is credited with the first use of the term "mental tests" (Cattell, 1890). We now begin to see an issue in test construction: whether to favor simple or complex processes.

Cattell, with Livingston Farrand, later president of Cornell University, published a study of the results of individual tests with 100 freshman students at Columbia University (Cattell & Farrand, 1896). The tests were largely of the types used by Galton: strength, reaction time, sensory discrimination.

The technical issue arose immediately that was to influence the later development of intelligence tests, with an outcome that affected their controversial nature. Hugo Münsterberg (1863–1916), who had taken his PhD with Wundt in 1885, had published at the University of Freiburg before migrating to Harvard University a paper on individual psychology describing some of the tests that he had given to school children (Münsterberg, 1891). All the functions he tested were broadly psychological, as distinct from sensory ones, for example, various aspects of reading, writing, and naming. As an illustration, one test required the writing of the color names of objects in the absence of the perceived object, such as writing "white" when the word "snow" appeared. He included memory for digits and letters after a single presentation, a test introduced by Jacobs (1887) and still used today. Binet and Henri began testing children in France with early forms of what was to evolve as the Binet-Simon intelligence test (Binet & Henri, 1894).

The tests of Münsterberg and of Binet and Henri contrasted with those of Cattell and Farrand, and arguments about the differences soon occurred. Cattell and Farrand, as noted, had used very simple tests, many of them sensory in nature: keenness of eyesight and hearing, perception of pitch and of weights, afterimages, reaction time. They preferred the *definiteness* of what they were measuring against the *vagueness* of the functions that Münsterberg and Binet and Henri were measuring. Of course, the tests selected by Cattell and Farrand might conceivably have turned out as good predictors of mental competence, but there had to be better evidence. In a second report from Columbia University, Clark Wissler (1901), later to become a distinguished anthropologist, who was a professor in Yale's Institute of Psychology in my graduate student days, tested 250 freshmen and 35 senior girls at Barnard College, and used Pearson's correlational method to relate their test performances to their academic grades. The correlations were disappointing, varying between −.28 and .39, although the grades in one college course correlated substantially with the grades in another college course. Wissler concluded that the tests must be measuring only special abilities because there was no evidence of any important functional relations between the activities employed.

In Germany, Hermann Ebbinghaus (1850–1909), who had invented the sentence-completion type of test item, came out on Binet's side as a result of his own experience, favoring the testing of more complex functions (Ebbinghaus, 1897). Despite Titchener's scant expressed interest in tests, one of his students, Stella E. Sharp (1899), studied the question of whether simpler or more complex functions should be tested. She was led to conclude, with Titchener's concurrence, that the more complex tests were more suitable. The controversy ended with victory on the side of vagueness or complexity as against the simpler functions. This conclusion set the tone for a high reliance on empiricism, rather than precise theory, in the development of intelligence tests, and the favoring of psychological content over more physical measurements (Baldwin, Cattell, & Jastrow, 1898).

There was more early interest in testing than was evident in the standard psychology textbooks of the period. The American Psychological Association in 1897, at the first of its annual meetings to have simultaneous sessions, devoted one of the two sessions to physical and mental tests. Hence, there came to be a respectable early interest in individual differences among the recognized experimental psychologists in America, as well as those in England, France, and Germany.

Spearman: The Beginning of Factor Analysis

A British psychologist and logician, Charles E. Spearman (1863–1945), a successor to Galton and Pearson, became interested in the theory and practice of intelligence testing before the first report on the Binet-Simon tests appeared (Spearman, 1904). Binet knew of Spearman's work and criticized it for its empirical inadequacies (Binet, 1905). However, Spearman's interpretation of intelligence as including a general factor (g) and special factors (s) influenced later developments. It is of interest how similar in some respects Spearman's conceptions turned out to be to Bain's impressionistic interpretation. Because of the paucity of Spearman's empirical work, and the practical orientation of those who were developing tests, Binet's work was far more influential until factor analysis came into its own in the 1930s.

The Binet-Simon Test in France

The test to have a lasting influence upon the individual appraisal of intelligence was announced in France by Alfred Binet (1857–1911) and Théodore Simon (1873–1961) in three published articles in L'Année Psychologique in the year after Spearman's initial published account, beginning with Binet and Simon (1905). Prior to the Binet-Simon test, both men had substantial experience in the measurement of individual differences, anthropometric as well as intellectual. Much of Binet's work had been done collaboratively, as noted, with Victor Henri (1872–1940), so that the Binet-Simon test, while highly original, was not the result of a sudden inspiration.

It should be recalled that, beginning with Binet, and continued in the later translations and revisions of tests of the Binet-Simon type, the testing was designed to be done with one person at a time by someone trained in the administration and interpretation of tests. A set of materials was provided, appropriate to the age of the child, including pictures about which questions were to be answered, familiar objects named or counted, form boards assembled. Many of the materials used in the test were familiar, and the effort in constructing the tests was to find problems that were not peculiar to the test situation, but that would be met by the child in the normal course of living. Hence the assumption was made that what has been learned from the common culture may indeed reflect the child's intellectual level. For example, vocabulary, involved in naming, sentence construction, and defining words, has obviously been learned, yet the level of vocabulary acquired by a child exposed to a normal environment became one of the most useful tests of intelligence.

In a later version, Binet and Simon (1908) introduced the concept of mental age. This was based on the readily understood principle that children's mental processes and store of knowledge become more complex with age, and a given child could respond on the test with answers similar to those of either a younger or an older child. Mental age as an index of retardation met the original purpose for which the test was constructed. The empirical assumption underlying the mental age scale was merely that average intelligence scores increased year by year, and the reference to age norms was readily comprehended by parents and teachers. It was the 1908 version that led eventually to the major American translations and adaptations of the Binet-Simon test. The scale was revised again in France in 1911, the year of Binet's death.

The American Versions of the Binet Scales

The tests were translated and given trials in many nations, but the history of use in the United States is our immediate concern. Versions of the Binet-Simon scale were soon published in America, the first by Henry H. Goddard (1866–1957), in a translation of the first Binet scale (Goddard, 1908). Goddard was another of the prominent early psychologists to be trained with Stanley Hall at Clark University, to which Hall had gone after Hopkins, where Goddard earned his PhD in 1899. He established one of the first psychological laboratories for the study of mental deficiency at the Training School at Vineland, New Jersey, and published the standard book for its day on *Feeblemindedness* (1914), fixing for a time the grades of idiot, imbecile, and moron on the basis of mental age levels. (The term "moron" was his invention.) He felt that mental age was a more useful measure than the relative scores of the IQ, a concept discussed further below, because the mental age gave a better indication of what the individual could be expected to do. He and his Vineland followers never adopted the IQ. Although he demonstrated that the higher grades of the mentally deficient could be trained for useful occupations, he believed that the level of intelligence was largely inherited. He supported this conviction by publishing a genealogical study of feeblemindedness through several generations of a family called by the pseudonym *The Kallikak Family* (1913). This was in the spirit of Galton's study of hereditary genius, except that it covered the lower end of the scale. It appeared to give support to a much earlier study of another inadequate family, the Jukes, by R. L. Dugdale (1877), a member of the New York Prison Association. Both of these family studies eventually provoked controversy because of their failure to give weight to environmental factors.

Other English translations and revisions of the Binet-Simon scales were made in the next few years. There was a second version by Goddard (1910) and then by three others: Huey (1910), Whipple (1910), and Kuhlmann (1912). The best known and most enduring through time was the revision made soon thereafter, by Lewis M. Terman (1877–1956), at Stanford University in a version called the Stanford-Binet published in 1916.

Terman had taken a degree with Sanford and Hall at Clark University in 1905, and he felt that he owed a great debt to Hall, even though Hall had discouraged him in his wish to study testing methods as a doctoral dissertation. His interest did not wane, however, and he soon began studies of intellectual differences. His first published study in the area, prior to familiarity with Binet's work, was a comparison of the intellectual processes of seven "bright" and seven "stupid" boys (Terman, 1906). At the suggestion of his friend E. B. Huey, who had made one of the early translations, he soon began a study of the Binet-Simon scales, and reported the impression gained through a study of 400 nonselected children (Terman, 1911); with H. C. Childs, he wrote another paper describing the revision and extension that was being worked on (Terman & Childs, 1912). The revision was published in 1916 in book form with supplementary materials. A later revision appeared in collaboration with Maud Merrill (Terman & Merrill, 1937) and another by Merrill after Terman's death (Terman & Merrill, 1960).

A contribution to the early Stanford-Binet came by way of the work on individual differences by a German psychologist, William Stern (1871–1938), whose PhD was earned with Ebbinghaus, under whose supervision his interest in individual differences may have arisen. Stern's books on individual differences were written while he was teaching at the University of Breslau. The first of these was entitled *Individual Differences* (1900), and was later revised with the title *Differential Psychology* (1911). Stern, in 1912, as reported in a later book in English translation (1914), had noted the possibility of using a quotient found by dividing the mental age (MA) by the chronological age (CA) as an index of intelligence. Terman adopted this in the Stanford-Binet, by defining Stern's ratio as an intelligence quotient or IQ, getting rid of the decimal by multiplying by 100 so that the average IQ would be set at 100.

Because the IQ could be interpreted as an index of growth in intelligence, based as it is on Binet's concept of mental age, an empirical (and theoretical) issue arose over the constancy of the IQ. For the IQ to remain approximately constant requires that the child of superior intelligence increase in mental age each year in proportion to the increased chronological age. Conversely, a child of below normal intelligence would have to fall farther and farther behind in mental age to maintain the same IQ. Arguments over the constancy of the IQ came to be superimposed on other questions about intelligence tests as measures of ability at any one time. Terman did not insist on absolute constancy and instead recommended retesting from time to time.

Although Terman is probably best remembered for the Stanford-Binet test and the concept of IQ, they represent but one aspect of his role in the measurement of individual differences. During World War I, Terman was deeply involved in the development of the Army Alpha and Army Beta intelligence tests, under the general supervision of Robert M. Yerkes (1876–1956). Shortly after the war, in 1921, Terman inaugurated his pioneer longitudinal study of a group of bright children from the early school years through adulthood, with a first volume appearing in 1925. He also extended the objective examination to what was learned in school in the form of the Stanford Achievement Test (Terman, Kelley, & Ruch, 1923). This led to a distinction between aptitude and achievement, which although conceptually plausible, failed to note that, in practice, an aptitude has to be inferred from related achievements (Humphreys, 1974).

Mental Measurement in World War I and Its Aftermath

The large-scale testing of the armed forces in the United States during World War I under Yerkes and others brought intelligence tests before the eyes of the public beyond anything that psychologists had previously studied or proposed. From September 1917 to January 1919 more than 1,750,000 men were tested by the Army Alpha, a test designed for group administration with men who could read and write English. The Army Beta was used for those who were either illiterate or non-English speaking. A major report on the army testing was later published (Yerkes, 1921). The tests had apparently proved useful for making practical decisions under the massive pressures of the war both for eliminating the unfit and for detecting candidates to be trained as officers. Later criticisms were to show that the tests were not as valid as they were thought to be for these purposes, but belief in them led to their enthusiastic adoption for a time after the war. The army tests encouraged the further development of pencil-and-paper tests that could be used with groups, saving the cost in time and expertness of individual testing. Such tests were under development by Terman's student, Arthur S. Otis, before the war, and Otis was able to join with Yerkes, Terman, Boring, and others, in the development of the army tests.

The Mounting Criticisms

After Terman had returned to Stanford University following the war, and just before he was to assume the presidency of the American Psychological Association in 1922, a storm broke out over the concept of intelligence measurement.

Two aspects of the intelligence test results during the war became widely discussed in the public press. The first was due to a confusion over the technical meaning of mental age; the second was based on the hereditarian bias which gave support to racial and ethnic interpretations based on test scores.

As a technical matter, the Army Alpha and Army Beta were not mental age scales and had not been based on the Stanford-Binet. However, during the war, as a young member of the research staff, Mark A. May (1891–1977), a Columbia PhD and later a professor at Yale and director of its Institute of Human Relations, had chosen to compare the results of the Army Alpha with scores on individual Stanford-Binet tests, a number of which had been gathered during the course of standardization of the army tests. The surprising result was that the MA of the American soldier, as computed from the Stanford-Binet, was between 13 and 14 years. How could a democracy function, the frightened public asked, if a nation of voters had the mentality of a child? Of course, tests had been constructed so that the average intelligence of a proper sample of the population can be nothing but average, but the peculiarities of the mental age concept, as applied to adults, were not known by the general public. Mental growth, as tested, levels off, so that an unselected public population has a mental age of about 15 years; the draftees in the army were only slightly below what might have been expected from a normal sample, because so many professionals and highly intelligent persons were excluded from the testing. These technical aspects were unknown to the alarmed public.

Walter Lippmann, a popular journalist and pundit, attacked the army test results in a series of seven articles in the *New Republic* between October 25 and November 29, 1922, and three more in 1923 (Lippmann, 1922, 1923). He attacked the army tests partly on technical grounds, that they had produced no evidence that the tests measured anything related to the problems of real life. They might identify a certain kind of ability, but it was improper to call that ability intelligence. Terman replied (1922a); he pointed out Lippmann's errors of fact and noted the extreme views that he assigned to the mental testers. Boring (1923) who had worked with Yerkes and Terman in constructing the tests, wrote another *New Republic* article, attempting to mediate the controversy, giving at the time what would now be called an operational view of measurement: Intelligence, as defined technically by the tests, is merely what the tests measure. That is, the tests were empirical instruments, devised and standardized according to established psychometric procedures, so that, when these procedural steps are understood, it is possible to define the measured aspects of intelligence by the scores that the tests yield. This did not satisfy the critics. The public controversy flared up and burned itself out in 18 months. A fuller account has been published by Cronbach (1975), covering later controversies as well.

Heredity and Environment: Nature versus Nurture

The second aspect of the post–World War I controversy—the hereditarian emphasis, with its assigning of low average intelligence to some racial and ethnic groups—led to more open attacks upon the tests. The opposition that Terman faced was, first of all, from a professional educator at Teachers College, Columbia, William C. Bagley (1922). Bagley saw himself as the defender of the common man by assuming that functional intelligence could be raised by education. He saw the whole ideal of democracy threatened by the implications of the testing movement. Terman replied, accusing Bagley of fighting a straw man (Terman, 1922b).

One of the books damaging to the psychologists' reputations—a favorite for the racists and a target for the critics—was published at the height of the controversy by a Princeton psychologist, Carl C. Brigham (1890–1943), carrying the neutral title of *A Study of American Intelligence* (1923). Brigham summarized the army tests, marshaling statistics to demonstrate their reliability, and stratified the scores of those tested according to nationality. He made much of the inferiority of some of the national groups that were then providing the largest number of immigrants, and indicated that his findings supported those of Madison Grant and other racists. Grant, a New York lawyer, had published his *Passing of the Great Race* (1916) with no mention of intelligence tests to support his doctrine of Nordic supremacy and his advocacy of eugenics programs. Brigham even sought Grant's help to determine the percentage of Nordic, Mediterranean, and Alpine stock in each of the nationalities and apparently accepted Grant's figures. There were also anti-Semitic overtones in the analysis, through Grant's and Brigham's classifying Jews as Alpine-Slavs, hence among those asserted to be of less intelligent national origins. However, in fairness to Brigham, it must be noted that he recanted 7 years later, declaring: "That study, with its entire superstructure of racial differences, collapses completely" (Brigham, 1930, p. 164). Unfortunately, that article did not get the attention that the earlier book had received.

Yerkes, in his formal report on the army tests, had not stressed the results with the foreign-born recruits, but he wrote an introduction to Brigham's book favoring the use of the army test data for Brigham's purposes, while omitting comments on Brigham's findings. Still, in the same year, Yerkes expressed himself strongly with respect to the hazards of selective immigration (Yerkes, 1923).

Some writers on the history of this period have asserted that psychological test scores and the claims of psychologists played an important role in the passage of restrictive legislation, particularly the Immigration Act of 1924 (e.g., Gould, 1981; Kamin, 1974). The issues are far from clear, however, for there was no unanimity among psychologists, and many other forces were at work to support the legislation. I leave it to other authors in this volume to comment on the debates which, as such, belong to a later date (e.g., Snyderman & Herrnstein, 1983), even though they bear upon the period that I am discussing.

Influences Outside Psychology

These were turbulent years as the debates on restrictive immigration and eugenics were carried on by geneticists, anthropologists, and sociologists, as well as by psychologists. At the beginning of the period, about the time of the First World War, the lineup was biology and psychology preferring hereditarian explanations, and cultural anthropology under Franz Boas and sociology under Charles Cooley moving toward environmentalist explanations ahead of the psychologists. It was not until a few years after the war that Watson became aggressively environmentalist and carried many American psychologists along with him.

An attempt by psychologists and educators to permit all sides to be heard was the appearance of a yearbook of the National Society for the Study of Education prepared by a committee that Terman chaired, with Galton's cliché in the title *Nature and Nurture* (1928). Part I carried the subtitle *Their Influence Upon Intelligence;* Part II had the subtitle *Their Influence Upon Achievement.* Terman, despite his own strongly hereditarian views at the time, proved to be a tolerant chairman, and the authors included those who leaned toward heredity and those who leaned toward environment.

A mass of research data was presented critically, with due regard for sources of error, and usually any attributions to heredity or to environment were tempered by comments upon the interactive possibilities. It was no longer a question of either-or; lingering preferences, and different types of data, led to residual disagreements as to the relative contribution of nature and nurture. Guy Whipple, the *Yearbook* editor for the Society, commented in the *Journal of Educational Psychology:*

> No one who reads the *Yearbook*—this is my impression at least—can put it away with the conviction that general intelligence is an absolutely fixed, immutable, innate capacity, but neither can put it away with the conviction that general intelligence is readily susceptible to environmental influence. The truth lies between these extremes. (Whipple, 1928, p. 392)

It appeared that the quarrelsomeness among the academics might be over, and what further clarification would come would be based upon critical research. However, any truce achieved was unstable because empiricism alone could not deal adequately with the ethical issues and the lingering uncertainties.

Psychometric Refinements in Intelligence Measurements

With the public debates somewhat quieted down, many psychologists turned to psychometric improvements of the tests. There were tests yielding more than one scale, as in the American Council on Education Psychological Examination prepared by L. L. Thurstone (1887–1955), beginning in 1924 with an "L" (linguistic) and a "Q" (quantitative) score, carried on in collaboration with Thelma Gwynne Thurstone. David Wechsler's Wechsler-Bellevue Adult Intelligence Scale appeared in 1939, with a deviation IQ not based on the concept of mental age, and including both a verbal IQ and a performance IQ. I shall not enter into a detailed account of these various refinements.

The most significant theoretical development was a new interest in factor analysis in America, proposed originally by Spearman in 1904. In England, Cyril Burt (1909) had followed Spearman, but in America Thorndike had rejected general abilities in favor of special abilities (Thorndike, Lay, & Dean, 1909). In England, William Brown (1910) had sided with Thorndike. A new initiative in America was taken by Truman Kelley in his book *Crossroads in the Mind of Man* (1928). Others entered the field, such as Karl Holzinger and Harold Hotelling, but the most influential at the time was Thurstone, in his *Vectors of the Mind* (1935) and *Multiple Factor Analysis* (1947). The supposedly most practical bearing on intelligence came from his *Primary Mental Abilities* in 1938. Unfortunately, the promise of factor analysis did not work out quite as decisively as hoped, but I have left this to other authors in this volume to comment on in the light of later developments.

The Nature-Nurture Issue Rises Again

Although the *Yearbook* of 1928 had seemed to usher in a period of tempered conflict and reliance on research findings to settle issues relating to intelligence, extremism is not easily vanquished. The nature-nurture issue surfaced strongly again in 1940.

A new yearbook of the National Society for the Study of Education appeared in two parts in 1940 (Stoddard, 1940). The general title, reflecting that of the 1928 yearbook, was *Intelligence: Its Nature and Nurture.* Part I carried the subtitle: *Comparative and Critical Exposition;* Part II: *Original Studies and Experiments.* The yearbook chairman was George D. Stoddard (1897–1981), at the time the director of the Child Welfare Research Station and dean of the Graduate College of the State University of Iowa, before becoming president of the University of Illinois.

The selection of Stoddard, known as an environmentalist, as the editor might have been viewed as a judicious choice to balance Terman's opposite bias as editor of the earlier yearbook. Sensitivity to issues of racial bias had been aroused in the years before 1940 by Hitler's anti-Semitism and his Nordic supremacy doctrines, and the education profession had joined the other social sciences and the behavioristic psychologists in a shift toward environmentalism. The old issues, however, were not dead.

Much of the controversy centered upon an ongoing dispute between the researchers at Iowa and Stanford, with the Iowa researchers tending to stress the environment, the Stanford ones the hereditary endowments. Actually there was a great deal of analysis in both parts of the yearbook that fell outside these disputes, but the many contributions by those not involved in the controversy were easily lost sight of.

The divergence of interpretations that highlighted the controversy were well represented in two chapters, one by Stoddard and Beth L. Wellman (1895–1952), a professor of child psychology associated with him in the Child Welfare Research Station at Iowa where she had received her PhD, the other by Florence L. Goodenough (1886–1959), a research professor at the Institute of Child Welfare at the University of Minnesota, who had earned her PhD under Terman at Stanford.

The chapter by Stoddard and Wellman (1940), entitled "Environment and the IQ," covered a series of studies from the University of Iowa, all supporting substantial changes in IQ associated with environmental stimulation. Included were a study providing evidence for changes in IQ as a result of nursery school training in the Iowa nursery schools. Another study showed the enhancement of initially deficient IQs of children in an orphanage previously lacking in psychological stimulation when individual help was provided. Still other research concerned the effects of schooling beyond the nursery school. A series of studies of foster children supported strong assertions that the environment of a good home into which children were adopted could produce dramatic changes in intelligence. The chapter was clearly in defense of the environmental thesis throughout.

Goodenough (1940) devoted many pages of her 59-page chapter on "New Evidence on Environmental Influence on Intelligence" to technical criticisms of the Iowa studies—the very ones reported so confidently in the Stoddard and Wellman chapter. In it she cited the analyses made by Quinn McNemar (1940), a psychologist-statistician working at Stanford with Terman. In addition to these criticisms, she also cited contradictory findings from studies done elsewhere—including the University of Minnesota—on similar topics.

A meeting was scheduled at Stanford University in 1940, when the *Yearbook* had just appeared, to discuss its findings, and Terman was invited to be the reviewer and critic. The meeting was held in the Cubberley Auditorium of the School of Education, with a panel of experts on intelligence on the platform and an audience consisting primarily of professional educators. Terman's address was to be followed by Stoddard's remarks as chairman of the *Yearbook*, and the panel was then to discuss the issues. The auditorium was packed. Terman launched a highly critical attack upon the University of Iowa studies, which bulked large in the *Yearbook* and which supported the environmentalist position. The audience of educators was offended by Terman's negative critique, which in addition to its distastefulness to an audience essentially environmentalist, appeared to be discourteous when uttered by a local and senior host (Terman) to a younger visitor (Stoddard) from another university (Iowa).

It so happened that, as a member of both the psychology and education faculties at Stanford, and not personally involved in the measurement of intelligence, I had been invited to chair the session. As Terman got further into his hour-long attack, Stoddard, with whom I was already well acquainted, who was sitting next to me on the platform, turned to me and said in a whisper that he could not take time to reply to all the points that Terman had raised because it would take as long as Terman's talk, so he intended to start out *as if* he were going to reply to all the points, but it would be up to me to interrupt him, so the panel discussion could go on. When Stoddard rose to reply and proceeded to answer point by point, he received an ovation and he obviously had a sympathetic audience. After he had made a few forceful replies, and was well launched upon his answers to the rest of Terman's criticisms, I interrupted him as he had proposed, amid boos from the audience.

To start the discussion in a less tense atmosphere, I called upon Mark May, who was seated on the platform in a row beside me. I invited him to tell about how he had computed the average mental age on the Stanford-Binet from the Army Alpha. I could not see from my position that he had dozed off, but he recovered, and gave an interesting and amusing talk about the consequences of what he had done. The panel discussion continued in a thoughtful manner, respectful toward both Terman and Stoddard.

The controversy, which appeared to be Stanford versus Iowa, continued for a time through the printed word outside the yearbook (McNemar, 1940; Terman, 1940; Wellman, Skeels, & Skodak, 1940). Again, the voice of an uncommitted person, not emotionally involved, was needed. The Social Science Research Council turned to Robert S. Woodworth (1869–1962), always a wise and sensitive middle-of-the-roader. He prepared a careful review entitled *Heredity and Environment: A Critical Survey of Recently Published Material on Twins and Foster Children* (Woodworth, 1941). He gave a balanced review of the evidence on both sides of the nature-nurture issue and did much to quiet the debate, at least within academic circles, for the next 25 years.

A later follow-up by Skodak and Skeels (1949) of the children from the Iowa investigations, siding with environment, illustrated again a major difference in emphasis between the methods preferred by those who favored the environment and those who favored heredity in their interpretations of the IQ data. The difference can be stated simply: Those who favor heredity tend to rely chiefly on *correlational* data, whereas those who favor environment rely chiefly on *changes in mean IQ*. The same body of data will yield opposite interpretations if emphasis is upon the data analyzed by one or the other of these procedures.

An illustration less controversial than intelligence testing can clarify why it is true that the two approaches appear contradictory. Consider the fact that throughout this century the mean adult heights of children have averaged higher than the heights of the parents (Meredith, 1963).* This is probably due to favorable conditions such as improved nutrition, less debilitation by intestinal parasites, and generally better hygienic

---

* One evidence of this is that during my period at Stanford University it has been necessary over the years to purchase an increasing number of longer beds for the women's dormitories to accommodate women students over 6 feet tall.

conditions and medical care. Were this all the information we had, we might confidently assert that adult height is primarily a function of favorable environment. If instead of mean heights of parents and children we turn to the correlational data, we find that tall parents still have taller children than shorter parents, and the parent-child correlations within a given population have remained essentially unchanged. Were this the only information we had, we would most surely be led to say that height was primarily hereditary. What is found in studies of intelligence is analogous.

Foster child studies, which commonly depend on the mean IQs of the foster children relative to what would be expected from their biological parental backgrounds, generally show higher IQs than would be expected, thus indicating the advantages gained through living in the homes carefully selected by the adoption agencies.

Twin data naturally fall into the correlational form of data analysis because investigators are interested in the resemblances between the members of twin pairs, such as identical (monozygotic) twins reared together or reared apart, and fraternal twins (dizygotic) also reared under different conditions. It is not surprising that in them the evidence tends to favor heredity.

Because I have chosen to end this discussion at mid-century, the Skodak and Skeels (1949) follow-up appears to be a good stopping point. My main conclusion must be that the years of hard and patient work by devoted scientists up to that date had resolved neither the technical and theoretical issues nor the problems of value inherent in the measurement of intelligence and in the interpretation of the obtained scores. It is these residual problems that provide the background for this symposium 35 years beyond mid-century.

As I now in writing this chapter look back over this gathering, I am pleased that after others had their opportunities to explore many facets of intelligence and its measurement, Lloyd Humphreys, who has been so thoughtful about these matters over the years, had an opportunity to give us his perspective before the symposium ended.

REFERENCES

Bagley, W. C. (1922). Educational determinism: Or democracy and the IQ. *School and Society, 15,* 373–384.

Bain, A. (1855). *The Senses and the Intellect.* London: Longmans, Green.

Baldwin, J. M., Cattell, J. McK., & Jastrow, J. (1898). Physical and mental tests. *Psychological Review, 5,* 172–179.

Binet, A. (1905). Analyse de C. E. Spearman, "The proof and measurement of association between two things" et "General intelligence objectively determined and measured." *L'Année Psychologique, 11*, 623–624.

Binet, A., & Henri, V. (1894). Le développement de la mémoire visuelle chez les enfants [The development of visual memory in children]. *Revue Philosophique, 37*, 348–350.

Binet, A., & Simon, T. (1905). Sur la nécessité d'établir un diagnostic scientifique des états inférieurs de l'intelligence [On the necessity of establishing a scientific diagnosis of the inferior states of intelligence]. *L'Année Psychologique, 11*, 163–190.

Binet, A., & Simon, T. (1908). Le développement de l'intelligence chez les enfants [The development of intelligence in children]. *L'Année Psychologique, 14*, 1–94.

Boring, E. G. (1923). Intelligence as the tests test it. *New Republic, 35*, 35–37.

Brigham, C. C. (1923). *A study of American intelligence.* Princeton, NJ: Princeton University Press.

Brigham, C. C. (1930). Intelligence tests of immigrant groups. *Psychological Review, 37*, 158–165.

Brown, W. (1910). Some experimental results in the correlation of mental abilities. *British Journal of Psychology, 3*, 296–322.

Burt, C. (1909). Experimental tests of general intelligence. *British Journal of Psychology, 3*, 94–177.

Cattell, J. McK. (1890). Mental tests and measurements. *Mind, 15*, 373–381.

Cattell, J. McK. (1929). Psychology in America. *Science, 70*, 335–347.

Cattell, J. McK., & Farrand, L. (1896). Physical and mental measurements of the students of Columbia University. *Psychological Review, 3*, 618–648.

Cronbach, L. J. (1975). Five decades of public controversy over mental testing. *American Psychologist, 30*, 1–14.

Davies, J. D. (1955). *Phrenology: Fad and science.* New Haven, CT: Yale University Press.

Diamond, S. (1980). Francis Galton and American psychology. In R. W. Rieber & K. Salzinger (Eds.), *Psychology: Theoretical-historical perspectives* (pp. 43–55). New York: Academic Press.

Dugdale, R. L. (1877). *The Jukes: A study in crime, pauperism, disease, and heredity.* New York: Putnam.

Ebbinghaus, H. (1897). Über eine neue Methode zu Prüfung geistiger Fähigkeiten und ihre Anwendung bei Schulkindern [Concerning a new method of testing intellectual abilities and their use in school children]. *Zeitschrift für Psychologie, 13*, 401–459.

Galton, F. (1883). *Inquiries into human faculty and its development.* London: Dent.

Galton, F. (1952). *Hereditary genius: An inquiry into its laws and consequences.* New York: Horizon Press. (Original work published 1869)

Goddard, H. H. (1908). The Binet and Simon tests of intellectual capacity. *Training School Bulletin, 5*, 3–9.

Goddard, H. H. (1910). A measuring scale for intelligence. *Training School Bulletin, 6*, 146–155.

Goddard, H. H. (1913). *The Kallikak family: A study in the inheritance of feeblemindedness.* New York: Macmillan.

Goddard, H. H. (1914). *Feeblemindedness: Its causes and consequences.* New York: Macmillan.

Goodenough, F. L. (1940). New evidence on environmental influence on intelligence. In G. D. Stoddard (Ch.), *Intelligence: Its nature and nurture* (pp. 307–365). *39th Yearbook of the National Society for the Study of Education, Part I.* Bloomington, IL: Public School Publishing Co.

Gould, S. J. (1981). *The mismeasure of man.* New York: Norton.

Grant, M. (1916). *Passing of the great race.* New York: Scribner's.

Hilgard, E. R. (1987). *Psychology in America: A historical survey.* San Diego: Harcourt Brace Jovanovich.

Huey, E. B. (1910). The Binet scale for measuring intelligence and retardation. *Journal of Educational Psychology, 1*, 435–444.

Humphreys, L. G. (1939a). Acquisition and extinction of verbal expectations in a situation analogous to conditioning. *Journal of Experimental Psychology, 25*, 294–301.

Humphreys, L. G. (1939b). The effect of random alternation of reinforcement on the acquisition and extinction of conditioned eyelid reactions. *Journal of Experimental Psychology, 25*, 141–158.

Humphreys, L. G. (1974). The misleading distinction between aptitude and achievement tests. In D. R. Green (Ed.), *The aptitude achievement distinction* (pp. 262–274). Monterey, CA: CTB/McGraw-Hill.

Jacobs, J. (1887). Experiments on "prehension." *Mind, 12*, 75–79.

Jastrow, J. (1892). Some anthropological and psychological tests on college students: A preliminary survey. *American Journal of Psychology, 4*, 420–427.

Kamin, L. J. (1974). *The science and politics of IQ.* Potomac, MD: Erlbaum.

Kelley, T. L. (1928). *Crossroads in the mind of man.* Stanford, CA: Stanford University Press.

Kimble, G. A. (1961). *Hilgard and Marquis' conditioning and learning* (2d ed.). New York: Appleton-Century-Crofts.

Kuhlmann, F. (1912). A revision of the Binet-Simon system for measuring the intelligence of children. *Journal of Psycho-Asthenics, Monograph Supplement.*

Lippmann, W. (1922). The mental age of Americans, etc. *New Republic, 32*, 213–215; 246–248; 275–277; 297–298; 328–380; 33, 9–11; 145–146.

Lippmann, W. (1923). Mr. Burt and the intelligence tests, etc. *New Republic, 34*, 263–264; 295–296; 322–323.

McNemar, Q. (1940). A critical examination of the University of Iowa studies of environmental influences upon the IQ. *Psychological Bulletin, 37*, 63–92.

Meredith, H. V. (1963). Changes in the stature and body weight of North American boys during the last eighty years. In L. P. Lipsitt & C. C. Spiker (Eds.), *Advances in child development and behavior* (Vol. 1, pp. 69–114). New York: Academic Press.

Münsterberg, H. (1891). Zur Individualpsychologie [Concerning individual psychology]. *Centralblatt für Nervenheilkunde und Psychiatrie, 4,* 196ff.

Seguin, E. (1856). Origin of the treatment and training of idiots. *American Journal of Education, 2,* 145–152.

Sharp, S. E. (1899). Individual psychology: A study in psychological method. *American Journal of Psychology, 10,* 329–391.

Skodak, M., & Skeels, H. M. (1949). A final follow-up of one hundred adopted children. *Journal of Genetic Psychology, 75,* 3–19.

Snyderman, M., & Herrnstein, R. (1983). Intelligence tests and the Immigration Act of 1924. *American Psychologist, 38,* 987–1000.

Sokal, M. M. (Ed.). (1981). *An education in psychology: James McKeen Cattell's journal and letters from Germany and England, 1880–1888.* Cambridge, MA: MIT Press.

Spearman, C. (1904). General intelligence objectively determined and measured. *American Journal of Psychology, 15,* 201–293.

Stern, W. (1900). *Über Psychologie der individuellen Differenzen (Ideen zu einer differentiellen Psychologie)* [Concerning psychology of individual differences (Ideas regarding a differential psychology)]. Leipzig: Barth.

Stern, W. (1911). *Die differentielle Psychologie in ihren methodischen Grundlagen* [The differential psychology in its methodological foundations]. Leipzig: Barth.

Stern, W. (1914). The psychological methods of testing intelligence (G. M. Whipple, Trans.). *Educational Psychological Monographs* (No. 13). Baltimore, MD: Warwick & York.

Stoddard, G. D. (Ch.). (1940). *Intelligence: Its nature and nurture. 39th Yearbook of the National Society for the Study of Education, Parts I, II.* Bloomington, IL: Public School Publishing Co.

Stoddard, G. D., & Wellman, B. L. (1940). Environment and the IQ. In G. D. Stoddard (Ch.), *Intelligence: Its nature and nurture* (pp. 405–442). *39th Yearbook of the National Society for the Study of Education, Part I.* Bloomington, IL: Public School Publishing Co.

Terman, L. M. (1906). Genius and stupidity: A study of some of the intellectual processes of seven "bright" and seven "stupid" boys. *Pedagogical Seminary, 13,* 307–373.

Terman, L. M. (1911). The Binet-Simon scale for measuring intelligence: Impressions gained by its application upon four hundred non-selected children. *Psychological Clinic, 5,* 199–206.

Terman, L. M. (1916). *The measurement of intelligence.* Boston: Houghton Mifflin.

Terman, L. M. (1922a). The great conspiracy, or the impulse imperious of intelligence testers, psychoanalyzed and exposed by Mr. Lippmann. *New Republic, 33,* 116–120.

Terman, L. M. (1922b). The psychological determinist, or democracy and the IQ. *Journal of Educational Research, 6,* 57–62.

Terman, L. M. (1925). *Mental and physical traits of a thousand gifted children. Genetic Studies of Genius* (Vol. 1). Stanford, CA: Stanford University Press.

Terman, L. M. (Ch.). (1928). *Nature and nurture: Their influence on intelligence. 27th Yearbook of the National Society for the Study of Education, Parts I, II.* Bloomington, IL: Public School Publishing Co.

Terman, L. M. (1940). Personal reactions of the Yearbook Committee. In G. D. Stoddard (Ch.), *Intelligence: Its nature and nurture* (pp. 460–467). *39th Yearbook of the National Society for the Study of Education, Part I.* Bloomington, IL: Public School Publishing Co.

Terman, L. M., & Childs, H. G. (1912). A tentative revision and extension of the Binet-Simon measuring scale of intelligence, Parts I, II, & III. *Journal of Educational Psychology, 3,* 61–74; 133–143; 198–208; 277–289.

Terman, L. M., Kelley, T. L., & Ruch, G. M. (1923). *Stanford Achievement Test.* Yonkers, NY: World Book.

Terman, L. M., & Merrill, M. A. (1937). *Measuring intelligence.* Boston: Houghton Mifflin.

Terman, L. M., & Merrill, M. A. (1960). *Stanford-Binet intelligence scale: Manual for the third revision, Form L-M.* Boston: Houghton Mifflin.

Thorndike, E. L., Lay, W., & Dean, P. R. (1909). The relation of accuracy in sensory discrimination to general intelligence. *American Journal of Psychology, 20,* 364–369.

Thurstone, L. L. (1924). *Psychological examination for high school graduates and college freshmen.* Washington, DC: American Council on Education.

Thurstone, L. L. (1935). *Vectors of the mind.* Chicago: University of Chicago Press.

Thurstone, L. L. (1938). *Primary mental abilities.* Chicago: University of Chicago Press.

Thurstone, L. L. (1947). *Multiple factor analysis.* Chicago: University of Chicago Press.

Wechsler, D. (1939). *The measurement of adult intelligence.* Baltimore, MD: Williams & Wilkins.

Wellman, B. L., Skeels, H. M., & Skodak, M. (1940). Review of McNemar's critical examination of Iowa Studies. *Psychological Bulletin, 37,* 93–111.

Whipple, G. M. (1910). *Manual of mental and physical tests* (Vols. 1–2). Baltimore, MD: Warwick & York.

Whipple, G. M. (1928). Editorial impression of the contribution to knowledge of the *Twenty-Seventh Yearbook. Journal of Educational Psychology, 19,* 392.

Wissler, C. (1901). *The correlation of mental and physical tests.* New York: Macmillan.

Woodworth, R. S. (1941). *Heredity and environment. A critical survey of recently published material on twins and foster children* (Bulletin No. 47). New York: Social Science Research Council.

Yerkes, R. M. (Ed.). (1921). *Psychological examining in the U.S. Army. Memoirs of the National Academy of Sciences,* No. 15.

Yerkes, R. M. (1923). Eugenic bearing of measurements of intelligence in the United States Army. *Eugenics Review, 14,* 225–245.

2

Models of Intelligence

JOHN HORN

A Few Words About Origins

First, I will acknowledge a huge debt to Lloyd Humphreys for his contributions to my thinking. He was my mentor when I was a graduate student in the psychology department at Illinois in the late 1950s and early 1960s. I was very fortunate to have been one of his students. Lloyd Humphreys has a powerful style of thinking. He looks complex problems straight in the eye, strips them of their frills and pretensions, and analyzes them bluntly, objectively, forcefully. He takes no sides except with truth, as he understands it, and he shows no fear of being wrong after his own best judgment has informed him that he is right. That kind of powerful thinking dramatically changes those it touches. It is also addictive. Scarcely a day has passed in my time in academe when Lloyd's ideas and style have not roared into my thinking and affected my teaching and research. I am very grateful for that influence. I am sure that my experience in this regard is not unique. Lloyd Humphreys has addicted many students and co-workers with his thinking. His unique style thus lives on and will continue to live on for many years.

This "Humphreys' effect" has been particularly profound in my work on human abilities. Those who know something about that work might assume that it stems primarily from Ray Cattell. There are good reasons for that assumption, but it is also true that my earliest serious study of intellectual abilities was done with Lloyd Humphreys, and a major portion of my thinking in this area derives from him. This may not be

Several people contributed to this chapter by doing some of the analyses or providing suggestions, many of which I have heeded. For such help I am particularly grateful to Mark Foster and Jack McArdle. Preparation of the manuscript was supported in part by grants from the National Institute of Aging (AG04704) and the National Institute of Child Health and Human Development (HD17552).

clear to a casual glance, but it is easily seen when one looks carefully at my work. I will point to some of this influence as I outline ideas about models of intelligence.

Three Major Kinds of Theories and Models

I will speak of a model of intelligence in much the same way as I might speak of a Lionel train as a model for the real thing. More often I will speak of a model as a particular expression of a theory about the real thing. A Lionel model of the California Zephyr is one model of ideas about that train; O and R makes another model of the Zephyr. A good model will represent the real thing in many important respects even as we recognize that in some ways the model is not the real thing.

My major point in this essay will be that today there is no single model for intelligence, and probably we should not expect to build such a model—because the real thing is not a single function. Several quite distinct things get labeled intelligence. These should be clearly distinguished. We should stop the practice of defining intelligence as just any old mixture of abilities that someone decides to call IQ or g; we should stop the practice of treating different mixtures as if they represent the same thing. The concept of intelligence has outlived its usefulness in science. That concept, not Lloyd Humphreys, should be retired.

Three Models for Intelligence: Compound, Mixture, and Essence

Most current ideas about intelligence can be represented with one or another of three basic kinds of theories. Chemical analogies—to compounds, mixtures, and essences—help reveal unique properties of these theories. Each theory pertains to individual differences.

Compound Models

Consider compound theories first. A compound (in chemistry) is a particular union of elements. In every quantity of water, for example, there is nothing but hydrogen and oxygen, each in a precise proportion of amount—two moles of hydrogen to one of oxygen. The two moles of hydrogen are necessary: there cannot be three moles or one mole (except in another compound, heavy water). In this same way a compound model of intelligence requires a particular union of intellectual capacities, each always present and each in the same proportion to other capacities.

The capacities of a compound theory of intelligence must function together as a unit and thus form a functional unity. If different intellectual capacities stem from a common core of genetic determinants; if they develop over a lifetime in a manner that indicates a unitary response to developmental influences; if they rise and fall in a jointly lawful manner under stimulations, treatments, and alterations of structure; if they have similar implications for adaptation, adjustment, and achievements, then the capacities for which these lawful relations are shown can be said to represent a functional unity.

Spearman (1904, 1927) specified a compound concept of a general factor he labeled g. His theory is an attempt to indicate the necessary and sufficient cognitive processes — eduction of relations and correlates — of a functional unity. His research was directed at showing the proportions of these processes — the number of moles — of each process in the compound. Spearman specified tests of a structural equation model derived from this theory. The tests are very demanding.

It is not in accordance with the design imperatives of the Spearman model to put together just any collection of ability measures, observe that these measures are positively correlated, calculate the first principal factor among these measures, observe that this is large, and conclude, as Jensen (1982, 1984), for example, has concluded, that these findings support Spearman's theory and the idea of using the first principal component and mixture-measures as "the working definition of g." The model for Spearman's theory is not the model of a first principal component for different mixtures of ability measures. The theory does not argue that different mixtures of subtests, such as are found in different IQ tests, represent the same g. Spearman was careful to specify necessary capacities of g. He insisted that any well-designed study to test his theory must be based on a careful selection of abilities to represent one, but only one, common factor.

The Spearman model is not specified to account for all the common variance, or even the major portion of common variance, of every kind of ability test that might be put into a battery. Spearman's model does not, and compound models in general do not, specify that there be a large first principal component among measures of a unitary g. Size of the first principal component is mainly a function of redundancy. If many tests measuring the same thing are included in a battery, the first principal component will be large. This largeness does not indicate whether or not variables represent necessary conditions of a compound theory. To calculate the first principal component among a collection of ability measures is not to produce an operational definition of Spearman's g or any other compound concept of intelligence.

Not correct, also, is an argument (Jensen, 1980, 1984) that because the major common factor in a battery of ability tests is usually highly correlated with the first principal component in that battery, the major common factor in one battery is the same as (or even highly correlated with) the principal component (or the major common factor) in another battery. This reasoning is incorrect because the sampling of tests in one battery need not represent, and in general does not represent, the sampling of tests in other batteries. The samples of abilities of different test batteries are different in analyses in which Jensen (1980) assumes they are not (Horn & Goldsmith, 1981). It is not correct to suppose that "any sizeable collection of complex tests . . . is a representative sample of the general population [of tests]" (Jensen, 1984, p. 95). Much less is it correct to suppose that one collection of subtests represents the same proportions of component processes of intellect as are found in other collections of subtests. The "g" that Jensen (1980) measures as the first principal component or IQ in one study is different from the "g" that he and others measure as a first principal component or IQ in other studies.

Mixture Models

A first principal component and typical omnibus tests designed to measure IQ represent models for mixture theories of intelligence. In chemistry a mixture is merely a collection of different ingredients. The ingredients need not stand in a particular proportion of one to the others. The quantities of one ingredient need not be precisely proportional to the quantities of other ingredients. Indeed, in one form of the concept of mixture, the ingredients need not be the same in different mixtures.

Godfrey Thomson (e.g., 1919, 1948) and Lloyd Humphreys (e.g., 1962, 1974, 1979) have been most clear in explicating the properties of the mixture theories of intelligence. Humphreys (1979) defined intelligence as "the entire repertoire of acquired skills, knowledge, learning sets, and generalization tendencies considered intellectual in nature that are available at any one period of time" (p. 106). Intelligence, according to this view, is a collection of many different abilities, possibly representing many different capacities. In different persons we see different collections of abilities mixed in different proportions. The number of elemental abilities that might, with justification, be included in such a mixture is very large, perhaps too large to ever hope to delimit. This largeness can be seen in the fact that new tests to measure new intellectual abilities can be created almost every day—indeed, are being created almost every day—as Humphreys (1979) pointed out.

The mixture concept of intelligence is rather like the concept of a "dinner": one can make a good dinner from any number of different ingredients, and we have the notion that dinners range from good to bad. But different good dinners are judged against different standards, just as are different bad dinners. There is no particular set of criteria in respect to which all dinners can be judged to be good or bad. No particular kind of dinner—no particular mixture— is, in general, better than all others. Much depends on the cook.

Essence Models

Essence theories in chemistry are early forms of theories of elements. Models representing essence theories of intelligence stipulate that all distinct intellectual abilities stem from one basic process, one element, the essence of intelligence. Such theories are well represented in the essays Eysenck brought together in his 1982 book titled *A Model for Intelligence*. The essence of a particular model that was most discussed in that book is a capacity for holding separate ideas and relations in the span of immediate awareness. In our earlier work, such a span was described as an essential *anlage* in a Spearman-like theory of a particular intelligence known as Gf (Horn, 1965).

A major hypothesis of an essence theory discussed in Eysenck (1982) stipulates that span of apprehension is indicated by quickness of response in tasks involving complex reaction time (CRT). Measures of CRT are obtained under conditions in which one must respond to one of several stimuli, each of which must be considered. In a simple reaction time task, on the other hand, one must simply respond to presence or absence of a particular kind of stimulus. Existing evidence suggests that as the natural log of the number of contingent stimuli one must consider in a CRT measure increases from 1 through 9, the correlation between the measure and an omnibus measure of intelligence increases more or less linearly (Jensen, 1982; Longstreth, 1986; Longstreth & Madigan, 1982).

Neurologic theory about span of apprehension suggests that it is a reflection of efficient confluence in neural transmission throughout the brain. In work reviewed in the Eysenck book, this efficient confluence is said to be indicated by shortness of latency of average cortical evoked potentials (LAEP) and smallness of variance in repeated recordings of evoked potentials over short periods of time (VAEP).

Essence theories can be quite correct, as far as they go, but be incorrect if they are assumed to go farther than they can go. Span-of-apprehension essence theories are correct and incorrect in this sense. Existing evidence certainly does not support a hypothesis that span of apprehension—or working memory (Ms), which is operationally (i.e., in measurements) the same—is an important part of whatever it is that researchers mean by intelligence. The evidence is equally clear in indicating that Ms is not all there is to intelligence, and is not identical to quickness in complex reaction time (CRT). The CRT correlates in the range of from .2 to .5 with measures of Ms, other measures of short-term apprehension and retrieval (SAR), long-term storage and retrieval (TSR), attentional capacity, creativity, concept formulation, and different forms of reasoning. The comparable correlations for measures of LAEP and VAEP are of about the same magnitude. There is overlap in measures of CRT, LAEP, or VAEP, and in the correlations of these measures with different indicators of intelligence, but the correlations are well below the reliabilities of measures (Eysenck, 1982; Schucard & Horn, 1972). Such evidence suggests that more than one "essence" is measured by the different operations that yield Ms, CRT, LAEP, and VAEP. The squares of the multiple correlation of these measures with measures of other features of intelligence are not equal to the squares of the reliabilities of the measures. Such evidence is clear in indicating that measures of working memory, complex reaction time, and cortical evoked potentials account for only a small proportion of the reliable variance in measures indicating important features of human cognitive functioning.

The Three Models in Perspective

A major problem with much writing and research on intelligence is that compound, essence, and mixture-models are not distinguished. They are treated as if they are interchangeable (Jensen, 1980). In one breath a Spearman compound model is said to represent several aspects of intelligence; in a next breath, CRT is said to be the essence of intelligence; in yet another breath, a mixture model is used as if it represented a Spearman model or other essence model. This will not do. The three models have different implications for measurement and outcomes of research. The construct validation that is supportive of one of these models is different from the validation needed to support the other models.

The major problem with compound and essence theories of a single intelligence is that the evidence of research simply does not support any such theory (Horn, 1985; Rimoldi, 1948). Plausibility arguments derived from current understanding of genetics, neurology, and human development also do not give credence to the idea that the variety of human abilities said to indicate intelligence, and individual differences in the abilities of intelligence, can be accurately represented by a theory of either a single essence or of a single compound.

As mentioned before, a theory stipulating that CRT is the essence of intelligence is not adequate because CRT does not accurately represent (predict, account for) the repertoire of intellectual abilities. CRT does not account for the covariance among such intellectual abilities as verbal comprehension, conjunctive reasoning, visual auditory awareness, short-term memory, and retrieval from long-term memory. It does not account for the intercorrelations among many of the "skills, knowledges, learning sets, and generalization tendencies" that Humphreys referred to as indicating human intelligence. Humphreys has pointed this out more than once. No essence model comes close to representing the entire repertoire of human abilities. It is unlikely that the common variance among human abilities can be explained in terms of a single essence of any kind.

Although CRT does not represent the essence of intelligence, it is not unreasonable in the light of today's evidence to suppose that a Spearman-like compound model can be shown to represent particular subsets of the repertoire of intellectual abilities and, in particular, a subset that includes measures of CRT. Such evidence would not support an essence theory, but the compound theory could be almost equally useful. It would not be a theory of general intelligence: it would not make the case that the compound is the source of human variability in all intellectual abilities. Better than theory of general intelligence, this modest theory would more adequately describe an important segment of cognitive functioning (Pelligrini & Glaser, 1979). There is need for such modest theories. The theory of Gf, as discussed later in this paper, comes close to being such a modest theory.

Evoked potential measurements also are not the essence of intelligence: they do not account for all, or even the major portion, of the common variance among measures that are said to indicate intelligence. This is true even after corrections for attenuation due to unreliability have been made (Horn, 1983). Our work with evoked potentials (Schucard & Horn, 1972) suggests that LAEP mainly represents a volitional form of activation, not the essence of intelligence. Attentional aspects of cognitive functioning are important. A compound theory that explains well how evoked potentials, activation, and attention are implicated in problem solving would be a contribution, even as it would not be a theory of general intelligence.

No compound model has been found to represent a broad spectrum of intellectual abilities. Results from well-conceived and well-executed studies designed to test major hypotheses of Spearman's compound theory have demonstrated that the model does not adequately represent the variability in human intellectual capabilities (see Horn, 1985b; Rimoldi, 1948, for reviews). It is a good theory because it is clear enough to have a test, but it is not a correct theory because it does not account for the phenomena. Results from studies designed to test Spearman's model indicate that several distinct capacities — several distinct intelligences — must be posited to account for the phenomena.

I attended a meeting recently at which Michael Commons suggested that humans might have 800,000 intellectual abilities. The figure is probably inflated to make a point, but in fact it may be reasonable. Humans do possess many, many intellectual abilities. The exact number is difficult to estimate. Estimating that number is rather like trying to count the number of stars in the Milky Way.

Some years ago, Humphreys pointed out to me that in a couple of hours most cognitive psychologists could make up a test to measure a new intellectual ability and that many psychologists doing this could generate a small infinity of human abilities. Such an infinity would be the "repertoire" of human abilities of the Humphreys's mixture theory of intelligence.

How can one talk about a myriad of abilities as representing one feature of an individual? Can one model represent a myriad?

A major problem with the mixture theories is that so many different models can be derived from such theory. Just as there are many star clusters one can "see" (from a particular perspective) in the Milky Way, so there are many mixtures one can "see" to be intelligence, and there is little basis for choosing between them. (Moreover, we probably "see" only the most obvious parts of the phenomena of human abilities, just as we see only the nearest and brightest stars in the Milky Way.) We do not know how to circumscribe the universe of abilities that should be regarded as intellectual. Because we cannot designate that universe, we are unable to sample representatively from it. Thus, although mixture theory does indeed describe what often is meant when the word intelligence is used, such theory does not get us to an agreed-upon operational definition of concepts. We need a way of specifying a particular mixture, or representative mixtures. We need a sampling theory for the repertoire of human abilities to which Humphreys refers. No theory today specifies such a mixture or a means for objectively sampling abilities to representatively identify the repertoire.

Models of mixture theories well represent today's practice of measuring intelligence, both in research and in applied situations, and such models have been with us for over 80 years. In clinical practice, education, guidance, selection, and common sense, we have continued to think of collections of different cognitive abilities as representing one thing — intelligence. Omnibus tests, each measuring a different collection of abilities, dominate in practice. Yet even when the same omnibus test is used, it will not in general measure the same component abilities in the same proportions in different people. Different component abilities are measured in different proportions in different people taking the same test, and this is most assuredly true when we use different omnibus tests or when we use what is labeled as the same test at different age levels. (The omnibus Stanford-Binet for infants, for example, is quite a different test than the omnibus Stanford-Binet one uses with 13-year-old children.)

Mixture theories have been useful, but it is time to move on. In science, theories are not so much wrong as they are outdated. They outlive their usefulness as more becomes known. With mixture theories as guides much has been learned about human cognitive functioning (as overviewed in Carroll & Horn, 1981, for example), but this knowledge points to the need to replace mixture theories with a variegated system of several compound and essence theories, each representing cognitive capability that is reminiscent of what has been referred to as intelligence. A system of several intelligences should guide research of the future. In this essay I will point to a small part of a large amount of evidence that leads to this conclusion.

In sum, then, the situation is this: no one essence or compound theory adequately describes the relations among all the abilities that indicate human intellectual capacities; there are many different mixtures of abilities that might be labeled intelligence, but to make these comparable there must be an adequate basis for sampling the domain of intellectual abilities, and no such basis is known to exist. To build the knowledge required for an adequate sampling theory of intelligence, there must be research on the major different abilities of the repertoire of abilities that can be considered to be intellectual.

Several segments of evidence should be taken into account in any adequate theory about variability in human cognition. The "real thing" of such models should be what we know about human abilities.

I will point to some of what is known about individual differences in abilities and the development of these individual differences. I will also point to some physiological correlates. I will suggest that if one looks carefully at these broad swaths of evidence, it will be found that a theory of general intelligence is not as useful for present-day scientific thinking as a theory of many intelligences.

Criticisms of Factor Analysis and Structural Equation Modeling

Factor analytic results point to the conclusion reached in the last section. Before presenting such results, however, it will be useful to detour for a moment to consider Humphreys's (1979) argument that factor analytic studies are little more than efforts to slice smoke. He points out that with very simple manipulation of facets of test design, one can create almost an infinity of abilities, and these can be factored in almost an infinity of ways. He points out, too, that higher order factoring affords no solution to this problem of an arbitrary infinity of factors among the Milky Way of human abilities: one is still slicing smoke even as bigger slices are being attempted. First-order and second-order factors reflect mainly only our procedures of test construction and our selections of tests to include in factor analytic studies. Whether or not a factor appears at a given order depends on the density of sampling of tests in a particular area of the smoke. A factor that appears at the first order in one battery will appear at the second order or third order or some other order in another battery.

I have no fundamental disagreement with these observations about the nature of factor analysis. I learned the smoke-slicing lesson back in my formative years with Humphreys; as I said earlier, it is difficult to forget the lessons he teaches. I do think it is reasonable, however, to fan smoke in ways that are meaningful and useful.

The Humphreys's lessons about factor analysis support the argument that first-principal component and IQ measures of intelligence should be banished from most scientific research. Principal component and mixture measures are examples of how one can overlap arbitrary collections of abilities to create homogeneously reliable and test-retest reliable measures that, however, represent no particular psychological attribute—no particular functional unity. The lessons of Humphreys also teach that stepping up to higher order solutions, as in Schmid-Leiman (1957) transformations, does not solve the problems stemming from the arbitrariness of collections of tests. Just as one can always calculate a first-principal component for the intercorrelations among any set of abilities, so one can always continue factoring at higher orders until only one factor is indicated, whence the results can be transformed via the Schmid-Leiman algebra to define a general factor operationally. But one can calculate this general factor for any mixture of abilities, and there is no assurance that the factor thus calculated in one arbitrarily formed battery is at all equivalent to a factor calculated in the same way in another such battery.

So factor analyses among ability measures can represent merely a slicing of smoke. Batteries need not be merely arbitrary collections of tests, however. It is possible to move smoke around in ways that show that we know where it is. Factor analysis and what is practically the same, structural equation modeling, are methods for demonstrating that one understands how to select samples of variables, samples of subjects, and analytic procedures that demonstrate regularities in performance. The latent variables (i.e., factors) demonstrated in a truly confirmatory study are, and should be, indications of the design that went into the selection of subjects and the construction and selection of variables; such design should yield results that need not have been found, but if found, support the substantive hypotheses on which the design is based. The design for selection of variables and subjects is the critical part of any factor analytic or modeling study regardless of whether or not the investigator is explicitly aware of this design. Factor analysis and modeling analyses are scientifically most useful when their application demonstrates that regularities thought to exist do indeed exist.

This line of argument thus leads to the view that researchers should be able to, and should, design confirmatory (factor analytic or modeling) studies that demonstrate precisely the directed and undirected relations among variables in a particular sample of subjects. (Features that should be attended to in such design are discussed in some detail in Horn & McArdle, 1980.) Fully confirmatory design is an ideal, however. The ideal is very difficult to maintain in the real world of conducting fallible studies on poorly understood phenomena with only limited resources.

At the present juncture of history in the study of human abilities, it is probably overly idealistic to expect to fit confirmatory models to data that well represent the complexities of human cognitive functioning: too much is unknown. Even when we can, a priori, specify a multiple-variable model that fits data in a general way—with chi-square three or four times as large as the number of degrees of freedom (df)—we cannot anticipate all the small loadings that must be in a model for a particular sampling of variables and subjects if the model is to "truly" fit data. Usually, we cannot take enough time with our subjects to get the high reliabilities and validities that must obtain if evanescent influences are to be largely eliminated and nonreplicatable relations are to be specified in advance, in accordance with the statistical demands of structural equations theory. To specify precisely which relations should be fixed exactly at zero or particular nonzero values (except for random error), and which relations invariably must be estimated, is beyond present-day knowledge (although perhaps not far beyond in some areas of research). The statistical demands of structural equations theory are stringent. If there is tinkering with the results to get a model to fit, the statistical theory, and thus the basis for strong inference, goes out the window. In such cases modeling analyses can be used to describe data in a particular sample (of variables and subjects), but the methods should not be used to suggest that results confirm and test substantive theory in the strong sense of the statistical tests of model fit.

In published reports of model fits, usually there has been tinkering to get a model to fit. In most such cases it is very difficult to assess the extent to which tinkering has been done and the extent, therefore, to which the inferential power of the analyses has been reduced. Under such conditions one should not give any greater credence to results from modeling analyses than one can give to results from comparably executed factor analytic studies of the older variety.

Factor analysis and modeling methods, as other forms of data analysis, have utility when used correctly. The methods are of use in demonstrating what we know about test construction and the ways people will respond to the tests we construct. Humphreys's criticisms provide descriptions of the limitations of such methods and identify studies in which these limitations were not properly considered. Investigators often expect too much from such methods. They expect the methods to do their thinking for them; this expectation is fruitless. One cannot simply throw everything that is called an ability into a battery and expect that by factoring that battery one will find the essences of human functioning—or the primary abilities. But one can design factor analytic or modeling studies that help indicate lawful patterns of covariation that can be verified and extended in other kinds of research.

This brings up a most important point: convergent confirmation of pattern is needed to support truly important scientific theory. The convergence should come from several different kinds of studies. It should support refutable hypotheses and validate constructs. Factor analytic—measurement model—studies are not sufficient to support adequate theory about cognitive functioning.

This is not a new idea. Thurstone (1947) emphasized it in his writings, and others since have pointed to it. The idea is extremely important, however; it deserves repeating. Scientific validation requires convergence of evidence from different sources.

Lack of convergence of evidence from different sources has led to the conclusion, stated earlier, that theory about general intelligence is not adequate to describe and explain the phenomena of human cognitive functioning. The tack Humphreys has taken in his recent research addresses this matter. He has proposed that the ideas and models of Spearman and Guttman be compared and, if in accordance with findings, combined. This is a correct response to the argument that the evidence does not support compound or essence models of general intelligence and that mixture models are too forgiving to provide adequate tests for competing hypotheses that can be specified on the basis of what is currently known. Simplex, circumplex, and hierarchical-order models of the kind Humphreys proposes, particularly when used with designs aimed at elucidating developmental patterns, provide a good basis for examining rejectable hypotheses. The approach is promising.

Results that Question the Utility of the Concept of Intelligence

I will now pull away from this detour into thoughts about factor analysis and lay out some of the empirical evidence that supports a conclusion that intelligence should not be the concept of choice for future research on human abilities. In the present discussion, I can point to only the tip of the iceberg of relevant evidence. The references cited will help to expose a bit more of this iceberg.

Structural Findings

I will begin with a few results from studies that Patricia Ellison, Mark Foster, David Prasse, Ralph Mason, and I have been doing of children who at birth were hospitalized in a neonatal intensive care unit. We have been able to obtain measures on these children at birth and at 6 months, 15 months, 4 years, and 7 years after their initial hospitalization. The results of Table 1 were obtained at the 7-year follow-up, using reliable measures designed to indicate fairly specific abilities. The scales are based on the items of the McCarthy (1972), the Kaufman and Kaufman (1983), and Wide-Range achievement tests, as well as tests that are less well known. We constructed the scales to be internally consistent, both logically and psychologically, and to have a modicum of psychometric internal consistency. The results shown in Table 1 are from one of several different samplings of variables designed to indicate whether or not the multifactor pattern of the table will emerge in objectively rotated, that is, analytically rotated, solutions. This pattern is found under several different conditions in which these design considerations were applied. The pattern is hardy.

In this essay we need not become involved in the details of theory specifying precisely what these factors indicate about human functioning. I have spelled out these details in other articles (Horn, 1982, 1985a, 1985b; Horn & Donaldson, 1980; Horn & Stankov, 1982). At the general level needed for the discussions of this book, the functions can be described as follows:

TABLE 1

Reference Vector Structure Coefficients (Correlations) and Primary Factor Inter-correlations for a Promax Solution Based on 7-Year-Olds (N = 154)

Descriptions of variables	Symbols	Gc	Gf	TSR	SAR	Gv	Ga
Identify synonyms	WEV	66					
Identify conventional spelling	WSP	65					
Read words	KRW	53		26			
Answer questions about reading	KCR	48		37			
Answer questions about numbers	MIN	34	40				
Show arithmetic skills	WAR	30	42				
Put pictures in series	KPS		51			25	
Short counts by number	MCS		39				
Group concepts	MCG		36	25			
Complete matrix analogies	KMT		33			26	
Repeat spoken words	MVM			30	28		30
Retrieve word for concept	KRI		29	55			
Retrieve numbers	KAR			34			
Retrieve words of categories	MVF			32			31
Name pictures	MWK	29		38			
Name places and people	KMP		32			25	
Repeat spoken numbers	KMN				64		
Touch silhouettes in order named	KMW				53		
Repeat (imitate) hand movements	KHM				29		
Repeat numbers in reverse order	MNB		28		27		
Assemble parts to match model	KTI					53	
Gestalt closure	KGC					50	
Copy figures	MDD					40	
Draw a child	MDC		36			40	
Repeat spoken syllables	MVM1						53
Repeat spoken sentences	MVM2						52
Follow spoken directions	MD						32
Do two-arm coordination tasks	MAC2						30
Do left-arm coordination tasks	MACL						34
Do right-arm coordination tasks	MACR						32

TABLE 1 (Continued)

Factor intercorrelations

	Gc	Gf	TSR	SAR	Gv	Ga
Gc	100	19	32	34	28	03
Gf	19	100	02	30	28	30
TSR	32	02	100	39	13	05
SAR	34	30	39	100	31	15
Gv	28	28	13	31	100	05
Ga	03	30	05	15	01	100

Note. Gc, crystallized knowledge; Gf, fluid reasoning abilities; TSR, long-term storage/retrieval; SAR, short-term acquisition/retrieval; Gv, visual thinking; Ga, auditory thinking.

Gc: A pattern of achievement and knowledge of a kind that is emphasized in acculturation.

Gf: A pattern of reasoning, seriating, sorting, and classifying.

TSR: A facility in retrieving information stored in long-term memory.

SAR: A pattern involving working memory, immediate awareness, alertness, and retrieval of material apprehended a short time before.

Gv: A facility for visualizing figures and responding appropriately to spatial forms.

Ga: A pattern of skills of listening and responding appropriately to auditory information. (This dimension, incidentally, is related to the auditory measures that Humphreys and his co-workers [Atkin et al., 1977a, 1977b] found to be most notably predictive of school achievement.)

My reason for bringing these factors to your attention is not to argue for these or any other particular interpretations, but rather to point out that although these results represent no more than fanning smoke, they illustrate that we can identify similar segments of smoke consistently under different conditions of analysis at different ages. We can do this in a way that leaves the intercorrelations among the factors not particularly high. More important, the correlations of these factors with other variables—variables obtained at earlier ages, for example—are consistently different. Also important, the factors obtained in samples of young children are similar to factors obtained through objective rotation in samples of adults, and for which, again, the different factors have different, scientifically interesting, correlations with outside variables. Let us turn to a somewhat more detailed look at some of this evidence.

Table 2 contains factor analytic results obtained with auditory variables in a sample of adults. In the studies that preceded the one summarized here, we (Stankov & Horn, 1980) demonstrated that a number of different factors are needed to account for the variability seen in auditory tests of cognitive abilities. The results of these studies have been replicated several times (Stankov, 1980; Stankov & Spilsbury, 1978). We have likened these factors to the primary mental abilities that had been indicated for visual tasks (Ekstrom, French, & Harman, 1979). The second-order dimensions of this table were identified within

TABLE 2

Dimensions Among Auditory and Visual Primary Abilities (N = 241 males)

Primary abilities	Symbol	Second-order factors				
		Ga	aSD	Gc	Gf	Gv
Auditory						
Discrimination among sound patterns	DASP	50			21	
Maintaining and judging rhythms	MaJR	35				29
Temporal tracking of sounds	Tc	29			26	20
Auditory cognition of relations	ACoR	23			24	
Auditory immediate memory	Msa	22			55	
Speech perception: Distraction/ distortion	SPUD		61			
Auditory acuity	Ac		39			
Listening verbal comprehension	Va		30	43		
Visual						
Verbal comprehension	V			50		
Semantic systems	EMS			51		
Semantic relations	CMR			47		
Induction	I			28	26	
Figural relations	CFR				57	
Visualization	Vz				46	24
Figural classes	CFC				20	40
Speed of closure	Cs		22			20
Flexibility of closure	Cf					50
Spatial orientation	S					47

Note. Based on Horn and Stankov (1982). Ga, auditory thinking; aSD, auditory sensory detection ; Gc, crystallized knowledge; Gf, fluid reasoning abilities; Gv, visual thinking.

a study in which such visual primary abilities were sampled along with the auditory primaries we had defined earlier.

The results of this table indicate that five distinct abilities are required to account for the covariabilities among a particular set of first-order factors. We designed our study to examine whether or not these factors would show up in an objectively rotated solution. We found that they did. These segments of smoke appear to be similar to the segments we could identify in samples of children. However one labels these factors and interprets them in detail, the results point to a need to acknowledge evidence of independence in patterns of abilities that psychologists and others accept as indicating intelligence.

The results of Table 3 add to the story. These results are from two studies in which the analyses were done with a variety of measures from the mainstream of research on information processing (e.g., Pelligrini & Glaser, 1979). In line with our studies of auditory abilities, these findings from studies of information processing indicate that we know how to fan smoke to show Gc, Gf, and Gv factors. In line with the childhood study, these results indicate a factor of short-term acquisition-retrieval (SAR) and a factor for retrieving information stored in long-term memory (the TSR dimension).

Speed of thinking, as variously defined, was the focus of the studies on which Table 4 is based. It is widely assumed that speed in solving difficult intellectual problems is virtually equivalent to the quality of thought about such problems, as revealed in, for example, the level of difficulty of the problems solved. In some theories, as discussed previously (Eysenck, 1982; Jensen, 1982), speed of thinking is thought to be the essence of intelligence. Teachers at all levels of education often give speeded tests to measure understanding of course content, presumably under the assumption that speed in dealing with the content measures the same abilities—or the same important abilities—as quality of thought about that content. Questioning this widely held view, however, are results from several different kinds of research. These results indicate that individual differences in speed of thinking are only lowly correlated with individual differences in power of thinking (e.g., Carroll, 1975; Horn, 1982; Horn & Bramble, 1967; Horn & Cattell, 1966; Morrison, 1960; White, 1982).

Artifactual correlations, generated in many studies of speed and power, have contributed to the belief that speed and power are equivalent. Such correlations are brought about partly through failure to define speed and power in operationally independent ways. Time-limit tests have been used to obtain speed scores based on the same items as are used to obtain power measures. In most studies, subjects have

TABLE 3
Dimensions Among Cognitive Processing Variables

Primary ability marker	Symbol	Latent dimensions				
		SAR	TSR	Gc	Gf	Gv
Short-term retention						
Recency (primary memory)	REC	30				
Murdock intercept (primary memory?)	MUI	58				
Primacy (secondary memory)	PRM	46				
Murdock slope (secondary memory)	MSP	56				
Memory span (forward, serial recall)	Ma	57				
Long-term retrieval						
Recall after Mandler sorting	REC		38		35	
Incidental recall	ICM		36		34	
Things fitting a definition	Fe		30	33		
Uses for objects	DMC		56			
Knowledge						
Vocabulary	V			75		
Remote associations	DMT			44	38	
Associations for a word	Fa			53		
Reasoning						
Esoteric word analogies	CMR			72		
Common word analogies	CHR			45	50	
Letter series	I			32	53	
Matrices	CFR				56	
Visualizing						
Paper folding	Vz				44	47
Gestalt closure	Cs				44	38
Reassembling cutouts (Hooper)	RCH				38	38
Matching figures	P					30

Note. Based on two studies by Horn, Donaldson, and Engstrom (1981). SAR, short-term acquisition/retrieval; TSR, long-term storage retrieval; Gc, crystallized knowledge; Gf, fluid reasoning abilities; Gv, visual thinking.

been encouraged to provide answer-choices even when they are not confident they have a correct answer. These conditions force artifactual correlations between measures of speed and power.

In the studies to which I refer in Table 4, these problems were avoided, or at least reduced, by using quite different sets of comparable items to obtain speed and power scores, by measuring power in terms of level of difficulty of problems actually attempted and solved, by mea-

TABLE 4
Dimensions Among Measures of Speed on Intellectual Tasks

Primary ability markers	Latent dimensions			
	Ga	CDS	Gc	Gf
Inspection speed				
Matching figures	77			
Finding a's and numbers	49			
Comparing lists of names	79			
Speed in providing correct answers				
Remote associations	35	55		
Analogies		63		
Letter series		46		
Paper folding		47		
Number correct				
Vocabulary			80	
Esoteric analogies			71	
Remote associations			51	47
Letter series			37	59
Matrices				60
Paper folding				49
Gestalt closure				58

Note. Based on Horn, Donaldson, and Engstrom (1981). Ga, auditory thinking; CDS, correct decision speed; Gc, crystallized knowledge; Gf, fluid reasoning abilities.

suring speed as quickness in actually solving (not merely attempting) problems of moderate difficulty, and by teaching subjects to give no answer to a problem if they are not satisfied that they have a correct answer.

Under these conditions of measurement in samples of adults, speed in obtaining correct answers to intellectual problems of nontrivial difficulty correlates at only a low level with the difficulty of problems correctly solved. A correlation of .20 indicates the typical finding of several studies of different intellectual abilities.

For the present discussion, the results of Table 4 are of use primarily for illustrating that speed of obtaining correct answers—correct decision speed (CDS)—is reliably separate from factors that have a strong claim to the name "intelligence," namely, Gf and Gc. Some people are considerably faster than others in providing correct answers to intellectual problems, but this is not highly indicative of the level of difficulty of problems solved.

This demonstration that CDS is largely independent from Gf and Gc threatens a claim that CRT is the essence of all intellectual abilities.

The research reviewed in Eysenck (1982) suggests that CRT correlates substantially with CDS; results such as those of Table 4 indicate that CDS does not share in all the common variance of other intellectual ability performances; this indicates that CRT, also, does not account for all the common variance among intellectual task performances. Indeed, most of the available evidence (e.g., Horn, 1976) indicates that it is unlikely that CRT is highly predictive of other intellectual abilities, although it is correlated with these other abilities.

The 11 reliable subtests of the Wechsler Adult Intelligence Scales (Wechsler, 1939), or WAIS, provide a well-known sample of abilities that are (believed to be) central to intelligence. We (McArdle & Horn, 1988) have done structural equation modeling analyses of the WAIS subscales in many large and distinct samples of subjects. We asked, in effect: "Can these subtests represent a compound model of intelligence?" We found that models that fit the data vary from one sample to another, but in every sample reliably independent abilities are indicated for the WAIS subtests. A one-common-factor model will not come close to providing a fit. This result is illustrated in Figure 1. The chi-square for fit (in a typical sample) is roughly 20 times as large as

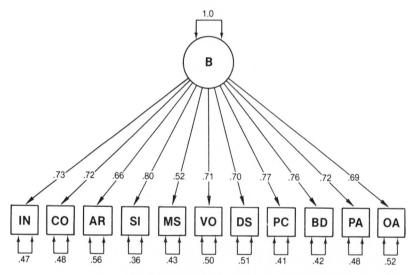

FIGURE 1. Fit for a single common factor for WAIS variables (chi-square = 2982, df = 152, Z = 60). Abbreviations of Wechsler Tests: IN, information; CO, comprehension; AR, arithmetic; SI, similarities; MS, memory span; VO, vocabulary; DS, digit symbol; PC, picture completion; BD, block design; PA, picture arrangement; OA, object assembly.

the degrees of freedom. Such results indicate that we are dealing with abilities for which the distributions, although positively correlated, are independent.

Moreover, although the Wechsler scales provide a widely used sample of intellectual abilities, this is only a very limited sample of the full Milky Way of intellectual abilities. If a one-factor model will not fit the narrow WAIS sample of abilities, it can hardly be expected to fit a sample that represents the full repertoire of human abilities to which Humphreys has referred.

Developmental Findings

The results of Figure 2 illustrate how the mixture model of intelligence, coupled with an assumption that the same g is measured in different mixtures, can create confusion. From young adulthood to old age there is (on the average, across many individuals) a monotonic decrease in some intellectual abilities and a monotonic increase in other abilities. Each of these kinds of abilities is a part of first-principal component and other (IQ) mixture-measures of intelligence. If a mixture-measure happens to be loaded with the abilities that decline with age, then investigators using that measure can argue that intelligence declines with age in adulthood; if most of a mixture-measure is made up of abilities for which there is aging increase, those who use that measure can argue that intelligence increases with age in adulthood; if the two kinds of abilities are about equally weighted in a mixture, then the pronouncement can be that intelligence reaches a plateau of growth in adulthood.

Several variations on these themes have been played in the published literature, with resulting controversy and effort to explain the so-called "contradictory" results. For example, many pages in the literature of adult development have been devoted to explanations for a belief that cross-sectional studies show aging decrease in intelligence while longitudinal results do not. This characterization of results is wrong on several counts (Horn & Donaldson, 1980), but one important count is that the apparent contradiction is created, at least in part, from the use of mixture-measures that were different in longitudinal studies from the mixture-measures in cross-sectional studies. The use of mixture-measures can create more subtle confusions than are illustrated by this example (Horn & Donaldson).

The results of Figures 3 through 6 illustrate other features of mixture-measures. The results on which these figures are based indicate independence among elementary abilities which, however, have some

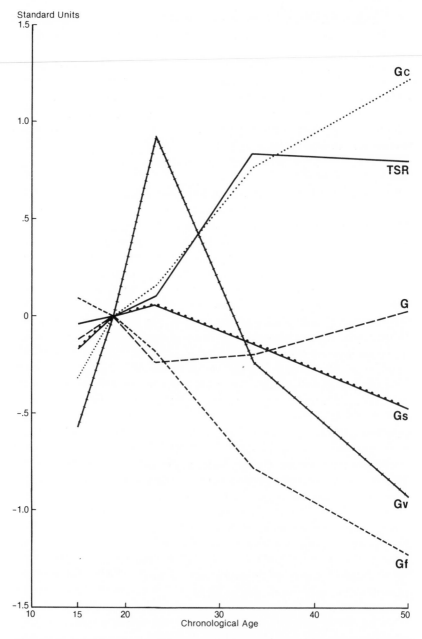

FIGURE 2. Adulthood age differences in dimensions of human intellect. Gc, crystallized knowledge; TSR, long-term storage-retrieval; G, omnibus intelligence; Gs, inspection speediness; Gv, visual thinking; Gf, fluid reasoning abilities.

claim to being regarded as among the major processes of intellectual abilities.

The rationale for the analyses of the studies of Figures 3–6 is illustrated in Figure 3. Here the prima-facie case is indicated for a claim that the aging decline of intelligence is due to aging loss of simple processes, such as are indicated by visual discriminations (vSD), short-term memory (SAR), and speed of discriminating (CDS).

Consider the visual discrimination process, vSD. Measured using procedures developed by Broadbent (1966), this indicates the breadth of a person's immediate awareness of stimuli. It is reasonable to suppose that if such awareness were lacking, there would be consequent distortion of perception in problems of the kind one must solve to score well on measures of Gf reasoning (i.e., a form of intelligence). Thus, if loss of visual-discrimination capacities occurred with aging, then this might be the underlying cause for any corresponding loss seen in Gf. The curve for decline of vSD, as shown in Figure 3, establishes the prima-facie case. Because the decline of vSD is about the same as the decline for Gf-reasoning, it appears that the decline of the latter could result from the decline of the former. Missing in such reasoning, however, is a demonstration that the decline of vSD accounts for the decline of Gf.

When this missing link is introduced by controlling for the part of Gf decline that can be accounted for with vSD decline, the results (illustrated in Figure 4) provide no support for a hypothesis that loss of sensory function is responsible for loss of the intellectual capacities represented by Gf-reasoning. Control for decline of vSD in the decline of Gf does not bring about a significant change: the change from 3.75 to 3.33 units of decline per decade is not significant. This same kind of result was obtained with a measure of auditory sensory discrimination.

Shown in Figure 5 are results suggesting that when there is control for short-term memory (SAR) and/or the abilities of organizing information in encoding (EOG), as measured using a paradigm developed by George Mandler (1968), the decline curve for Gf is significantly reduced (from 3.75 to 1.66 or 1.87 units of decline per decade). Such results support a hypothesis that individual and aging differences in Gf-reasoning involve, in part, an elementary process of immediate memory and encoding organization. The SAR factor is broader than working memory, which we equate with elementary span of apprehension.

The results for EOG and SAR are not independent. Indeed, EOG can be viewed as a component or subprocess of SAR. Our results

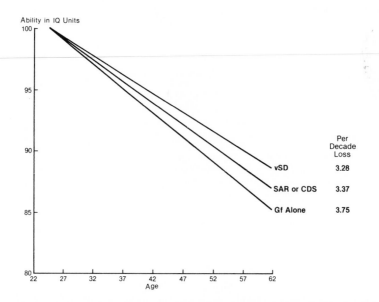

FIGURE 3. Aging decline of four variables: vSD, visual sensory detectors; SAR, short-term acquisition-retrieval; CDS, correct decision speed; Gf, fluid reasoning abilities.

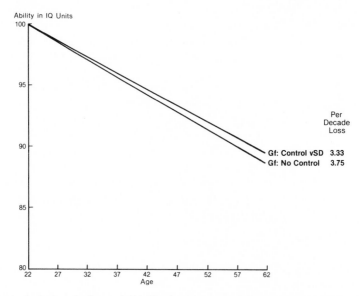

FIGURE 4. Aging decline of Gf (fluid reasoning abilities) after control of vSD (visual sensory detectors).

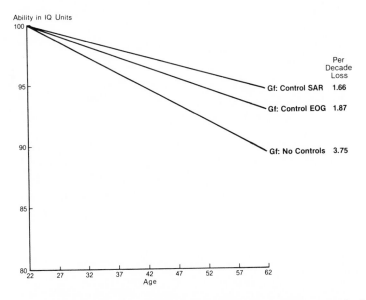

FIGURE 5. Aging decline of Gf (fluid reasoning abilities) after control of SAR (short-term acquisition-retrieval) and EOG (encoding organization).

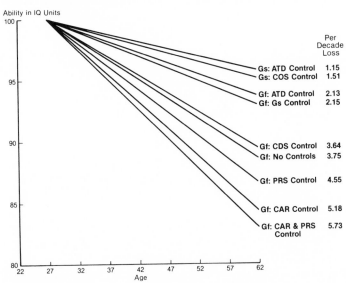

FIGURE 6. Aging decline of Gf (fluid reasoning abilities) and Gs (inspection speediness) after control of particular variables: CDS, correct decision speed; ATD, attention division; COS, concentration on slowness; PRS, persistence; CAR, carefulness.

indicate, however, that control for EOG produces roughly the same reduction in the decline curve for Gf as is produced by SAR (varying a bit from one study to another, as seen in Horn, Donaldson, & Engstrom, 1981). Adding one of these controls to the other does not significantly increase the effect. The suggestion is that EOG is the major element of SAR that is associated with the aging decline of Gf-reasoning.

This is not to say, however, that EOG accounts for all the variance in SAR or all the aging decline of SAR or of SAR in Gf. EOG accounts for only the part of SAR in Gf that declines with age, and only about one-half the aging decline of SAR, as such.

Several findings are illustrated by the results summarized in Figure 6. First, these results indicate the extent to which the decline of Gf can be described in terms of aging changes in speed of performance.

As mentioned in the discussion of factor analytic results, an interesting finding of our studies suggests that speed in obtaining correct answers to problems of nontrivial difficulty (CDS) has very little relation to the level of difficulty with which one copes in dealing with the reasoning problems that define Gf. Results depicted in Figure 6 tell this story again, this time in terms of development: control for CDS has very little influence on the decline curve for Gf (i.e., the change of the decline curve is from 3.75 to 3.64, which is not significant).

In contrast to control for CDS, control for a simple factor of inspection speediness, Gs, does account for some of the aging decline of Gf. The change from 3.75 to 2.15 units of decline per decade is significant.

The results thus suggest that the speed of intellectual functioning that is represented by Gs is implicated in the quality of reasoning measured in Gf. Such findings support a refinement of the hypotheses of Jensen and others writing in the Eysenck (1982) book. The refined hypotheses stipulate that Gs is an element of Gf.

These findings are also consistent with results on which Birren (1974) has based theory stipulating that loss of speed of intellectual functioning is the principal feature of decline of intellectual abilities with aging in adulthood.

We have obtained results that question the notion that speediness, per se, is the culprit responsible for the loss of Gf. Indeed, our reasoning runs the other way: that loss of elementary processes of Gf-reasoning capacity results in slowness of intellectual functioning.

As shown in the top part of Figure 6, most of the aging decline of Gs itself is accounted for by control of capacities for maintaining close concentration (COS) and dividing attention (ATD). When COS and ATD are controlled in Gf-reasoning, there is control also for the decline of Gs and the associated decline of Gf. The part of Gf decline that is associated with Gs is accounted for by decline of capacities represented by COS and ATD.

The summary of Figure 6 suggests that the decline of Gf-reasoning does not result because older adults are more careful and persistent than younger adults. To the contrary. These results add to the reasoning that slowness of thinking comes about as difficulties of Gf-reasoning occur and are recognized by the person.

We find that older adults work longer than younger adults before abandoning a difficult problem. In the power tests used to measure Gf, the subjects are taught that some problems do not have solutions; they are taught that when a problem that seems to be unsolvable is encountered in the test, one should put a dash in the space for the answer and go on to the next problem. Under the press of such instructions, adults will abandon difficult problems that do have solutions (as viewed by the test constructors), and measures of the level of difficulty of problems attempted and solved can be obtained. Under these conditions, too, we obtain a measure of the average (over many problems) amount of time a person will work on a problem before deciding that the problem is unsolvable. This is the measure labeled PRS (persistence) in Figure 6. PRS increases as age increases in adulthood: older persons work longer than younger persons before abandoning a difficult problem.

Older adults also give fewer incorrect answers to problems of non-trivial difficulty. The number of incorrect answers accumulated over several tests given under speeded conditions is the CAR (carefulness) variable of Figure 6. Several years ago, Fruchter (1950, 1953) showed that CAR measures something different from what is measured with a number-correct score. The results of Horn and Bramble (1967) indicate that it is useful to accumulate the CAR score over several different kinds of ability tests. Then CAR measures a fairly pervasive tendency to err on the side of slowness in favor of being sure that only correct answers are given. Older adults, more commonly than younger adults, adopt this strategy.

CAR and PRS are reflected in slowness of performance in timed tests, particularly if the respondent is given no opportunity to provide an "abandon" response in problems for which no solution is found. Because older adults score higher than younger adults on CAR and PRS, it is reasonable to suppose that older adults score lower than younger adults on Gf-reasoning primarily because they work more slowly and thus get fewer problems correct. Our power measures of Gf are not counts of how many problems are solved, however; they are averages of the difficulty levels of problems attempted (i.e., not abandoned) and correctly solved. When Gf is measured in this way, and persistence and carefulness are controlled in the decline of Gf, the decline is not reduced, it is increased, as can be seen in the results of Figure 6. The findings thus indicate that carefulness and persistence are qualities that enable older adults to perform better on power measures of Gf than they would perform if these qualities were not allowed to operate: when the qualities associated with CAR and PRS are removed by statistical control, there is significant increase in the aging decline of Gf-reasoning.

As concerns the main point of this essay, the importance of the findings I have just reviewed is not to be found in particular results, but in the repeated indications that what we see as intelligence, and tend to regard as whole, is in fact a mosaic of many distinct units. In the sense in which Cronbach has so eloquently described construct validity in this volume, each of these units can be expected to have a construct validity of its own. To work out the science of these validities is a proper job for future research.

Table 5 adds another wrinkle to the evidence outlined previously. The table contains a summary of results from analyses in which several different sets of variables were controlled simultaneously in study of

TABLE 5
Summary of Processes Involved in Decline of Gf
Over the "Vital Years" of Adulthood

Process label	Symbol	Brief description of process
Concentration	COS	Maintaining close attention, as in very slow behavior
Encoding organization	EOG	Classifying incoming information in ways that facilitate subsequent recall
Incidental memory	ICM	Remembering small things (i.e., things that would seem to be insignificant)
Eschewing irrelevancies	EIR	Not attending to what has proved to be irrelevant
Dividing attention	ATD	Attending to other things while remembering a given thing
Working memory	MSB	Holding several distinct ideas in mind at once
Hypothesizing	HYP	Forming ideas about what is likely
Inspection speediness	Gs	Speed in "finding" and "comparing"

Note. Based on Horn, Donaldson, and Engstrom (1981). Choose your favorite three: Almost any three will do the job of all under crossvalidation.

the aging decline of Gf-reasoning. An important conclusion derived from these analyses is that different sets of three or four control variables produce essentially the same result, and that no more than four control variables are needed to produce the effect—aging decline accounted for—produced by all the variables. Such results indicate that there is overlap in the measurements obtained with different variables. Ostensibly different operations of measurement get at the same basic intellectual processes. Operationally independent measures such as working memory, concentration, dividing attention, inspection speediness, etc., do not carry entirely independent variance in accounting for the aging loss of Gf. The same can be said for several other combinations of four of the variables shown in the table.

Such results will not surprise researchers who do multiple-variable analyses, but many researchers still do not do such analyses. They should. Results such as those of Table 5 indicate that although various forms of attention, concentration, speediness, etc., can be defined operationally in ways that seem to indicate that they would measure quite distinct processes, it will be found that they do not. This is the other side of the argument that g is all; ostensibly different paradigms usually do pertain to (i.e., measure) some of the same things. Moreover, there are usually several different ways to talk about three or four basic processes that can account for a particular outcome (Horn, 1982, 1985b; Horn et al., 1981). This is one reason why we should not get carried away with the explanation of any particular study. This is why, too, we should not be overly impressed with results from tinkering with modeling analyses until a particular configuration is shown "to fit the data very well" (Horn & McArdle, 1980). We have shown that tinkering with random data (Horn, 1967) and random tinkering with real data (Horn & Knapp, 1973, 1974) can lead to results that psychologists will accept as fitting data very well.

Another important point is illustrated in Table 5. This is the finding that although the processes of the table account for much of the aging decline of Gf-reasoning, they do not account for all of it. The precise proportion of the decline that is accounted for by different sets of processes varies from study to study—partly as a function of the reliabilities of the measures and the extent of the variability in the subject sample—but, roughly, only about one-half of the aging loss of Gf can be reliably accounted for with variables of the kind that are illustrated in Table 5. There is much about Gf, and the aging decline of this complex function, that has yet to be described.

Other Major Features of Cognitive Abilities

The results outlined in the previous section of this paper indicate that Gf is a mixture of separate processes in the same sense, formally, as general intelligence is a mixture. No compound theory of Gf has been constructed. Gc, also, is a mixture. Yet Gf and Gc represent broadly different sets of intellectual capacities (and each of these sets might, with justification, be called intelligence). Gf and Gc have different courses of development over the life span. Each is developmentally different from Gv, visual intelligence; Ga, auditory intelligence; SAR, short-period apprehension and retrieval; TSR, long-term storage and retrieval; and Gs and CDS. But each is subject to the same criticisms I leveled at theories of general intelligence. Each is a mixture. All the major "intelligences"—Gv, Ga, SAR, TSR, and Gs—are mixtures.

These ideas about intelligence are rather like ideas one can have about a ragbag that contains other ragbags. In research on human cognition most of the last 80 years has been spent studying the big ragbag that we now see contains other ragbags, within which there are yet other ragbags. For the next 80 years there are good reasons to move away from earlier preoccupations and devote most research to study of the bags within the big bag. That big bag is not a proper unit for analyzing its contents.

The ragbags of Gc, Gf, Gv, Ga, Gs, SAR, and TSR represent much of the human variability identified as indicating intelligence. There are, however, important pockets of variation that are not well represented by these concepts.

Gc is the most heterogenous of the ragbags within the big bag. It includes knowledge in all of many areas that are regarded as separate disciplines in schools and colleges—history, the arts, mathematics, the physical sciences, the social sciences, business and economics, etc. Each of these areas of knowledge could be identified as an important factor of intellectual ability in much the same way as TSR is identified as such a factor. In educational guidance, particularly, there are good reasons for distinguishing such factors of knowledge. The model representing the Educational Testing Service theory of intelligence includes such factors.

A quantitative factor, in particular, is often distinguished in educational and vocational guidance and prediction. By the time children have reached junior high school in our culture, individual differences in a broad range of quantitative skills—a Gq dimension—can be seen to stand apart from individual differences in the broad pattern of other knowledge that characterizes Gc. Looked at in terms of development in childhood and in terms of predictions in academic and vocational settings, Gq has construct validity that is different from the construct validities of Gf, SAR, TSR, Gv, Ga, Gs, and Gc-sans-quantitative-knowledge. Gq represents an important feature of cognitive functioning.

Response to novelty (RTN) also appears to be an important feature of cognitive functioning that is not well represented by the concepts discussed earlier in this essay. I was at a meeting recently in which Joseph Fagan displayed an impressive array of evidence indicating that, in infants, RTN (or is it better labeled preference for novelty?) is indicative of what is meant by intelligence in young children. In his work, a typical correlation between measures of RTN in infancy and omnibus measures of intelligence, obtained in childhood, was about .40.

At the same meeting, Robert Sternberg suggested that RTN is a motivational concept. According to this view, a child is programmed to respond to rewards, becomes bored with the usual, finds this to be unpleasant, and finds that the novelty of dealing with new complexities is a reward that moves one away from the unpleasant condition. If response to novelty is not punished over the course of development, it will continue to be rewarding and one will move from seeking novelty that resolves one complexity, and becoming bored with that, to seeking more novelty at a higher level of complexity. In this way, through reward, the child can move to ever-higher degrees of resolving complexity. Resolving complexities is an important feature of human intelligence. Michael Commons argued eloquently for this position.

Thus, RTN appears to be an important feature of human thinking—at least in infants and children. By no means all of what is meant by intellectual functioning is indicated by such measures. RTN accounts for some, not all, of the variance of what is measured in omnibus measures of general intelligence; it accounts for an even smaller portion of the variance of all intellectual abilities.

Intelligence in Perspective

Sometimes it is argued that general intelligence is indicated by extensive evidence suggesting that the intercorrelations among ability measures are almost always positive (e.g., Horn, 1967). Guilford (1964) questioned this argument with results showing that the intercorrelations among some intellectual abilities are near zero or possibly even negative. Even if the intercorrelations are always positive, it does not follow that this is indicative of general intelligence. Humphreys has reminded us that Godfrey Thomson (e.g., 1919, 1948) demonstrated that positive manifold among variable intercorrelations is not compelling support for a hypothesis that the variables represent a unitary concept. There are many ways in which quite different influences can overlap to produce manifestations that are positively correlated but do not represent a functional unity.

Positivity among intercorrelations does not indicate the boundaries of a domain of function. Many intellectual abilities are positively correlated, to be sure, but many nonintellectual variables are positively correlated with intellectual abilities. For example, measures of athletic skills usually are positively correlated with intellectual abilities. One does not argue on this basis that athletic skills are necessary components of general intelligence (although in work with infants motoric skills may be included in omnibus measures that are treated as measures of intelligence). It is clear that for many scientific and practical reasons athletic abilities and cognitive abilities often should be distinguished. Similarly, although artistic and musical abilities, preferences, motivation, and temperament are correlated positively with intellectual abilities, there are good practical and scientific reasons for distinguishing these domains from the domain of cognitive abilities.

Positive intercorrelations among broad samples of human attributes may call for a concept of general organization of behavior, as in Hebb's (1949) theory. There may be psychologists who would argue that such a theory is a theory of intelligence. A model representing such a theory would not be a model for Spearman's (1927) theory of g, however, for the same reason that a model for an omnibus test of IQ is not a model for g. A theory that general organization of behavior is intelligence is an extreme form of theory that emphasizes the term "general" in general intelligence. Such theory may be useful for some purposes, but for cognitive research of the future it is probably not a good guide.

Another powerful argument in favor of retaining the concept of general intelligence stems from evidence that often in prediction one linear combination of separate abilities works as well as another involving a different set of separate abilities (Hunter, 1986; Hunter, Schmidt, & Jackson, 1982; McNemar, 1964). Usually, no more than about five separate tests will have significant beta-weights in the prediction of almost any criterion. Frequently, with no significant decrease in prediction, one test can be replaced with another test (Hunter, 1986). A spatial test, for example, can replace a memory test with no significant decrease in the multiple correlation. This is often true even when the criterion is judged to be one that involves the abilities of the replaced test—when, for example, the criterion is thought to involve spatial abilities and a memory test replaces a spatial test. There are exceptions to this kind of finding, but the result is prevalent, as Hunter emphasizes. It is said to indicate that only a general factor among diverse measures is required in prediction. Such a general factor is often interpreted as general intelligence.

A major difficulty with this line of argument is that criterion measures are not usually differentiated at all, or are not differentiated in the manner of the predictor battery. The criterion typically is measured as a global rating or with a global, omnibus test. If behavior ratings are used to identify the criterion, usually the raters are not trained to distinguish different abilities in the performance of a job. Rarely is there any evidence that raters can or do distinguish different abilities in a criterion. If several tests are used to obtain a criterion measure, typically the tests are not designed to measure the same separate functions that enter in the predictor battery, and usually the separate criterion measures are combined into one measure in any case. The criterion measures of different jobs appear to be similar. Evidence is not presented to show that criteria are distinct along separate ability dimensions of the kind that are entered in predictor batteries.

In these ways, criteria are defined as hodgepodge general factors. It is not surprising that under these conditions one hodgepodge predictor battery predicts hodgepodge criteria as well as another. Such evidence does not indicate whether or not criteria involve distinct factors that can best be predicted with distinct predictors. The different hodgepodges of the predictors are equivalent to different omnibus IQ tests. They do not represent a model of Spearman's theory of g any more than first-principal components represent this model. Such evidence of predictor studies is largely tangential to questions about the nature of human intellect.

It is often argued that evidence from behavior genetics forces acceptance of a theory of general intelligence. It seems, in fact, that some researchers have emotional needs to believe that "g exists and is inherited."

Jensen (1973) has likened the heritability of what he calls g or IQ (really just different mixture measures) to the heritability of a polygenetic trait. He has referred to the quasi-normal distribution of IQ measures and the regression of IQ scores for related people—as from parent to child—as evidence in support of this theory. These arguments are misleading.

The alleles of perhaps nine genes, transmitted independently, may add up to determine a polygenetic trait such as skin color: if you get none of these genetic determiners, you are sheet-white; if you get all nine, you are jet-black; the colors of most people are between these extremes, distributed in accordance with a symmetrical binomial, an approximation to a normal distribution.

There could be an attribute called intelligence that conforms to this kind of theory, but a finding of a normal distribution for measures of IQ neither supports nor threatens such a theory. What are added to produce a normal distribution for a polygenetic trait? Gene determiners. What are added to produce a normal distribution of IQ scores? Responses to items. There is no known isomorphism between these two kinds of elements — alleles of genes and responses to items — and there are no compelling reasons to suppose that such isomorphism might exist. The influences that determine which items are put into an IQ test are not at all similar to the influences that determine gene selection in reproduction.

The adding of item responses in a psychological test produces a linear composite. If the items of such a composite are not highly correlated and/or if the difficulties of the items are distributed in a bell-shaped manner, the measures produced by these operations of measurement will be distributed in a bell-shaped, approximately normal manner, as Humphreys demonstrated to me when I was in graduate school (Horn, 1963). This will occur regardless of whether the measured attribute is determined by gene influence, by the environment, by both, or indeed, by chance. If the items of a linear composite measure were dichotomous, for example, and people chose their answers to the items by a flip of a coin, the distribution for the resulting linear composite scores would be a symmetrical binomial, approximately normal. Findings of approximately normal distributions for IQ measures merely indicate that linear composite measures are obtained under conditions of low item intercorrelations and symmetrical distribution of item difficulties. Such findings say nothing about combinations of gene influences. They neither support nor threaten a hypothesis stipulating that the underlying attribute — the attribute of theory — is genetically determined. A trait produced by genes can be distributed in a thoroughly non-normal way when the distribution for a linear composite measure of that trait is thoroughly normal. Similarly, a polygenetic trait that is normally distributed at the genotypic level can be measured in a manner that yields a thoroughly non-normal distribution. A finding of normal distribution for a composite measure of IQ is irrelevant to claims that the measures represent a unitary polygenetic trait.

Environmental influences can be thought to combine independently and thus to produce a normal distribution. But in this case, too, a finding of a normal distribution for a composite measure neither supports nor refutes a claim that the trait is determined by environmental factors.

Regression to the mean of high or low measures of IQ in one class of people (e.g., children), relative to similar measures on another class of people (e.g., parents), does not support claims that the measures are genetically determined (nor does it threaten such a theory). Such regression is no more than a restatement of the fact that the two arrays of measures are less than perfectly correlated. Such regression provides no more support for a polygenetic theory of intelligence than it provides for a theory that the environments of related people are similar. The less-than-perfect correlation could occur because variables derive from different but overlapping sets of genes, but it can just as well occur because variables derive from different but overlapping kinds of environmental influences—or influences associated with measurement, per se. A finding of regression to the mean of children's IQ scores relative to their parents' IQ scores is no more evidence in favor of a polygenetic theory of intelligence than it is evidence that IQ scores are determined by environmental influences. The finding does not contribute to evidence that there is a unitary trait of intelligence.

One should not read these arguments as saying that there is no evidence to support hypotheses that intellectual capacities are, to some extent, inherited. That is not the argument. There are intractable problems of separating environmental and genetic determinants in studies with humans, but in this respect research in behavior genetics is no different from research in other important areas of the behavioral sciences. With qualifications—recognition of the impossibility of fully separating environmental and genetic influences—well-designed behavior genetics analyses of differences in ability correlations between identical twins, fraternal twins, ordinary siblings, parents and children, other related people, and unrelated people, living together and living apart through formative years of development, support the commonsense notion that intellectual traits are in some degree inherited (Loehlin, 1977; Loehlin, Lindzey, & Spuhler, 1975). The arguments of previous paragraphs do not dispute this evidence. Those arguments simply point to the fact that findings of normal distribution for IQ, particular correlations between IQ scores for related people, and regression to the mean for such correlations do not constitute evidence of heritability.

The evidence of heritability for omnibus measures of IQ is not good evidence for a claim that there is a unitary trait of general intelligence. Analogies to facial beauty may help to illustrate this point. Individual differences in omnibus measures of intelligence are analogous to individual differences in global assessments of facial beauty.

One can define facial beauty—using features of nose shape, space between eyes, the turn of the lips, etc.—in a manner that yields a positive manifold for the correlations among the defining features, and one can calculate a first-principal component to combine these features, just as intelligence can be defined as a mixture of abilities for which there is a positive manifold among the intercorrelations and for which a first-principal component can be calculated. There is a reasonable agreement in our society about who has, and who does not have, facial beauty, and such agreements would probably correlate positively with a first-principal component among facial features of beauty, just as reasonable agreement can be found in ratings of who is and who is not intelligent, and such ratings correlate positively with the first-principal component among ability measures. But when we examine what goes into the principal component and ratings for beauty—as viewed through physiology, biology, genetics, sociology, anthropology, and psychology—we find that it is unlikely that what we see in facial beauty is a unitary or polygenetic trait. At the level of measurement, we find beautiful faces that have long, thin noses—Meryl Streep, for example—and beautiful faces that have short, wide noses—Sally Fields. At the level of genetics, we know that several distinct features of noses, eyes, cheeks, coloring, etc., are inherited independently. These distinct features yield distinctly different physiognomies that we identify with the single label, "beautiful face." If we consider beauty from an anthropological or sociological perspective, we realize that what is highly regarded as beautiful in one society is not so highly regarded in another society.

Evidence indicating heritability for a mixture-measure of intelligence can support a claim that the mixture is genetically determined, just as similar evidence can support a claim that beauty is genetically determined, but this evidence is not pointedly relevant to the argument that the measures represent unitary, polygenetic traits. In recognizing that beauty, per se, is not what one inherits, one need not deny that various features of beauty are genetically determined and that mixtures—quite different mixtures—of these traits can have high heritability. If the different features that go into assessments of beauty are separately inherited, as is likely, then different mixtures of these features in different configurations of beauty will indicate heritability. Under such conditions, different definitions of beauty can yield similar heritabilities. Similarly, if the distinct components that go into mixture-measures of intelligence are separately inherited, then the heritabilities for different mixtures can be high and numerically similar. This is not evidence that there is any functional unity in any of the mixtures.

The complexity of faces is analogous to the complexity of brains that lie behind faces. Brains are similar to faces: at first, they can all look the same, but on closer examination, it can be seen that each one is different. The brain is often regarded as the basis for intelligence. The thought is that a unitary, mass action of the brain underlies and accounts for a unitary attribute of intelligence. But just as facial beauty is not unitary, so individual differences in brains and neurological function are not unitary. A theory of mass action of the brain is probably not a good analogical theory for intellectual functioning.

Mass action is no longer a major guiding light of neurological research. The brain supports several quite separate functions (Cowan, 1979; Dunant & Israel, 1985; Eccles, 1977; Hubel, 1979; Iverson, 1979; Kety, 1979; Thompson, 1985). Most modern-day research is directed at understanding these functions.

There are many distinguishable neurotransmitters, for example, and these are not distributed diffusely throughout the brain, but are located in particular centers and along separate pathways. The norepinephrine, dopamine, and serotonin systems play quite different roles in the aging of human abilities and in other dramas of human development and function. The norepinephrine system centers around the locus ceruleus, branching largely into the hypothalamus and adjacent areas. It is closely associated with arousal of neurological functions—arousal such as appears to be manifested in Gf (for review, see Iverson, 1979; and Horn, 1982, 1985b). The dopamine system, on the other hand, seems to be centered around the substantia nigra and corpus striatum. It is linked to a complex of events associated with such outcomes as Parkinson's disease. The serotonin system also has a distinct place of function in the brain and distinct associations in behavior. See Thompson (1985) for a detailed but introductory description of these neurotransmitter systems.

Anatomical analyses indicate distinct functions associated with different sections of the brain. The left and right hemispheres, for example, are associated with different aspects of intellectual function, and a growing mound of evidence suggests that the top-to-bottom and front-to-back divisions of the brain are even more important indicators of distinct ability functions than is the left-to-right division (Blackwood & Corsellis, 1976; Bourne, Ekstrand, & Dominowski, 1971; Prohovnik, 1980).

Brains involve distinct components, each based on different genetic determinants and each having a different role to play in sensation, perception, learning, and the manifestations we see as abilities. Different configurations of these distinct features produce different capacities, and different perceptions and cognitions of the same information. Just as there are many different configurations of facial features that provide examples of a "beautiful face," so there are many configurations of features of brains that exemplify the "good brain" that might be thought to underlie good intelligence. Language can unite this diversity in the single word "intelligence" much in the way that it can unite quite different facial features in the word "beautiful," but we should not think that this use of language represents scientific laws of function. Studies of how the brain functions, and of different brains, do not support any known theory of general intelligence. To the contrary.

It is sometimes argued that it really does not matter whether or not we stick with the mixture concept of intelligence: research with IQ and principal component measures can net worthwhile results. So why all the fuss?

It is true, of course, that worthwhile results can be obtained with research based on mixture-measures. Much of what is currently known about human abilities was learned under the press of such research. Even today, some questions can be effectively addressed with mixture-measures (Humphreys, 1981; Jensen, 1984). As McNemar (1964) pointed out, conglomerate measures can be efficient and practical predictors of conglomerate criteria.

But having acknowledged this, it remains true that for many scientific and practical purposes, mixture-measures are inadequate and can be misleading. When different (nonequivalent) elements are treated as equivalent, inconsistent findings are likely to emerge, and much wasted effort can be generated. Consistent operational definitions are needed to establish dependable scientific laws. Such definitions should be based on evidence and plausibilities that are indicated by evidence. The evidence of today indicates that there are several distinct intelligences, each having distinct genetic, physiological, and environmental determinants, distinct courses of development, distinct predictive validities, and distinct implications for understanding human functions, human adjustment, human adaptation, and human happiness. The distinctions surely can make a difference. At the very least, it is premature to suppose they do not.

Summary

The evidence thus adds up. Humans evince many cognitive abilities, and these can be grouped in many ways. Any one of these groupings might be said to indicate intelligence as this is defined in one or another verbal definition and the preferences of a particular author. It is unlikely that any of these groupings corresponds to a functional unity. It is doubtful that there is functional unity among most of the abilities that are said to indicate intelligence. Although the word "intelligence" can continue to be useful in everyday language, this use does not represent sound scientific theory.

The domain of intellectual abilities can be described at any of several different levels of abstraction. In considering which level is best, objectives should be carefully considered. In some work, rather narrow concepts and measures should be used. In other work, broad concepts, such as outlined in this essay, will be of most value. For the next few years, particularly in developmental psychology, probably it will be most worthwhile to work with broad concepts. As the overall picture begins to be seen clearly, it will become most useful to explore the details of particular cognitive processes.

Figure 7 suggests that the broad concepts discussed in this chapter stand in hierarchical relation to each other. Each of the abilities of this figure is broad enough to represent what has been described as intelligence. Yet each is distributed independently in individual differences. It is likely that the abilities derive from different environmental and genetic determinants and have different implications for refined predictions of outcomes.

There is reason to believe that Gf and Gc, for example, derive from separate sets of genes, the influences of which are manifested early in development (Horn, 1985a). Piaget (1947, 1973) may have identified such early manifestations in his descriptions of assimilation and accommodation. The suggestion is that from an early age some individuals are best structured to readily bring information into their cognitive systems, whereas others are best structured to mull and reorganize information that (less readily) enters their systems. Such predilections shape individual development from infancy onward.

Many environmental influences must pile on top of genetic shaping and produce much variation in particular abilities. The independence we see in the broad abilities of Gf, Gc, Gv, Ga, SAR, TSR, and Gs (and possibly CDS, Gq, and RTN) reflects independent environmental influences, independent genetic determiners, and the independence of these two broad classes of influences.

Yet it is true that to some extent genetic and environmental determiners must work together. Genetic influences will, in a probabilistic manner, be more highly associated with some environmental patterns than with others. A readiness to bring information into cognitive structures will tend to facilitate the acculturation that results in Gc. Self-

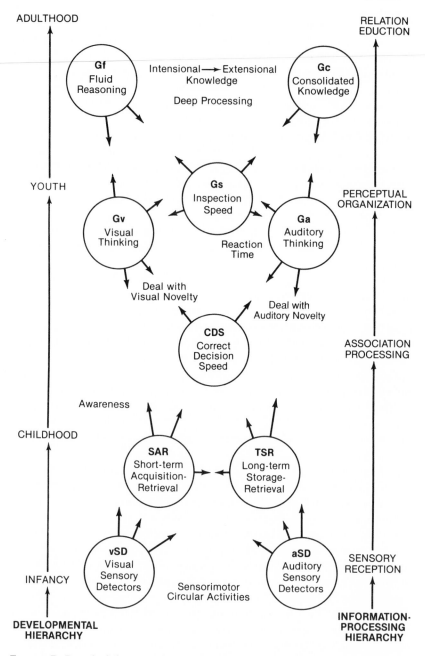

FIGURE 7. Broad abilities within developmental and information-processing hierarchies.

dictated learning experiences, stemming from early readiness to reorganize information, can result in relatively extended development of Gf. Different nutritional and physical injury factors will affect different genetic and learning predilections in different ways. Neurological injuries in adulthood are known to have a more profound influence on Gf than on Gc—at least in the short run of a few years.

These kinds of hypotheses need to be considered for each of the broad abilities for which we have evidence of independence (Cattell, 1971; Vandenberg, 1971). SAR, for example, can stem from genetic factors that are different from those that affect TSR. Different genetic determiners would chart a somewhat different course of optimal and typical development of SAR and TSR over the life span. The same would be true for each of the abilities shown in Figure 7. Each comparison of one of these capacities with the others presents a series of questions about how the distinctions emerge and how they affect adjustment and adaptation.

The hierarchies suggested in Figure 7 are intended to indicate the interdependence among independent capacities. Along an information-processing hierarchy, one can see that often, at least, sensory detection must precede preceptual organization in the expression of an ability; perceptual organization, in turn, often must set the stage for comprehending complex relationships. Along a developmental hierarchy, the organizations of the lower part of the figure emerge before, and influence, emergence of the organizations of the upper part of the figure.

It is true also that the abilities of the upper part of the figure determine expressions of the abilities of the lower part of the figure; the hierarchy of the figure should not be regarded as representing only unidirectional influences.

There is much to learn about the relations suggested in Figure 7. To move ahead with this learning, research should move away from the idea that different conglomerates of abilities represent a singular "something" labeled intelligence. If there is such a singular something that has major features of a sound theory of intelligence—a compound or essence theory—almost certainly it has a narrower operational definition than is implicit in mixture-measures of IQ. It might be shown that a principle of function (e.g., nerve conduction speed, Reed, 1984) binds a particular configuration of basic capacities. Such a narrowed concept of intelligence could be useful. But research to establish such a concept must derive from careful examination of the covarying patterns of different abilities. Such research cannot derive merely from continued faith in the idea of general intelligence.

This chapter illustrates that much of what I have learned since I was a graduate student studying with Lloyd Humphreys has led me to abandon theories about cognition that were most influential in those days. Today, the concept of general intelligence is useful mainly as a contrast—a way of talking about what human thinking is not. It is the anti-image of human intellectual functioning, not the image. For help in developing that view of the matter, as well as for help in improving my thinking in many other ways, I thank Lloyd Humphreys.

REFERENCES

Atkin, R., Bray, R., Davidson, M., Herzberger, S., Humphreys, L., & Selzer, U. (1977a). Ability factor differentiation, grades 5 through 11. *Applied Psychological Measurement, 1,* 65–76.

Atkin, R., Bray, R., Davidson, M., Herzberger, S., Humphreys, L., & Selzer, U. (1977b). Cross-lagged panel analysis of 16 cognitive measures at four grade levels. *Journal for Research in Child Development, 48,* 944–952.

Birren, J. E. (1974). Psychophysiology and speed of response. *American Psychologist, 29,* 808–815.

Blackwood, W., & Corsellis, J. A. (Eds.). (1976). *Greenfield's neuropathology.* London: Arnold.

Bourne, L. F., Ekstrand, B. R., & Dominowski, R. L. (1971). *The psychology of thinking.* Englewood Cliffs, NJ: Prentice-Hall.

Broadbent, D. E. (1966). The well-ordered mind. *American Educational Research Journal, 3,* 281–295.

Carroll, J. B. (1975). *Speed and accuracy of absolute pitch judgments* (Research Bulletin No. RB-75-35). Princeton, NJ: Educational Testing Service.

Carroll, J. B., & Horn, J. L. (1981). On the scientific basis of ability testing. *American Psychologist, 36,* 1012–1020.

Cattell, R. B. (1971). *Abilities: Their structure, growth and action.* Boston: Houghton Mifflin.

Cowan, W. M. (1979). The development of the brain. *Scientific American, 241,* 112–133.

Dunant, Y., & Israel, M. (1985). The release of acetylcholine. *Scientific American, 252,* 58–66.

Eccles, J. C. (1977). *The understanding of the brain.* New York: McGraw-Hill.

Ekstrom, R. B., French, J. W., & Harman, M. H. (1979). Cognitive factors: Their identification and replication. *Multivariate Behavioral Research Monographs, 79*(2).

Eysenck, H. J. (Ed.). (1982). *A model for intelligence.* New York: Springer-Verlag.

Fruchter, B. (1950). Error scores as a measure of carefulness. *Journal of Educational Psychology, 41,* 279–291.

Fruchter, B. (1953). Difference in factor content of rights and wrongs scores. *Psychometrika, 18,* 257–263.

Guilford, J. P. (1964). Zero intercorrelations among tests of intellectual abilities. *Psychological Bulletin, 61,* 401–404.

Hebb, D. O. (1949). *The organization of behavior.* New York: Wiley.

Horn, J. L. (1963). Equations representing combinations of components in scoring psychological variables. *Acta Psychologica, 21,* 184–217.

Horn, J. L. (1965). *Fluid and crystallized intelligence.* Unpublished doctoral dissertation. University of Illinois, Urbana-Champaign.

Horn, J. L. (1967). On subjectivity in factor analysis. *Educational and Psychological Measurement, 27,* 811–820.

Horn, J. L. (1976). Human abilities: A review of research and theory in the early 1970s. *Annual Review of Psychology, 27,* 437–485.

Horn, J. L. (1982). The aging of human abilities. In B. B. Wolman (Ed.), *Handbook of developmental psychology* (pp. 847–870). New York: Prentice-Hall.

Horn, J. L. (1983). Comment croire un homme sage? [On believing a wise man]. *Revue Canadienne de Psycho-Education, 12,* 132–143.

Horn, J. L. (1985a). Intellectual ability concepts. In R. L. Sternberg (Ed.), *Advances in the psychology of human intelligence* (Vol. 3, pp. 35–77). Hillsdale, NJ: Erlbaum.

Horn, J. L. (1985b). Remodeling old models of intelligence: Gf-Gc theory. In B. B. Wolman (Ed.), *Handbook of intelligence* (pp. 462–503). New York: Wiley.

Horn, J. L., & Bramble, W. J. (1967). Second order ability structure revealed in right and wrong scores. *Journal of Educational Psychology, 58,* 115–122.

Horn, J. L., & Cattell, R. B. (1966). Refinement and test of the theory of fluid and crystallized intelligence. *Journal of Educational Psychology, 57,* 253–270.

Horn, J. L., & Donaldson, G. (1980). Cognitive development in adulthood. In O. G. Brim & J. Kagan (Eds.), *Constancy and change in human development* (pp. 445–529). Cambridge, MA: Harvard University Press.

Horn, J. L., Donaldson, G., & Engstrom, R. (1981). Apprehension, memory and fluid intelligence decline in adulthood. *Research on Aging, 3,* 33–84.

Horn, J. L., & Goldsmith, H. (1981). Reader be cautious: *Bias in Mental Testing* by Arthur Jensen. *American Journal of Education, 89,* 305–329.

Horn, J. L., & Knapp, J. R. (1973). On the subjective character of the empirical base of Guilford's structure-of-intellect model. *Psychological Bulletin, 80,* 33–43.

Horn, J. L., & Knapp, J. R. (1974). Thirty wrongs do not make a right: Reply to Guilford. *Psychological Bulletin, 81,* 502–504.

Horn, J. L., & McArdle, J. J. (1980). Perspectives on mathematical/statistical model building (MASMOB) in research on aging. In L. W. Poon (Ed.), *Aging in the 1980s* (pp. 503–541). Washington, DC: American Psychological Association.

Horn, J. L., & Stankov, L. (1982). Auditory and visual factors of intelligence. *Intelligence, 6,* 165–185.

Hubel, D. H. (1979). The brain. *Scientific American, 241,* 44–53.

Humphreys, L. G. (1962). The organization of human abilities. *American Psychologist, 17,* 475–483.

Humphreys, L. G. (1974). The misleading distinction between aptitude and achievement tests. In D. R. Green (Ed.), *The aptitude achievement distinction* (pp. 262–274). Monterey, CA: CTB/McGraw-Hill.

Humphreys, L. G. (1979). The construct of general intelligence. *Intelligence, 3,* 105–120.

Humphreys, L. G. (1981). The primary mental ability. In M. P. Friedman, J. P. Das, & N. O'Connor (Eds.), *Intelligence and learning* (pp. 87–102). New York: Plenum Press.

Hunter, J. (1986). Cognitive ability, cognitive aptitude, job knowledge, and job performance. *Journal of Vocational Behavior, 29,* 340–362.

Hunter, J. E., Schmidt, F. L., & Jackson, G. B. (1982). *Meta-analysis: Cumulating research findings across studies.* Beverly Hills, CA: Sage Press.

Iverson, L. L. (1979). The chemistry of the brain. *Scientific American, 241,* 134–149.

Jensen, A. R. (1973). *Educability and group differences.* New York: Harper & Row.

Jensen, A. R. (1980). *Bias in mental testing.* New York: Free Press.

Jensen, A. R. (1982). Reaction time and psychometric g. In H. J. Eysenck (Ed.), *A model for intelligence* (pp. 93–132). New York: Springer-Verlag.

Jensen, A. R. (1984). Test validity: g versus the specificity doctrine. *Journal of Social and Biological Sciences, 7,* 93–118.

Kaufman, A. S., & Kaufman, N. L. (1983). *Kaufman Assessment Battery for Children (K-ABC).* Circle Pines, MN: American Guidance Service.

Kety, S. S. (1979). Disorders of the human brain. *Scientific American, 241,* 202–218.

Loehlin, J. C. (1977). Psychological genetics from the study of human behavior. In R. B. Cattell & R. M. Dreger (Eds.), *Handbook of modern personality theory* (pp. 163–180). New York: Wiley.

Loehlin, J. C., Lindzey, G., & Spuhler, J. N. (1975). *Race differences in intelligence.* San Francisco: W. H. Freeman.

Longstreth, L. E. (1986). The real and the unreal: A reply to Jensen. *Intelligence, 10,* 181–191.

Longstreth, L. E., & Madigan, S. (1982). Sex differences in the correlation of memory span with scan and other episodic memory tasks. *Intelligence, 6,* 37–56.

Mandler, G. (1968). Organized recall: Individual functions. *Psychonomic Science, 13,* 230–236.

McArdle, J. J., & Horn, J. L. (1988). *Intelligence and aging: A meta-analysis of repeated-measures studies of the WAIS.* In preparation.

McCarthy, D. (1972). *McCarthy Scale of Children's Abilities.* New York: The Psychological Corporation.

McNemar, Q. (1964). Lost: Our intelligence? Why? *American Psychologist, 19,* 871–882.

Morrison, J. R. (1960). *Effects of time limits on the efficiency and factorial composition of reasoning measures.* Unpublished doctoral dissertation, University of Illinois, Urbana-Champaign.

Pelligrini, J. W., & Glaser, R. (1979). Cognitive correlates and components in the analysis of individual differences. In R. Sternberg & K. Detterman (Eds.), *Human intelligence* (pp. 61–88). Norwood, NJ: Ablex.

Piaget, J. (1947). *The psychology of intelligence.* London: Kegan Paul.

Piaget, J. (1973). *The child and reality: Problems of genetic psychology.* New York: Grossman.

Prohovnik, I. (1980). *Mapping brainwork.* Malmo, Sweden: CWK Gleerup.

Reed, T. E. (1984). Mechanism for heritability of intelligence. *Nature, 311,* 417.

Rimoldi, H. J. (1948). Study of some factors related to intelligence. *Psychometrika, 13,* 27–46.

Schmid, J., & Leiman, J. M. (1957). The development of hierarchical factor solutions. *Psychometrika, 22,* 53–61.

Schucard, D. W., & Horn, J. L. (1972). Cortical evoked potentials and measurement of human abilities. *Journal of Comparative and Physiological Psychology, 78,* 59–68.

Spearman, C. (1904). "General intelligence," objectively determined and measured. *American Journal of Psychology, 15,* 201–293.

Spearman, C. (1927). *The abilities of man: Their nature and measurement.* New York: Macmillan.

Stankov, L. (1980). Ear differences and implied cerebral lateralization on some intellective auditory factors. *Applied Psychological Measurement, 4,* 21–38.

Stankov, L., & Horn, J. L. (1980). Human abilities revealed through auditory tests. *Journal of Educational Psychology, 72,* 21–44.

Stankov, L., & Spilsbury, G. (1978). The measurement of auditory abilities of sighted, partially sighted and blind children. *Applied Psychological Measurement, 2,* 491–503.

Thompson, R. F. (1985). *The brain: An introduction to neuroscience.* New York: Freeman.

Thomson, G. A. (1919). On the cause of hierarchical order among correlation coefficients. *Proceedings of the Royal Society, A, 95,* 400–408.

Thomson, G. A. (1948). *The factorial analysis of human abilities* (3d ed.). Boston: Houghton Mifflin.

Thurstone, L. L. (1947). *Multiple factor analysis.* Chicago: University of Chicago Press.

Vandenberg, S. G. (1971). What do we know today about the inheritance of intelligence and how do we know it? In R. Cancro (Ed.), *Intelligence: Genetic and environmental influences* (pp. 182–218). New York: Grune and Stratton.

Wechsler, D. (1939). *The measurement of human intelligence.* Baltimore: Williams and Wilkins.

White, P. O. (1982). Some major components of general intelligence. In H. J. Eysenck (Ed.), *A model for intelligence* (pp. 33–54). New York: Springer-Verlag.

3

Protecting General Intelligence: Constructs and Consequences for Interventions

SANDRA SCARR

In 1971, Lloyd Humphreys defined intelligence as "the entire repertoire of acquired skills, knowledge, learning sets, and generalized tendencies considered intellectual in nature that are available at any one time" (p. 31). Humphreys set two criteria for useful definitions of intelligence: First, that the terms of the definition, in conjunction with other terms in the theory, lead to testable hypotheses; second, that the definition be tied directly to available measuring devices, such as IQ tests. In elaborating his view, Humphreys further defined intelligence as encompassing the totality of cultural acquisitions. He rejected Spearman's notion of "mental energy" in favor of Thomson's multiple bond approach, and chose to discuss intelligence as "a unitary disposition to solve intellectual problems" (1971, p. 32).

Humphreys distinguished his view from an older operationalism (intelligence is what IQ tests measure) by proposing additional criteria for the measurement of intelligence. First, tests should have suitable reliabilities, and they should be intercorrelated to such an extent that their intercorrelations are part of the main distribution of such correlations to qualify as adequate representatives of the domain. By this criterion, so-called culture-fair tests do not qualify. Second, knowledge of the constitutional bases of learning is important, not as a definition of intelligence but as substrates for learning. Third, he distinguishes between intelligence as acquired knowledge, and performance on tests in which the person may not display the knowledge he or she has, a distinction usually made between learning and performance, but made here between acquired knowledge and performance.

Tests measure acquired behavior, not biological substrates, a distinction that Humphreys emphasizes because he believes that test scores

74

are inappropriately used to infer both biological and environmental causation. Although, he says, it is perfectly reasonable to assume that individuals and species differ in the biological and psychosocial underpinnings of their intelligent behavior, test scores are only indirect indices of such differences. Thus, one should be cautious in interpreting the origins of test score differences. Furthermore, test score differences are not designed to assess the causes of differences so much as the nature of those differences.

Big cultural changes, Humphreys notes, make for big changes in test scores. The malleability of average scores on entrance tests across generations is illustrated by the change in armed forces' scores from World Wars I to II and from World War II to 1963: a change of 1.5 standard deviations or the equivalent of 22 IQ points. (Humphreys sounds almost optimistic when he cites these results.) One assumes that general knowledge of the culture spread in these 50 years, through schooling and communications, to millions of citizens who had little access in the early years of the century to the knowledge sampled on tests.

In his recent work, Humphreys (1984) still defends the nature of general intelligence and its usefulness to the world. He is disillusioned by the lack of consensus among psychologists about the definition of intelligence as described on the Stanford-Binet and Wechsler tests, but he claims that members of the American Psychological Association cannot agree on *anything* psychological! *Cognizant* psychologists will agree, he claims, that the intellectual domain sampled by standard tests is what we who understand intelligence mean by the term. Personally, I hope he is right.

In his chapter in the 1984 book, Humphreys again rejects attacks on general intelligence and calls the first-order factors of tests, often called primary abilities, a misnomer.

> The first-order factors, mistakenly called *primary* and connoting psychological importance, constitute in a wide range of talent relatively minor perturbations in the measurement of general intelligence. They are primary only in the sense that they be extracted first. Properly defined in terms similar to the overlapping bonds of Godfrey Thomson (i.e., the repertoire of skills and knowledge labeled *intellectual* by cognizant psychologists), general intelligence is better considered primary. (p. 54)

The evidence he has amassed on military and high school samples about the efficacy of general intelligence for human affairs is impressive, as we all know. Perhaps no concept in the history of psychology has had or continues to have as great an impact on everyday life in the Western world.

Humphreys's view of intelligence contains two biases with which I heartily agree: a hardrock empiricism, and a practical view of how the concept of intelligence is useful to society. My own biases in discussions of intelligence include concerns with genetic variation in general intelligence that must underlie differences in intelligent behaviors, and a practical bent toward improving people's performance on socially useful tasks, such as schooling, parenting, and jobs. In keeping with the second of Humphreys's predilections, I will focus this chapter on the practical applications of the concept of general intelligence.

Preserving General Intelligence from Encroachments

Two threats to a theory of general intelligence and its practicality have emerged in recent years: One has led socially concerned scientists toward the dissection of intelligence into segments that have neither meaningful measurement nor demonstrated social utility, and a second lumps all manner of human virtues under the banner of several intelligences.

Underlying the acceptance or rejection of a theory of general intelligence is, I think, a more fundamental cultural context for ideas. Ideas about intelligence must fit into a larger, implicit view of human nature held by a culture. Ideas about human nature change with the times (Borstelmann, 1983). In times of optimism, human nature is presumed to be perfectible, and individual differences attributable to easily remedied differences in experience. In pessimistic times, human nature is seen as difficult to change or even immutable. From such general cultural views flow ideas about intelligence; competing ideas about intelligence are judged within the larger cultural context (Scarr, 1985b).

A second consideration in judgments about the appropriateness of theories of intelligence is their implications for change or improvement. A primary principle of behavioral change is that the more limited the domain or more specific the behavior to be changed, the easier it is to effect the desired change. The more general or more inclusive the domain to be changed, the more difficult the intervention and the less likely its success. Theories of general intelligence imply a very large and heterogeneous domain of knowledge and behaviors to be changed, if individuals are to be perfected. Very specific, particulate theories of intelligences imply that faulty behaviors or deficient knowledge can be more easily remedied. Thus, a theory of general intelligence fits better a culture and period of relative pessimism about human perfectibility.

Implicit in each theory of intelligence and associated constructs is a theory of intervention to improve people's functioning in real life situations. Various theories of intelligence imply either more or less optimistic ideas about intervention. The relative optimism or pessimism implied by various theories of intelligence can account for their shifting popularity, for, as the culture goes, so goes intelligence. In times when humanity is considered perfectible through human efforts, theories that imply obstacles to perfectibility are unpopular. When pessimistic views about humankind are culturally accepted, theories that imply that changes in human behavior are difficult to accomplish are far more acceptable.

The cultural relativity of intelligence leaves theories, and the interventions they imply, at the mercy of the historical times and cultural places. Is this an accurate reflection of where we are and have been in this century? Indeed, I think so. One has only to recall the translation of Binet's hopeful developmental ideas at the turn of the century into the hardened geneticism of Terman and Goddard in the 1920s. Then, reflect on the rejection of general intelligence under the domination of behaviorism's specifically learned, S → R connections. Today, we see the return of concern with human nature as a modifier of our preoccupation with nurture over the past 50 years. In the present climate, ideas about general intelligence are more acceptable than they have been in the past 50 years.

Are all views of intelligence as general or specific, perfectible or intransigent, equally useful? Despite my constructivist epistemology (Scarr, 1985b) in which all ideas have cultural-historical contexts, I do think there are criteria of usefulness that are violated by the abandonment of a theory of general intelligence. I do not believe it has proved useful, for example, to think that existing interventions with the mentally retarded will make them into normally functioning, intelligent adults, even if one *can* teach them some useful, specific skills. The retarded still suffer a deficit in general intelligence, higher levels of which lead others to learn more from their exposure to the same environments and to generalize and apply their knowledge from one situation to another (Campione, Brown, & Ferrara, 1983).

I do not think that is has proved useful to consider cultural differences in intelligence, measured by knowledge of the majority culture, as deficits in discrete information that can be easily compensated. The Headstart program may have changed some children's adaptation to the school environment, but it has not done wonders for their knowledge of the majority culture, in all of its many manifestations that are sampled on IQ tests (Consortium on Longitudinal Preschool Programs, 1983).

Culturally prescribed optimism about our ability to change intellectual functioning has led erroneously, I think, to the depreciation of the importance of general intelligence in human functioning. Two approaches to the redefinition of intelligence are both based on this faulty optimism that leads to dead ends in both theory and practice. One is the particulate view in which general intelligence is dissected into tiny parts that could be items on IQ tests or correlates thereof. The other is the lumper theory in which everything good in human behavior is called intelligence. I have labeled the lumper view, *cognition über alles.*

In the last year, the lumper trend has become popular: Call it intelligence and it will be socially valued, regardless of what behavioral domain it belongs to (Gardner, 1983). I have criticized the *cognition über alles* theory elsewhere (Scarr, 1985a), so that I will not dwell here on the problems of calling all human virtues intelligence. Briefly, there are many human virtues that are not sufficiently rewarded in our society, such as goodness in human relationships, and talents in music, dance, and painting. To call them intelligence does not do justice either to theories of intelligence or to the personality traits and special talents that lie beyond the consensual definition of intelligence. Nor does calling all human virtues intelligence readjust social rewards, the goal toward which I believe such theories are pointed.

In this chapter, I shall dwell on the excessive dissection of intelligence that I see as the major threat to the integrity of the concept of general intelligence in my field, developmental psychology. More important, the dissection of general intelligence leads to erroneous conclusions about the nature and efficacy of interventions.

Particulate Intelligence: Part-Whole Problems

One dissection of general intelligence uses index variables, or items that belong to an IQ test, without acknowledging their relation to the whole. Usually the items seem to have face validity for some kind of everyday adaptation. Behaviors that are sampled by tests of general intelligence, such as knowledge and skills with cultural relevance, are taken as specifically learned skills. Investigators select a specific intellectual, linguistic, or social piece of knowledge or skill and study its relations to other variables. Although there is no scientific law against such a practice, I will show that the inferences usually drawn from such studies are misleading, because they ignore the part-whole relation of specific knowledge and skills to general intelligence. I do not want to criticize any researchers in particular, so I will invent summary examples of the kind of research that isolates intellectual items and gives them causal status. Then, I will parody my own research.

A second set of variables often selected for isolated study consists of those not sampled on IQ tests but substantially correlated with test scores. In this category are many examples of social perception, social competence, and even personality.

Knowledge and Intelligence

Take, for example, a study that hypothesizes that parents' knowledge of child development causes better child development: Parents who know more about the course of development will provide more appropriate environments for their children (books, educational toys, stimulating activities) than parents with less knowledge of child development. The hypothesis also states that children reared by knowledgeable parents will develop better intellectual skills than children reared by less knowledgeable parents.

Imagine a study in which parents were given a test of knowledge of contemporary facts about child development and their children were given a test of intelligence. Lo and behold, we find that knowledgeable parents have smarter children. The inference usually drawn from this result is that parents should be taught what is currently believed about child development so that they may become better parents who promote the intellectual development of their children. The specific-knowledge model of parent-child effects is shown in Figure 1.

But knowledge of one domain is positively correlated with knowledge of other domains. Knowledge of contemporary child development is doubtless correlated with knowledge of musical composers, world geography, and the engineering of bridges. I do not know of any theory of child development, however, that posits that parents' knowledge of composers, geography, or bridges per se is causally related to children's intellectual development, unless one concedes that general knowledge is important in child rearing. Indeed some investigators do. (These investigators usually ignore the implications of general cultural knowledge for a theory of general intelligence.) They highlight that knowledgeable parents (a) provide their children with role models, and (b) serve as information transmitters to their children. In this model, and those to follow, single-headed arrows indicate causal paths in the direction of the arrowheads, and double-arrow paths indicate correlations

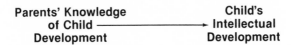

FIGURE 1. A specific-knowledge model of parent-child effects.

without causal direction. The model of such developmentalists is shown in Figure 2.

Implicit in this model of knowledge transmission is a simple intervention: Give parents more knowledge and they will produce more knowledgeable children, a desirable outcome for everyone concerned.

Another possible model of parent-child transmission of intelligence and general cultural knowledge stresses the knowledge pathway as a cause of parent-child correlations in intelligence, as shown in Figure 3.

In this model, knowledge acquired by parents is transmitted to children; knowledge is the basis for inferences of intelligence in both parents and children; and therefore, the intelligence of parents and children is correlated. Because intelligence is merely an inference from general knowledge, the implicit intervention is still to help parents acquire knowledge that they will then transmit to their children, who will simultaneously become more intelligent.

Problems with Assumptions

Most developmental investigators have a fundamentally different epistemology from that of investigators of intelligence. The former believe that information is discrete and environmentally transmitted from parents to children. Knowledgeable parents provide more information for their children to learn than do less knowledgeable parents. Intelligence experts believe that general cultural knowledge is one of the best indicators of some more general intellectual ability, which is

FIGURE 2. Knowledgeable parents produce knowledgeable children. Figures 2–6 and 8–10: copyright 1985 by the American Psychological Association. Reprinted by permission of the publisher (Scarr, 1985b).

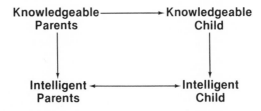

FIGURE 3. Knowledgeable parents, who are intelligent, produce children who are knowledgeable and also intelligent. © 1985 APA (Scarr, 1985b).

why cultural knowledge of all sorts is sampled on most IQ tests. Intelligence researchers believe that knowledgeable parents are more intelligent and that more intelligent parents have more intelligent children, who learn more about their cultural environments, not only from their parents but from the world at large. One possible model is shown in Figure 4.

The implicit implications of this model of intelligence for intervention are not encouraging; therefore, this is not the first approximation to the knowledge-intelligence connection for psychologists who want to intervene to improve people's educational and occupational functioning. Most psychologists recognize that improving general intelligence with deliberate interventions is a formidible task. Regardless of its "truth" value, this model does not win popularity contests.

Still another model stresses the transmission of intelligence per se, with intelligence usually considered genetically transmissible, but it posits that knowledge, though the product of intelligent parents' learning histories, is transmitted as knowledge to their more intelligent children. This model is illustrated in Figure 5.

In this model, general intelligence is posited to be the cause of knowledge acquisition; intelligence is transmitted from parent to child, and intelligent parents also transmit more knowledge to their children through socialization. Unlike the model demonstrated in Figure 4, in-

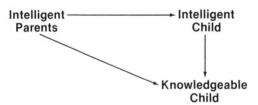

FIGURE 4. Intelligent parents produce children who are intelligent and also knowledgeable. © 1985 APA (Scarr, 1985b).

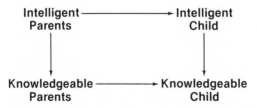

FIGURE 5. Knowledgeable, intelligent parents produce knowledgeable, intelligent children. © 1985 APA (Scarr, 1985b).

tervention seems possible to make parents more knowledgeable and therefore to improve their children's functioning in part. How much improvement takes place will depend on the path coefficients in the model.

A Multitude of Models

All of these models and others can account for the common observations, to wit: Intelligent parents tend to have intelligent children; knowledgeable parents tend to have knowledgeable children; intelligent parents tend to have knowledgeable children; and knowledgeable parents tend to have intelligent children. In any developmental model of parent-child effects, the nature of transmission and the nature of the intelligence-knowledge connection must be specified by theories. Choices among such partial models are not often empirically resolved, because all models are, in some theoretical contexts, true. How one construes the problems, accounts for the observations, and attempts to persuade others of the validity of one's model are the everyday problems of working scientists.

There is, however, an extremely important consequence of holding one or another model of intelligence and knowledge. Effective interventions depend on the accuracy of models to predict the payoff (Scarr, 1982). Path, or partial regression, coefficients are the best estimates we can have of the effectiveness of redistributing *existing* environments among *existing* genotypes. A seemingly easy maneuver to avoid the consequences of this claim is to say that novel interventions, those that have not been tried in the past, will render such path coefficients obsolete. If a radical new treatment, such as vaccination for measles, is being considered, then I can agree: Previous estimates of the importance of genetic variability in susceptibility to the disease and environmental variations in exposure will no longer predict which children will succumb to the disease. But, nearly all of our current interventions depend on redistribution of what are considered good practices to members of the populations who currently experience what we consider bad practices. In these cases, the estimates of intervention effects from path models certainly do apply.

Therefore, wishful thinking about knowledge transmission will not suffice to justify expensive and bothersome intervention programs, if the sole or major paths of parent-child influence are through intelligence and not through knowledge per se. Because developmental and intelligence investigators tend to have different causal models in mind and different epistemologies, competing models are rarely tested against one another. This is not to say that they cannot be tested competitively, only that they rarely are. I will show later that competition can be a healthy goad to our ideas about intelligence and knowledge and a prerequisite for effective interventions.

Other examples of items like those on IQ tests that are given causal status in developmental research can be found in language studies. Parents who speak to their children with larger vocabularies, in more complex sentences, with longer utterances, are often found to have more verbally complex and fluent children. Similarly, parents who use more sophisticated reasoning techniques with their children are said to induce more complex reasoning skills in their offspring. And so forth. In such studies, measures of parental and child behaviors taken in interactional situations are drawn from the same domain of behaviors that is sampled by items on tests of general intelligence.Therefore, it is hardly surprising that parental behaviors are found to *correlate* with child behaviors. What is surprising is the investigators' willingness to attribute causality exclusively to the behavioral interactions.

Indirect Sampling of General Intelligence

Let us examine other kinds of knowledge and skills that are not sampled directly on tests of general intelligence but that are correlated with IQ test scores. Whether such behaviors *really* belong to the domain of general intelligence, and whether they should be sampled on IQ tests, are matters of judgment and purpose (Scarr, 1986).

Preserving intelligence, as distinct from nonintellective skills or traits, depends on both the theoretical and practical purposes of the inves-tigator. If one wants to argue that competent people must have both intelligence and social skills, which *are* correlated, one may prefer to lump behaviors into a competence domain by stressing their interre-latedness. If, on the other hand, one wants to distinguish intellective processing from social skills, one may want to emphasize distinctiveness over correlations. In either case, the observations are the same, even if the theoretically determined "facts" are different. For the present, however, let us look at the confusions that arise for intervention from the failure to acknowledge that many social behaviors are intellectual correlates.

Peer Relations

As an example, the literature on peer relations considers children who are popular or who are isolated or rejected by their peers. Dif-ferences in social status among these children are described as differ-ences in knowledge of how to get along with others, how to time one's exchanges, how to listen and talk in satisfying dialogues, how to make a smooth entry into an ongoing group interaction, and how to protect oneself from aggression without committing unjustified attacks on others. In short, popular children have good social skills, and unpopular children have poor social skills.

Now, it also turns out that popular children usually have good school achievement and ability scores, whereas rejected children are often labeled as learning disabled, held back in school, and placed in remedial classes. Children who are liked by peers are also liked by teachers; children who are disliked by peers are not the teachers' favorites either. Most often the correlations between social skills with peers and teachers, and school achievements are relegated to a minor result section, because the implicit model in research on peer relations is as indicated in Figure 6.

This model stresses the poor peer relations of some children as the cause of both their more generally poor school adjustment and their poor school achievement. Implicit in this model is an intervention strategy: If one could improve their peer relations, one would also improve their relations with teachers and their school achievement and ability scores.

One can easily imagine another model or two (or 10) to account for the same data. One model could emphasize the crucial nature of school achievement for school adjustment with both teachers and peers. In such a model, children who do not read or do mathematics well suffer poor relationships with teachers and peers in the school setting. They are rejected by their higher achieving peers and disliked by teachers, who find them unsusceptible to their best teaching efforts.

The intervention strategy implied by the model in Figure 7 is that improving a child's academic skills will improve his social adjustment with both peers and teachers. The causes of poor social adjustment in school, therefore, are seen as primarily academic.

Another model of the same data stresses the importance of intelligence for both academic achievement and social skills with teachers and peers. This model is shown in Figure 8.

An intervention strategy implied by this model might advise schools

Poor Social
Status with ─────────────→ Poor School
Peers   Adjustment and
                             Achievement

FIGURE 6. Poor peer relations cause poor school achievement and poor school adjustment. © 1985 APA (Scarr, 1985b).

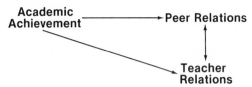

FIGURE 7. Poor academic achievement causes poor school adjustment and poor relations.

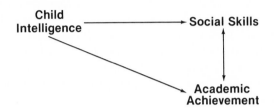

FIGURE 8. Low intelligence causes poor school achievement and poor peer relations. © 1985 APA (Scarr, 1985b).

to reduce the intellectual variability among peers in a classroom and to give teachers more realistic expectations of the social skills that children with different levels of intelligence are likely to have. Because general intelligence is such a broad concept of functioning, it is difficult to imagine direct interventions that would aim to improve g directly.

The correlations among peer and teacher social relations and school achievement lend themselves to competing interpretations, which are rarely considered in the same articles. One of the principal reasons for the neglect of competing models is the wishful thinking of good-hearted interventionists: It is far easier to fix a child's peer relationships or even more general social skills than to fix low intelligence or learning deficits.

Parent-Child Relations

A similar phenomenon can be seen in parent-child relations. As we saw in the earlier section on behaviors that are essentially items on an IQ test, there are many possible models of parental effects on children. In the domain of social behaviors, which are not usually sampled on IQ tests, the same dangers of inference lurk. In a recent paper (Scarr, 1985b), I reviewed some data on the "effects" of parent management techniques on children's intellectual, language, and social development. The data are from a longitudinal study of mothers and children from the ages of 24 to 42 months. I applied competing models to the observed correlations in parent and child behaviors. Some models have more optimistic implications for intervention than others, but that does not make them useful.

In that study I took both proximal measures of the interactions of parents and their children at Times 1 and 2 (24 and 42 months, respectively). I also took more distal measures of parent and child characteristics—knowledge and skills that are not bound by the interactional situations being observed and rated. Having been influenced by trait theories of intelligence and personality, I tested cross-situational traits and situational variables in competing models of parent-child reciprocal influence.

Parental Predictors

First, let us look at two proximal parental variables: maternal control of child rated from a 15-min observation of a teaching situation, and scores from an interview with mothers about their methods of disciplining their children in the face of typical misbehaviors. Both measures have suitably high reliabilities and have been scored to yield a positive to negative dimension of parental management techniques. At the positive end are reasoning, explaining, and other verbal ways of dealing with young children. At the negative end is physical punishment. In the middle are various moderate to severe forms of admonishment. Figure 9 shows the relationships of maternal discipline and control to child IQ.

The prediction of children's Stanford-Binet IQ scores over an 18-month period (Time 1 to Time 2) is quite good. Positive control techniques observed as well as positive discipline scored from the discipline

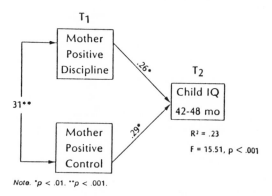

FIGURE 9. Proximal maternal behaviors as predictors of child's IQ. © 1985 APA (Scarr, 1985b).

interview significantly predict child IQ concurrently (rs = .42 to .49) and 18 months later (R^2 = .23).

Psychologists with a proximal model stop there, write their papers and "prove" that positive parental management has a beneficial effect on intellectual development. The inference usually drawn from this sort of result is that parents who do not manage their children in positive ways could have more intelligent children if they did. The implications for intervention with parents are clear: If only psychologists could help all parents to behave positively toward their children, their children would turn out to be brighter. As the editor of a developmental journal, I received many papers of this sort.

As an investigator, however, I cannot resist examining the result outlined in Figure 10. When two more distal variables (mother's WAIS vocabulary score and her education) are put into the equation, mother's IQ dominates the prediction of her child's IQ. Mother's IQ determines in large part how she behaves toward her child in the teaching situation and contributes to her discipline techniques. Her educational level is of little importance to her behavior or to her child's IQ, once her own IQ is estimated from her vocabulary score. The only significant predictor of the child's IQ at 3.5 to 4 years of age is mother's WAIS vocabulary.

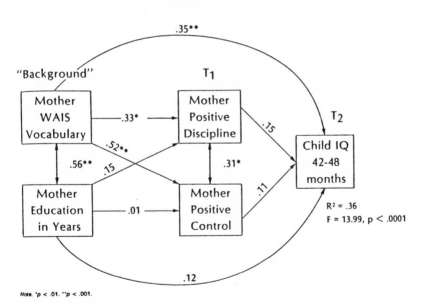

Note. *p < .01. **p < .001.

FIGURE 10. Proximal and distal maternal predictors of child's IQ. © 1985 APA (Scarr, 1985b).

The most striking findings in Figure 10 are the intimate connections between mother's intelligence and her behaviors toward her child. Intelligent mothers use more positive discipline and control techniques. And, of course, the overall prediction of child IQ is greatly improved by the addition of mother's vocabulary to the equation.

The implications of this result for improving children's intellectual functioning by intervention in mother's control and discipline techniques are dismal. Even if one could dramatically improve mother's positive behaviors toward her child, her improved behavior would have little payoff in the child's IQ score. Whereas the proximal results promised some payoff for children's intellectual outcomes, more distal variables undercut that model.

Perhaps, this result is peculiar to IQ. Let us look at child's communication skills, a score from the Cain-Levine Social Competence Scale (Cain, Levine, & Elzey, 1963), answered by the mothers. Again, mother's positive control and discipline techniques at Time 1 predict the child's communication skills at Time 2. If *only* all mothers would manage their children in more positive ways, their children would be better able to carry messages, remember instructions, answer the telephone, and tell stories.

But again, the importance of these proximal predictors pales in comparison to mother's vocabulary score, as shown in Figures 11 and 12. Children with good communication scores have mothers with high WAIS vocabulary scores. Any importance of maternal management techniques is mediated by maternal IQ. Mothers who are smarter behave in more benign ways toward their children, and their children have better verbal skills. Improving mother's discipline and control

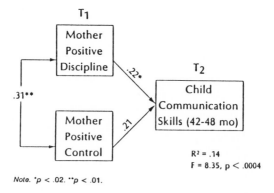

FIGURE 11. Proximal maternal predictors of child's communication skills.

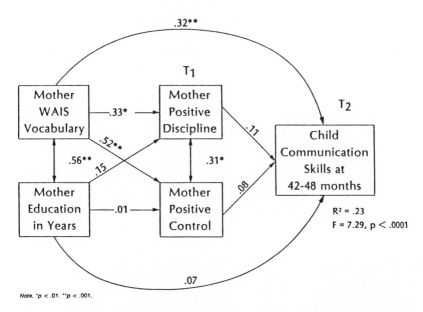

FIGURE 12. Proximal and distal characteristics of mothers as predictors of child's communication skills.

techniques will not dramatically improve children's language skills, even though the proximal results seemed to offer this hope.

Do these results apply only to cognitive outcomes for children? Let us look at social adjustment. The Childhood Personality Scale (Cohen & Dibble, 1974) was rated by both mothers and observers. The average of their scores was entered into a principal components analysis, which resulted in one, large dimension of social adjustment—high expressiveness and attention and low apathy and introversion—as seen in Table 1.

TABLE 1

Social Adjustment Factor: Combined Ratings of the Childhood Personality Scale by Mothers and Raters

Component	Rating
Attention	.61
Expressiveness	.76
Introversion	−.81
Apathy	−.80

Note. The eigenvalue is 2.26. Copyright 1985 by the American Psychological Association. Reprinted by permission of the publisher (Scarr, 1985b).

Figure 13 shows that positive maternal discipline predicts a well-adjusted child. Mothers who handle their children in benign ways have children who are more expressive and attentive and less withdrawn. The relationship between positive maternal discipline and child adjustment is sustained after the two maternal IQ and education variables are entered into the equation. This model is shown in Figure 14. Maternal vocabulary does not make a statistically reliable contribution to child's social adjustment, apart from its contribution to her discipline techniques. Changing mothers' discipline and control techniques *could* have some payoff for children's social adjustment.

Thus, we can see that the proximal variables of maternal control and discipline techniques can mask the relationships between maternal IQ and child's intellectual skills but contribute directly to the child's social adjustment. With a theoretical model that included only proximal variables, we could not have perceived a difference in the prediction of children's social and intellectual outcomes. Without testing proximal versus distal variables, we would not have invented differential models for social and intellectual development and potential forms of intervention.

Child Predictors

Now let us examine children's effects on parents, again longitudinally. What effects do what characteristics of children have on their parents' behaviors toward them? I present only the full models to save space.

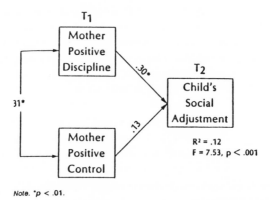

FIGURE 13. Proximal characteristics of mothers as predictors of child's social adjustment.

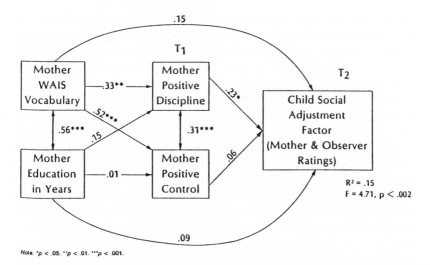

FIGURE 14. Proximal and distal maternal predictors of child's social adjustment.

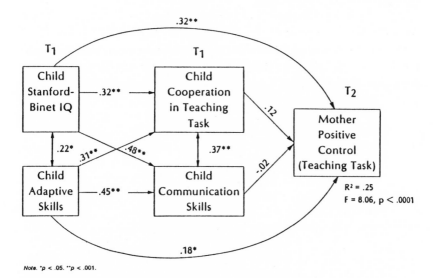

FIGURE 15. Proximal and distal characteristics of children as predictors of maternal control techniques.

One can see in Figure 15 that cooperative children are also those who score higher on the Stanford-Binet and have better communication and adaptive, self-help skills. In the model with only proximal variables, one would have "found" that children's cooperation in the teaching task was very important in "determining" how their mothers control them while teaching the toy sort ($r = .37$ over 18 months from test to retest). In the full model, however, one can see that intelligent children "cause" their mothers to behave in positive ways toward them.

Children who are intelligent also have mothers who discipline them in positive ways, according to their mothers' replies to 15 vignettes of typical child misbehaviors. The correlation of child IQ with mother's discipline techniques is .40, both when the child is 24 and 48 months of age. Nothing children are observed to do proximally controls this much variance in mother's behavior toward them, as shown in Figure 16. Although there are positive and statistically reliable relationships between children's proximal behaviors and maternal handling, they are better explained, one might say mediated, by the child's IQ. Little variance is explained by the proximal effects of children's behaviors on their mother's behaviors.

Actually, I don't believe that intelligent children directly cause their mothers to behave more positively toward them, because the model does not take into account the mother-child IQ connection or the connection between maternal intelligence and maternal behaviors.

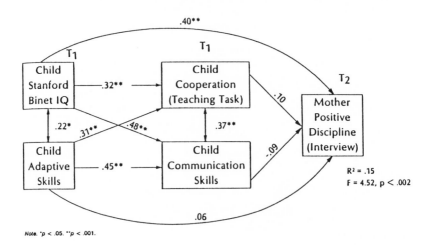

Note. *p < .05. **p < .001.

FIGURE 16. Proximal and distal characteristics of children as predictors of maternal discipline techniques.

Mothers who are intelligent have children who are intelligent; intelligent mothers behave in more benign and positive ways toward their children, who may also evoke more positive handling from their mothers. The world of parent-child interaction is fraught with inferential pitfalls.

I can "demonstrate" with the same data that bright children cause their mothers to be better educated. As Figure 17 shows, high-IQ two-year-olds with good communication skills produce mothers with higher educational levels, regardless of whether or not the children cooperate in a teaching task. Implausible, you say! I agree that this model is implausible, because we have independent information about the educational histories of adults that makes it very unlikely for a mother to obtain more education or to drop out of school according to her preschooler's IQ score. To imagine that preschoolers' intelligence determines their mothers' educational levels violates criteria of plausibility—and ultimately our credibility. But imagine the intervention that could be launched to raise mothers' educational levels! Because the same results can be shown for children's "effects" on their mother's IQ scores, we could aspire to improve the intelligence of mothers by making their children smarter!

Models of maternal and child behaviors can be constructed from

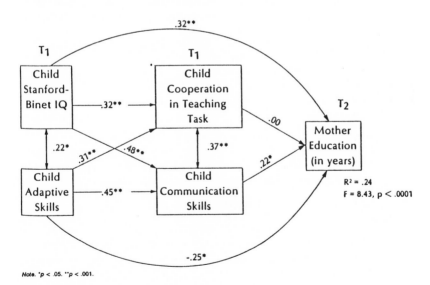

Note. *p < .05. **p < .001.

FIGURE 17. Proximal and distal characteristics of children as predictors of maternal educational levels.

isolated samples of intelligent behaviors and their correlates to "prove" just about anything a theory could want. Only when there is information independent of the model and the immediate data used to test it, do we see the implausibility of some constructions, as with preschoolers' IQ scores determining their mothers' educational levels. In most cases of peer, teacher, and parent-child relations, we do not have compelling information that rules out models. Rather, we have competing models that are seldom put into competition.

What, Then, Is Intelligence?

If general intelligence is implicated in many parent-child, peer, teacher, and other human connections, what shall we make of the efforts to dissect it and to isolate it from other human characteristics? A major reason for the unpopularity of the construct general intelligence is the difficulty it implies for intervention. But this problem does not invalidate the concept; it just makes other models more attractive to contemporary investigators, who are loathe to conclude that invidious comparisons among individuals cannot be overcome by determined interventions. A current competitor for the theory of general intelligence is that of multiple intelligences.

Multiple Intelligences

A serious consideration for intelligence theorists is the definition of the domain of intelligent behaviors. Should correlated kinds of behaviors, such as social skills, be included in the definition? Howard Gardner (1983) has proposed a theory of multiple intelligences that rejects any general intelligence in favor of a more inclusive definition of multiple, uncorrelated *intelligences.* His intelligences include musical talent, athletic abilities, personal relations, spatial skills, and the usual quantitative and verbal abilities. Should acute social perceptions, such as reading cues from facial expressions and understanding others' emotions, be considered part of intelligence? Is the ability to move with grace and verve a sign of intelligence? Is creating good painting and sculpture evidence for intelligence?

Surely, the answers to these questions are yes, if one considers the moderately to severely retarded, whose understanding of human relationships, and ability to perform in music, dance, and the graphic arts are usually limited. The Special Olympics were invented to give the mentally handicapped a chance to win, when they cannot compete with people of normal intelligence and greater physical abilities. Research on the mentally retarded does not usually stress their personal insightfulness or artistic abilities. By this observation, there are few human endeavors that could not be included in the domain of intelligence, if one considered all of the correlates of g. If we ignore Gardner's counter-factual claim that such intelligences are uncorrelated, then their inclusion in the domain of intelligence can be useful for some purposes.

Are the samples of intelligence on the most common, culturally loaded tests so broad, however, as to preclude discriminant validity for other human endeavors? Where to draw the lines among intelligence, personality, emotion, and so forth? As noted early in this chapter, many specific behaviors are either *sampled* on or *correlated* with other knowledge and skills that are sampled on IQ tests. Is this evidence for the ubiquitous influence of general intelligence or of a theory that includes too much?

For some purposes, lumping many human talents into a single domain may be useful, especially if one focuses on the practical importance of the concept, social competence. Getting along well in school, with peers, and in many occupations such as sales, public relations, counseling, and the like, requires personal attributes of extraversion, self-confidence, low anxiety, and social perceptiveness, all of which are positively correlated with each other and with traditional intelligence in the general population.

I have argued (Scarr, 1981a, b) that assessments used to predict children's functioning in school ought to sample more broadly from these related areas of personality than from only the traditional intellectual abilities, because effective functioning in the school context requires more than verbal and numerical intelligence. Similarly, Robert Hogan (1985) stresses the importance of social knowledge and skills to occupational success. Indeed, David Wechsler (1974) described intelligence as one aspect of personality, which for him was the more generic concept for human adaptive functioning.

Arguments against lumping intelligence into the broader domain of personality center on the loss of precision. A broad adaptational view that includes intelligence with other aspects of personality that affect one's overall ability to get along well in the world of people, jobs, and personal pursuits may not suit an information-processing or problem-solving theory that focuses on the internal processing of restricted kinds of information. The processing of meaning from human facial expressions may require quite different procedures from processing verbal syllogisms. Both are legitimately useful human skills, but a theory about one may not promote research on the other. A theory about both may be at so abstract a level as to be untestable and fail to provide empirical guidance. There is room in the world of intelligence theories for useful ideas about facial expressions *or* syllogistic reasoning.

Correlated Pluralism

Denial that many aspects of human personality, including intelligence, are correlated is folly. As Paul Meehl remarked many years ago, all good things are correlated. Wishful thinking about the independence, and presumably compensatory distribution, of human abilities, advances neither science nor practice. The hope of the multiple intelligence theorists seems to be that being good at one kind of activity does not guarantee excellence in another, and that being poor in verbal and numerical intelligence does not mean that you cannot be a genius in some other area. Alas, the world is not that just.

Neither laypeople nor experts in this country think of intelligence as a set of independent talents or skills (Sternberg, Conway, Ketron, & Bernstein, 1981). Rather than multiple, independent intelligences, as Gardner (1983) or more extremely, Guilford (1967) have proposed, most psychologists and laypeople seem to have a hierarchical model in mind, a model with *g* and several levels of more specific but correlated abilities of the sort Humphreys and others have proposed. A hierarchical model that recognizes the role of general intelligence in human behavior seems to fit our contemporary culture well. The idea of a hierarchical model of some kind, with general intelligence at the apogee of the pyramid, has been entrenched in all theories of intelligence since Thurstone's allegedly independent, primary mental abilities failed to replicate in population samples. Even theorists, such as John Horn (see present volume), who stress several kinds of abilities, do not deny that they are correlated, and thus a part of the general intellectual domain.

In my opinion, the breadth of the personality-intelligence domain will not be settled on logical or theoretical grounds but on criteria of usefulness. For some purposes, a more restricted definition will serve the analysis of specific information-processing skills. For other purposes, a more inclusive definition will foster the exploration of broader human adaptations. Arguments about definitions of intelligence, apart from their purposes, are vacuous and futile, as thousands of pages in professional journals will attest.

The critical issue in defining intelligence is that each theory of intelligence implies some form or forms of intervention, and each intervention promises a payoff in some desired change. If the intervention does not deliver that payoff when tested, it should be replaced by other interventions implied by other theories that do deliver on their promises.

Effects of Intervention

Not all promises about the effects of intervention are positive or optimistic. Models that stress the role of general intelligence in human affairs promise that specific interventions will have little payoff beyond the immediate behaviors they address at the time they are addressed. For example, teaching parents to use positive behavior management strategies with their young children will not generalize to help those parents manage their children as adolescents, because the specific parental behaviors taught to parents of preschoolers must be different from those that are appropriate with adolescents.

Parents who are more intelligent seem more likely to adjust their parenting techniques to the developmental level of the child, even without specific training. Less intelligent parents can benefit from specific training in parenting techniques with given children at given ages, but a theory that stresses the role of general intelligence in parenting behaviors would predict that the less intelligent parents must be trained again and again to match their behaviors to the demands of parenting their other children and the same offspring when they are at different developmental ages.

A theory of parenting that does not refer to general intelligence might predict that parent training will be generalized, once the principles of parenting had been grapsed (Ramey, Sparling, Wasik, & Bryant, 1979). I submit that there is little evidence in the literature on which to base this hope. Parent training, when evaluated, has shown little generality and little carry-over (e.g., Ramey, Bryant, Sparling, & Wasik, in press). The alternative prediction is that only specific behaviors with specific applications have been learned; that is, parents can now cope with the four or five behaviors targeted for change in this specific child at this specific age. I find this neither an optimistic position nor one that is distinguishable from the intervention results predicted by a model of general intelligence. Specific knowledge models without the promise of generalization are merely black-box theories that ignore the role of general intelligence in benign parenting.

Similarly, a model of peer relations that addresses only the situational behaviors of isolated and rejected children can probably show some efficacy in improving the children's social skills in those situations at that given age. But a model of general intelligence underlying social skills predicts that such interventions will have little generality across time and situations.

How, Then, To Intervene?

The basic problem in theories of intelligence, and hence their implications for interventions to improve intelligence, is that their concepts of individual differences look in the wrong places. Attention is directed to sources of variation that account for small portions of the intellectual variation, while avoiding scrutiny of those sources of variance that could pay off for interventions. Most psychologists can reluctantly accept the finding that genetic variation accounts for about half of the intellectual variation, however measured, in the general population (although not among highly selected university samples with whom intellectual intervention is not an issue, anyway). Most psychologists look for the other half of the intellectual variation in differences among families — in social class, cultural practices, parenting styles, educational levels of parents, and the like. Unfortunately, that is not where most of the environmental variance can be found. Our theories address a small minority of environmental variation that occurs *between families* and not the majority of the environmental variance that occurs *within families:* that is, the differences in environments of children who live in the same family. That knowledge leads us to quite different ideas about effective intervention. First, though, it is necessary to detour into theories and facts about individual differences in intelligence — their causes and remedies.

Siblings and Strangers

Let me illustrate the problem of accounting for individual differences in intelligence with data from family studies. Studies of sibling similarities and differences reveal that siblings, reared together all of their lives and sharing about half of their genes, have IQ test scores that are correlated about .45. Adopted children reared together from early infancy to late adolescence are no more similar than randomly paired members of the population (Scarr & Weinberg, 1978, 1980, 1983). Thus, rearing together in the same adoptive home does not make you intellectually similar to your brothers and sisters at the end of the child-rearing period, whereas being genetically related by half of your genes does.

But how similar are biological siblings? The typical sibling correlation for IQ test scores is about .45 when corrected for attenuation (Scarr & Weinberg, 1978). If the IQ correlation between biological siblings is .45 and the standard deviation of the IQ measure is 15 points, which is typical of such measures, then the average absolute difference between siblings is 13 IQ points, a difference of nearly one standard deviation.

This value is calculated by a general formula that assumes a normal distribution, an assumption that is met by IQ scales (Jensen, 1980, p. 459):

$$/\bar{d}/ = (2\sigma\sqrt{1 - r}/\sqrt{\pi})$$

where $/\bar{d}/$ is the average absolute difference between siblings' scores, σ is the standard deviation of the scores, r is the correlation between the siblings, and π is 3.1416.

Given that randomly paired people in the population have scores that are not correlated, their average IQ difference is 17 points, compared with the biological sibling difference of 13 points—not a very impressive increase for being a randomly chosen mate.

Adopted adolescent siblings, reared together since infancy, have negligible correlations in IQ (−.03 in our study and .02 in another large study) on the same intelligence scales, so that their average difference is close to that of the general population.

Brothers and sisters who have had objectively similar experiences with divorce, parental unemployment, abuse, and authoritarian child rearing practices (or lack of same) do not turn out to have similar intelligence. If the siblings are unrelated but reared together, there is no reduction in their average difference over randomly paired people. If the siblings are genetically related, there is a 24% reduction in their differences—statistically significant in most studies but not very impressive. Somehow, there is a mismatch between the nature of theories and the data about individual differences in intelligence.

Most standard psychological and sociological concepts about families involve environments that siblings share and that therefore *cannot* account for the vast differences among them. Parental occupations, parental beliefs about child rearing, parental education and intelligence, family size, rural-urban residence, income, and so forth are measures of characteristics that are common to all children in the family. If the goal of the research is to explain individual differences, the theories do not even contain concepts that can address the majority of the variance to be explained.

Unfortunately, investigators do not always make clear what variance they are attempting to explain. A prime example of this confusion between group and individual variances is found in the birth-order literature. Ironically, theories about the effects of sibling constellations (birth order, age spacing, age, and sex of siblings) are the only well-developed theories of individual differences between siblings (Scarr & Grajek, 1982). The confluence model (Zajonc & Markus, 1975; Zajonc, Markus, & Markus, 1979) is the only operational model that has attempted prediction of sibling IQ scores by a set of constellation variables, most notably birth order. The spectacular model-fits in regression models of IQ on birth order are achieved with *average* IQ scores for thousands of young men at each birth order. Thus, the model eliminates individuality by averaging out all other sources of individual differences.

In models of family constellation variables fit to *individual* IQ values, birth order accounts for 2%–4% of the total IQ variation (Brackbill & Nichols, 1982; Galbraith, 1982; Grotevant, Scarr, & Weinberg, 1977). Thus, the confluence model can account for 90+% of 2%–4% of the individual IQ variation.

One crafty strategy to produce seemingly impressive results is the universal practice in developmental psychology of studying only one member per family and attributing the results to differences in parenting practices or other parental characteristics. On the face of it, attributing causality to environments that are shared by siblings but that differ among families would seem to require a test of within- versus between-family models. So far, investigators have largely escaped the logical consequences of this nonsequitur. Of course, investigators of IQ variation among college sophomores and police recruits are also guilty of sampling one child per family, but they less often attribute causality to the parental environment. The variance they seem to want to account for is a small portion of the total variance, anyway. Again, these studies account for only tiny fractions of the total intellectual variation.

An old morality tale about a drunk and a lost coin has him looking for the coin on the pavement in the light cast by a street lamp, even though he knows the coin is lost somewhere in the dark alley. When asked why he is looking on the pavement if he knows the coin is in the alley, he replies that's where he can see. And so it is, I fear, with research on individual differences in intelligence; we explore those places where our theories illuminate the terrain, and not the dark areas where the important data lie but where there are no ideas to light the search. If you are now persuaded that most of the environmental variance in intelligence can be found *within* families (that is, among siblings), why then do we study variation *between* families? The problem is that we have no adequate theories about the causes of individuality among members of the same family. There is no light to guide the search, even if we know the coin is there. At this time, however, some investigators are trying to find a light for the sources of individuality.

Environmental Variations Within the Family

Although most investigators would agree that siblings experience somewhat different environments when growing up in the same family, there is little theory to guide research on the critical features of those environmental differences. Rowe and Plomin (1981) reviewed the causes of environmental variation among siblings and classified them into five types: accidental factors of each sibling's experiences, like Bandura's (1982) random experiences; sibling interaction in which each affects the other; family compositions; differential parental treatment; and extrafamiliar sources, such as teachers, peers, and television. The correlation between any one of these potential sources of sibling differences and any behavioral difference is very small, however. Even more discouraging is Rowe and Plomin's finding that no common environmental factor can be extracted to account for more than a tiny fraction of the vast behavioral differences that siblings display on all behavioral measures.

Rather than despair, Rowe and Plomin (1981) and Scarr and McCartney (1983) advise that understanding how family environments affect individual members will require behavior genetic designs with at least two siblings per family and more than one degree of genetic relatedness. Recent research on siblings' perceptions of family relations and parental treatment (Daniels & Plomin, 1986) shows that children in the same families perceive different parental treatment, especially in affection and to a lesser extent in control. There are "his" and "her" parents, just as there are "his" and "her" marriages.

Of course, research on children's perceptions of family treatment and relations is just one way to examine within-family effects. We have not yet begun to explore how differences in family environments, measured by an observer, relate to differences among them. Nor have we considered seriously the possibility (in my mind, the probability) that differences in parental treatment are instead largely caused by differences in children's talents, interests, and personalities, or by the match or mismatch between parental and child characteristics (Buss & Plomin, 1984; Scarr, 1985b; Thomas & Chess, 1977).

Parents may be differentially responsive to their children, depending on the children's characteristics and depending on the flexibility of parents in dealing with children with different attributes (Bugenthal & Shennum, 1984). Some "difficult" children may be hard for most parents to foster to normal personality development, while other "easy" children in the same families may escape parental despair and irascibility (Plomin & Daniels, 1984), but corroborating data are hard to find (Daniels, Plomin, & Greenhalgh, 1984).

Children are also likely to differ in the degree of their vulnerability (Garmezy, 1983) to environmental stresses, making parental treatment more of an issue for some children than others. For all of these reasons, family environments need to be conceptualized in finer grain than is now the mode (Wachs, 1983; Wachs & Gruen, 1982). And, more important, children need to be conceptualized as providing different events for parental treatment and as being differentially responsive to those treatments.

Behavior Genetic Challenges to Intelligence and Intervention

Seemingly unbeknownst to most psychologists, behavior geneticists who study intelligence have arrived at a startling consensus about two major points:

1. The heritable portion of intellectual variation is a demonstrable 35% to 60% of the total variance.

2. Most of the nonerror variance in intelligence is due to *individual experiences*—those not shared by members of the same family, neighborhood, or social class—and therefore unaccounted for by any contemporary theory of intelligence.

The basis for estimations of heritable variation in intelligence is twin and family studies of parents and children (genetic $r = .50$) and of brothers and sisters who are either related as identical twins (genetic $r = 1.00$), as fraternal twins, as ordinary siblings (genetic $r = .50$), or as adopted siblings (genetic $r = .00$). Assuming that all of the members of families have been reared together and that there is modest assortative mating between parents for IQ, the formula for calculating the heritability of intellectual measures in the population is straightforward:

$$h^2 = 2(r_{ia} - r_{ib})$$

where h is the estimate of heritability based on the comparison of r_{ia} for pairs of persons genetically related by 1.00 and r_{ib} for pairs related by .5., or r_{ia} for pairs genetically related by .5 and r_{ia} for pairs genetically unrelated, .00.

Each comparison controls for environmental similarity (for twins, see Scarr & Carter-Saltzman, 1980; for adoptees, see Scarr, Scarf, & Weinberg, 1980) and estimates half of the genetic variance (hence, the multiplier). If there is significant assortative mating, adjustments can be made in the multiplier to reflect the lower genetic variance within the family and the greater genetic variance between families.

Comparisons of family resemblances can also take differences in rearing environments into account, as when identical twins reared apart are compared with those reared together. From comparisons of family resemblances by genetic and environmental relatedness, models can be fit to estimate the degree of genetic and environmental variability in IQ measurements. Furthermore, the genetic and environmental components of variance can be divided into within- and between-family components, to reflect the degree to which assortative mating and common rearing environments affect the sources of personality variation in the population.

Twins and Siblings, Together and Apart

In a previous paper (Scarr & McCartney, 1983), we reviewed evidence about how identical or monozygotic (MZ) twins come to be more similar than fraternal or dizygotic (DZ) twins, and biological siblings more similar than adopted siblings on nearly all measurable characteristics, at least by the end of adolescence (Scarr & Weinberg, 1978). We also reviewed the evidence on the unexpected similarities of MZ twins reared in different homes. All of these data can be fit nicely to our theory of declining family influences and increasing individuality.

Representative findings from twin and family studies of intelligence are presented in Table 2. Twin and sibling resemblances on IQ scales show a pattern that parallels their genetic resemblances. Minor variations on the genetic pattern are apparent in the slightly higher correlations of DZ twins than ordinary siblings (but then twins are the same age when tested) and the slightly higher correlations of MZ twins raised in the same homes than those reared in different homes.

For laypeople, the most fascinating results are the unexpectedly great similarities between MZ twins reared in different homes. Bouchard (1981, 1984) reported on the intellectual resemblance of a sample of 30 pairs of adult MZ twins reared apart for most or all of their lives, and found, as did Juel-Nielson (1982), Newman, Freeman, and Holzinger (1937) and Shields (1962), that MZ twins reared largely apart are almost as similar in tested intelligence as MZ twins reared together. The IQ correlations of MZs reared in different homes average .76; those of MZs reared in the same home, .83.

In contrast to the considerable similarity of MZ twins reared apart or together, fraternal or DZ twins and ordinary siblings are much less similar. The average IQ correlation of DZ twins is .55 and of siblings, .45. For adopted siblings, rearing together from the early months after

TABLE 2

IQ and Degrees of Relatedness: Similarities of Genetically Related and Unrelated Persons Who Live Together and Apart

Relationship	Correlation	Number of Pairs
Genetically identical		
Identical twins together	.86	1,300
Identical twins apart	.76	137
Same person tested twice	.87	456
Genetically related by half of the genes		
Fraternal twins together	.55	8,600
Biological sisters and brothers	.47	35,000
Parents and children together	.40	4,400
Parents and children apart	.31	345
Genetically unrelated		
Adopted children together	.00	200[a]
Unrelated persons apart	.00	15,000

Note. Adapted from Plomin and DeFries, 1980.
[a] Based on data from Scarr and Weinberg (1978) and Teasdale and Owen (1984) on older adolescents and comparable in age to other samples in this table. Younger adopted children resemble each other with correlations around .24, based on samples of 800 pairs.

birth to adolescence results in a median correlation of .00 (Scarr & Weinberg, 1978).

Heritabilities calculated from the twin and family data range from less than half to more than three-quarters of the total IQ variation. If the MZs reared in different homes are compared with the genetically unrelated adopted siblings reared in the same home, the comparison is between individuals with all of their genes but none of their rearing environment in common and individuals with none of their genes but all of their rearing environment in common. The difference in their correlations is an estimate of heritability (.76 − .00 = .76). The comparison of MZ and DZ median correlations of .83 and .55, respectively, yields a heritability coefficient of .56. By contrast, the comparison of the biological with adopted siblings' median correlations yields an estimated heritability of .90. How can this be?

Others as well as I (Carey & Rice, 1983) have pondered the discrepancy between the twin and family data. We wondered about the possibly reduced within-family environmental variance that MZ twins may experience, being the same sex, same age, and looking and acting much alike. Fraternal twins and siblings, on the other hand, are not so similar in appearance or behavior. Adopted siblings, as predicted by their lack of genetic resemblance, bear little intellectual resemblance to each other. None of this speculation about sibling versus twin results really addresses the unusual similarity of MZs reared in different homes or the lack of similarity of adopted children reared together. A theory of declining family effects and increasing individuality will address these observations.

Similar to heritability estimates, one can calculate the effects of being reared in the same home, neighborhood, and social class by holding genetic resemblance constant and varying degree of shared environment. A comparison of MZ twins reared together with others reared apart yields a modest effect for common rearing environments (.83 − .76 = .07). A comparison of DZ twins' resemblance with that of ordinary siblings gives an estimate of the effects of "twinness" or unusually similar environments (.55 − .45 = .10), a slightly positive effect. Adopted children reared together (.00), compared with genetically unrelated members of the population reared apart (.00), suggests no effect whatsoever for between-family environmental differences. In all cases, the environment has a small effect.

An environmental theory of main effects cannot account for the stunning findings from research on adoptees, siblings, and identical twins. Our theory of genotype → environment effects *can* account for these data by predicting the degree of environmental similarity that is experienced by the co-twins and siblings, whether they live together or not.

Individual Differences in Experience

Each of us encounters the world in different ways. We are individually different in the ways we process information from the environment, which makes our experiences individually tailored to our interests, personality, and talents. Human beings are also developmentally different in their ability to process information from the environment. Each of us at every developmental stage gains different information from the same environments, because we attend to some aspects of our environments and ignore other opportunities for experience. Each individual also processes information against a background of previously different experiences — not different environments but different experiences gleaned from those environments.

I propose that these differences in experience — both developmental changes and individual differences — are caused by genetic differences. Over development, different genes are turned on and off, creating maturational changes in the organization of behavior, as well as maturational changes in patterns of physical growth. Genetic differences among individuals are similarly responsible for determining what experiences people do and do not have in their environments. What is attended to and what is ignored are events that are correlated with individual differences in interests, personality, and talents. Thus, I argue that individual and developmental differences in behavior are more a function of genetic differences in individuals' patterns of development than of differences in the *opportunities* available in most environments (Scarr & McCartney, 1983).

A Model of Genotypes and Environments

As in most developmental theories, transactions occur between the organism and the environment; here they are described by the correlation between phenotype and rearing environment. In most models, however, the source of this correlation is ambiguous. In our model, both the child's phenotype and rearing environment are influenced by the child's genotype. Developmental changes in the genetic program prompt new experiences through maturation. Before the full phenotype is developed, the person becomes attentive to and responsive to aspects of the environment that previously were ignored or had other meanings. For example, just before puberty, many children become attentive to the attractiveness of the opposite sex. Little do they know what is to come, but they are responding to preliminary, changing relationships with peers that will change their biological and social lives for many years to come. What is "turned on" in the genotype affects an emerging phenotype both directly through maturation and through prompting new experiences. Similarly, transitions from infancy to childhood— from sensorimotor to conceptual intelligence—rely more on the genetically programmed maturation of the brain than on any shift in environments available to the child. Most babies have been talked to and given information they cannot process for want of concepts; when they become toddlers they begin to understand more of what has been and is happening around them. Intellectual changes in the aging do not merely reflect a shift in environmental opportunities open to retired citizens. Aging is also a biologically programmed stage of life in which some mental processes, such as speeded performance, slow down, while others, such as acquiring cultural knowledge, maintain their vigor.

It follows from the preceding argument that the transactions we observe between phenotypes and environments are merely correlations, determined by developmental changes in the genotype. Thus, in this theory, the course of development is a function of genetically controlled, maturational sequences, although the rate of maturation can be affected by some environmental circumstances, such as the effects of nutrition on sexual development (Watson & Lowry, 1967) and the living circumstances of the elderly on their intellectual changes.

An Evolving Theory of Behavioral Development

Plomin, DeFries, and Loehlin (1977) described three kinds of genotype-environment correlations that I believe form the basis for a developmental theory. The theory of genotype → environment effects we proposed has three propositions:

1. The process by which children develop is best described by three kinds of genotype → environment effects: (a) a *passive* kind whereby the genetically related parents provide a rearing environment that is correlated with the genotype of the child (sometimes positively and sometimes negatively); (b) an *evocative* kind whereby the child receives responses from others that are influenced by his or her genotype; and (c) an *active* kind that represents the child's selective attention to and learning from aspects of the environment that are influenced by his or her genotype and indirectly correlated with those of the child's biological relatives.

2. The relative importance of the three kinds of genotype → environment effects changes with development. The influence of the passive kind declines from infancy to adolescence, and the importance of the active kind increases over the same period.

3. The degree to which experience is influenced by individual genotypes increases with development and the shift from passive to active genotype → environment effects, as individuals select their own experiences. Genetic similarity determines environmental similarity, and increasingly so across development.

Proposition 1: The Passive, Evocative, and Active Processes

The first, *passive* genotype → environment effects, arises in biologically related families and renders all of the research literature on parent-child socialization uninterpretable. Because parents provide both genes and environments for their biological offspring, the child's environment is necessarily correlated with his or her genes, because the child's genes are correlated with the parents' genes, and the parents' genes are correlated with the rearing environment they provide. It is impossible to know *what* about the parents' rearing environment for the child determines *what* about the child's behavior, because of the confounding effect of genetic transmission of the same characteristics from parent to child. Not only can we *not* interpret the direction of effects in parent-child interaction, as Bell (1968) argued, we also cannot interpret the *cause* of those effects in biologically related families.

An example of a positive passive kind of genotype-environment correlation can be found in social skills. Parents who are very sociable, who enjoy and need social activity, will expose their child to more social situations than parents who are socially inept and isolated. The child of sociable parents is likely to become more socially skilled, for both genetic and environmental reasons. The children's rearing environment is positively correlated with the parents' genotypes and therefore related to the children's genotypes as well.

An example of a negative passive genotype-environment correlation can also be found in sociability. Parents who are socially skilled, faced with a child who is a social isolate, may exert more pressure and do more training than they would with a socially more adept offspring. The more enriched environment for the less able child represents a negative genotype → environment effect (see also Plomin et al., 1977). There is, thus, an unreliable, but not random, connection between genotypes and environments when parents provide the opportunities for experience.

The second kind of genotype → environment effect is called *evocative*, because it represents the different responses that different genotypes evoke from the social and physical environments. Responses to the person further shape development in ways that correlate with the genotype. Examples of such evocative effects can be found in the research of Lytton (1980) and the review of Maccoby (1980). Smiley, active babies receive more social stimulation than fussy, difficult infants (Wachs & Gandour, 1983). Cooperative, attentive preschoolers receive more pleasant and instructional interactions from the adults around them than uncooperative, distractible children. Individual differences in responses evoked can also be found in physical attractiveness; people who are considered attractive by others receive more positive attention and are thought to be more pleasant, desirable companions (Berscheid & Walster, 1974).

The third kind of genotype → environment effect is the *active*, niche-picking or niche-building sort. People seek out environments they find compatible and stimulating. We all select from the surrounding environment some aspects to which to respond, learn about, or ignore. Our selections are correlated with motivational, personality, and intellectual aspects of our genotypes. The active genotype → environment effect, we argue, is the most powerful connection between people and their environments and the most direct expression of the genotype in experience.

Examples of active genotype → environment effects can be found in the selective efforts of individuals in sports, scholarship, relationships — in life. Once experiences occur, they naturally lead to further experiences. David Buss (1985) argues that mate selection is a niche-selection process by which personal similarities make for compatibility and lead to further environmental shaping of personal characteristics. I agree that phenotypes are elaborated and maintained by environments, but the impetus for the experience comes, I think, from the genotype.

Proposition 2: Developmental Changes in Genotype → Environment Effects

The second proposition states that the relative importance of the three kinds of genotype → environment effects changes over development from infancy to adolescence. In infancy much of the environment that reaches the child is provided by adults. When those adults are genetically related to the child, the environment they provide in general is positively related to their own characteristics and their own genotypes. Although infants are active in structuring their experiences by selectively attending to what is offered, they cannot do as much seeking out and niche-building as older children; thus, *passive* genotype → environment effects are more important for infants and young children than they are for older children, who can extend their experiences beyond the family's influences and create their own environments to a much greater extent. Thus, the passive genotype → environment effects wane when the child has many extrafamilial opportunities.

In addition, parents can provide environments that are negatively related to the child's genotype, as illustrated earlier in social opportunities. Although parents' genotypes usually affect the environment they provide for their biological offspring, this effect is sometimes positive and sometimes negative, and therefore not as direct a product of the young child's genotype as later environments will be. Thus, as stated in Proposition 3, genotype → environment effects increase with development, as active forms replace passive ones. Genotype → environment effects of the *evocative* sort persist throughout life, as we elicit responses from others based on many personal, genotype-related characteristics from appearance to personality and intellect. Those responses from others reinforce and extend the directions our development has taken. High intelligence and adaptive skills in children from very disadvantaged backgrounds, for example, evoke approval and support from school personnel who might otherwise despair of the child's chances in life (Garmezy, 1983). In adulthood, personality and intellectual differences evoke different responses in others. Similarities in personal characteristics evoke similar responses from others, as shown in the case of identical twins reared apart (Bouchard, 1981). These findings are also consistent with the third proposition.

Proposition 3: Genetic Resemblance Determines Environmental Similarity

The expected degree of environmental similarity for a pair of relatives can be thought of as the product of a person's own genotype → environment path and the genetic correlation of the pair. Figure 18 represents a model of the relationship between genotypes and environments for pairs of relatives who vary in genetic relatedness. The symbols G_1 and G_2 represent the two genotypes, and E_1 and E_2 their respective environments. The similarity in the two environments (Path a) is the product of the coefficient of each genotype with its own environment (Path x) and the genetic correlation of the pair (Path b). On the assumption that individuals' genotypes are equally influenced by their own genotypes, the similarity in the environments of two individuals becomes a function of their genetic correlation.

This model can be used to describe the process by which MZ twins come to be more similar than DZ twins, and biological siblings more similar than adopted siblings. For identical twins, for whom $b = 1.00$, the relationship of one twin's environment with the other's genotype is the same as the correlation of the twin's environment with that twin's own genotype. Thus, one would certainly predict what is often observed: that the hobbies, food preferences, choice of friends, academic achievements, and so forth of the MZ twins are very similar (Scarr & Carter-Saltzmann, 1980). Kamin (1974) proposed that all of this environmental similarity is imposed on MZ co-twins, because they look so much alike, a proposal that fails utterly to account for the close similarities of identical twins reared apart. We propose that the responses that the co-twins evoke from others and the active choices

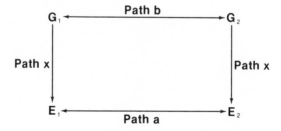

FIGURE 18. A model of environmental similarity based on genetic resemblance.

they make in their environments lead to striking similarities through genotypically determined correlations in their learning histories.

The same explanation applies, of course, to the greater resemblance of biological than adopted siblings. The environment of one biological sib is correlated to the genotype of the other as one-half the coefficient of the sibling's environment to his or her own genotype, because their genetic correlation $b = .50$, as described in Table 3. The same is true for DZ twins. There is virtually no genetic correlation between unrelated children adopted into the same household, so that their resemblances in behavioral characteristics are also predicted to be low, because they will not evoke from others similar responses nor choose similar aspects of their environments to which to respond.

Changing Similarities Among Siblings

It is clear from Matheny, Wilson, Dolan, and Krantz's (1981) longitudinal study of MZ and DZ twins that the DZ correlations for intelligence of .60 to .75 are higher than genetic theory would predict in infancy and early childhood. For school-age and older twins, DZ correlations were the usual .55. Similarly, the intelligence correlations of a sample of late-adolescent adopted siblings were *zero* compared with the .25 to .39 correlations of the samples of adopted children in early to middle childhood (Scarr & Weinberg, 1978). How can it be that the longer you live with someone, the less like them you become?

The theory put forward here predicts that the relative importance of passive versus active genotype-environment correlations changes with age. Recall that passive genotype-environment correlations are created by parents who provide children with both genes and envi-

TABLE 3
Similarity of Co-Twins' and Siblings' Genotypes and Environments for Intelligence

Subjects	Genetic correlation	Correlations in the environments of related pairs	
		Positive passive genotype → environment effects in early development	Active genotype → environment effects in later development
MZ twins	1.00	High	High
DZ twins	.50	High	Moderate
Biological siblings	.50	Moderate	Moderate
Adopted siblings	.50	Moderate	Low

ronments, which are then correlated. Certainly in the case of DZ twins, whose prenatal environment was shared and whose earliest years are spent being treated in most of the same ways at the same time by the same parents, the positive, passive genotype → environment effect is greater than that for ordinary sibs. Of course, biological and adopted siblings do not, as a rule, share the same developmental environments at the same time because they usually differ in age. The passive genotype-environment correlation still operates for siblings, because they have the same parents, but to a lesser extent than for twins. Table 3 shows the predictions of the model for intelligence.

Correlations for intellectual competence in MZ twins do not decline when active genotype-environment correlations outweigh the importance of the passive ones, because MZ co-twins typically select highly correlated environments anyway. On the other hand, DZ pairs are no more genetically related than sibs, so that as the intense similarity of their early home environments gives way to their own choices, they select environments that are less similar than their previous environments and about as similar as those of ordinary sibs.

Adopted sibs, on the other hand, move from an early environment, in which parents may have produced similarity, through positive, passive effects or through compensatory, negative ones, to environments of their own choosing. Because their genotypes are not correlated, neither are their chosen environmental niches. Thus, by late adolescence, adopted siblings do not resemble each other in intelligence, personality, interests, or other phenotypic characteristics (Grotevant et al., 1977; Scarr, Webber, Weinberg, & Wittig, 1981; Scarr & Weinberg, 1978).

Biological siblings' early environments, like those of adopted children, can lead to trait similarity as a result of positive, passive genotype → environmental effects. As biological siblings move into the larger world and begin to make active choices, their niches remain moderately correlated, because their genotypes remain moderately correlated. There is no marked shift in the intellectual resemblance of biological sibs as the process of active genotype → environment replaces the passive one.

Identical Twins Reared Apart

The most interesting observation is of the unexpected degree of resemblance between identical twins reared mostly apart. With the theory of genotype → environment effects, their resemblance is not surprising. Given the chance to attend selectively to and choose from varied opportunities, persons with identical genotypes are expected to make similar choices. They are also expected to evoke similar responses from others and from their physical environments. That they were reared in different homes and different communities is not important; differences in their development could arise only if the experiential opportunities of one or both were very restricted, so that similar choices could not have been made.

According to previous studies (Juel-Nielsen, 1980; Newman et al., 1937; Shields, 1962) and the recent research of Bouchard and colleagues at the University of Minnesota (Bouchard, 1981, 1984), the most dissimilar pairs of MZ twins reared apart are those in which one was severely restricted in environmental opportunity. Extreme deprivation, and perhaps unusual enrichment, can diminish the influence of genotype on environment and therefore lessen the resemblance of identical twins reared apart.

Making Genotype-Environment Correlations

J. McVicker Hunt, a thoroughgoing environmentalist, called for a *match* between environment and child — a meeting of the minds, as it were. Others would call this a positive correlation between person and environment. Based on quite different theoretical considerations, our theory calls for such relationships between interventions and persons, beginning in the earliest years of life. Because we hypothesize that children, adolescents, and adults choose their own experiences and evoke different reactions from others, the intervention strategy implied is that of offering a variety of possibilities that may match experience to the person. The major reason for our theory's prediction of the effectiveness of a matched person-and-environment is the incorporation of Hunt's idea about the match of environmental input to the developmental level of the child, but our theory also focuses on individual variability in the ways different people experience the same environment.

Most attempts to improve intellectual functioning address the average problems of the average person. There are certain tricks-of-the-trade, such as mnemonic strategies, self-control routines, and behavior management techniques that can make a difference in one's life. There are even metacognitive strategies, such as "check your answer again," that can increase efficiency and accuracy in problem solving in school. Teaching 13 ways to solve matrix-reasoning problems is another such aid. Tutoring high schools students on how to improve their SAT scores is still another.

The known interventions that our theory implies are not radical departures from current good practice, I am sorry to say. In fact, the theory of genotype → environment effects predicts that interventions with average people who are not personally or experientially impaired will have only small effects on their position in the distribution of intellectual differences, because most people in the mainstream of Western societies manage to get from their environments what they can manage to learn. The background opportunities for individuals in our society include preschool education for most children, free and mandatory public education from 5 to 16 years of age, free public libraries, music and art in the schools, community colleges, business training courses, and a host of support groups such as YMCA, YWCA, Boys and Girls Clubs, Big Brothers and Sisters, and Junior Achievement for socially advantaged and many disadvantaged youngsters. Is it any wonder that individual differences in intelligence are found to arise in large part from genetic differences rather than from systematic differences in environmental opportunities available to children from different families? It is against this background of opportunities that interventions must show their effectiveness. (The widespread availability of such opportunities underlies the phenomenal rise in the average intellectual level of the U.S. population in the last 50 years.)

Before readers jump to conclusions about my political posture, let me hasten to add that some children, especially minority children, do *not* have the same array of opportunities to participate in the myriad opportunities available to majority group children. When opportunities to find one's niche—those activities that are compatible with one's intelligence, interests, and personality—are lacking, then interventions that provide those opportunities will have beneficial effects on children's intellectual outcomes.

Even so, interventions with the disadvantaged rarely affect the distribution of individual differences among participants. Each person is responsive to the opportunities provided within his or her own genotypic range of reaction. The mean of the group can be raised, but interventions have never been shown to overcome individual differences. Rarely are there important interactions between intellectual level and learning opportunities that favor the less able; usually those who know more learn more from real-life environments. (Here I am ignoring classroom experiments with instructional techniques that limit what children can learn or bore bright children into a stupor.)

This theory does imply that general intelligence develops out of the many opportunities individuals can use to make their own environment, through having an impact on others and through choosing what to learn about in the vast array of possibilities. Making one's own environment is a function of both developmental level and individual differences in ability to learn from those exposures. Interventions with general intelligence should be evaluated against this background of individual differences in responsiveness to experiences.

Putting Interventions to the Test

Competing models about the role of general intelligence in parenting and peer relations are testable. Even if alternative models of intelligence are not often tested, the interventions that are implicit in each theory can be tested. Put simply, a theory of intelligence can be tested by the *usefulness* of the intervention it implies. As Urie Bronfenbrenner is fond of saying, quoting his own mentor, "If you want to understand something, try to change it." To date, I will put my bet on a theory of general intelligence that underlies important human affairs, with the pessimism that implies about the far-flung effects of situational and timebound interventions.

Lloyd Humphreys has stuck tenaciously for many years to a view of general intelligence that has come in and gone out of cultural favor. In my view, he is to be congratulated for his perspicacity.

REFERENCES

Bandura, A. (1982). The psychology of chance encounters and life paths. *American Psychologist, 37,* 747–755.

Bell, R. Q. (1968). A reinterpretation of the direction of effects in studies of socialization. *Psychological Review, 75,* 81–95.

Bersheid, E., & Walster, E. (1974). Physical attractiveness. In L. Berkowitz (Ed.), *Advances in experimental social psychology.* New York: Academic Press.

Borstelmann, L. J. (1983). Children before psychology: Ideas about children from antiquity to the late 1800s. In P. H. Mussen (Ed.), *Handbook of child psychology* (Vol. 1, pp. 1–40). New York: Wiley.

Bouchard, T. (1981, August). *The Minnesota study of twins reared apart: Description and preliminary findings.* Paper presented at the annual meeting of the American Psychological Association, New York.

Bouchard, T. J., Jr. (1984). Twins reared together and apart: What they tell us about human diversity. In S. W. Fox (Ed.), *Individuality and determinism* (pp. 147–184). New York: Plenum Press.

Brackbill, Y., & Nichols, P. (1982). A test of the confluence model of intellectual development. *Developmental Psychology, 18,* 192–198.

Bugenthal, D. B., & Shennum, W. A. (1984). Difficult children as elicitors and targets of adult communication patterns: An attributional-behavioral transactional analysis. *Monographs of the Society for Research in Child Development, 49*(1).

Buss, A. H., & Plomin, R. (1984). *Temperament: Early developing personality traits.* Hillsdale, NJ: Erlbaum.

Buss, D. M. (1985). Toward a psychology of person-environment (PE) correlation: The role of spouse selection. *Journal of Personality and Social Psychology, 47,* 361–377.

Cain, L. F., Levine, S., & Elzey, F. F. (1963). *Cain-Levine Social Competency Scale.* Palo Alto, CA: Consulting Psychologists Press.

Campione, J. C., Brown, A. L., & Ferrara, R. A. (1983). Mental retardation and intelligence. In R. J. Sternberg (Ed.), *Handbook of human intelligence* (pp. 392–492). New York: Cambridge University Press.

Carey, G., & Rice, J. (1983). Genetics and personality temperament: Simplicity or complexity? *Behavior Genetics, 13,* 43–63.

Cohen, D. J., & Dibble, E. (1974). Companion instruments for measuring children's competence and parental style. *Archives of General Psychiatry, 30,* 805–815.

Consortium on Longitudinal Studies. (1983). *As the twig is bent . . . : Lasting effects of preschool programs.* Hillsdale, NJ: Erlbaum.

Daniels, D., & Plomin, R. (1986). Differential experience of siblings in the same family. *Developmental Psychology, 21,* 747–760.

Daniels, D., Plomin, R., & Greenhalgh, J. (1984). Correlates of difficult temperament in infancy. *Child Development, 55,* 1184–1194.

Galbraith, R. (1982). Sibling spacing and intellectual development. *Developmental Psychology, 18,* 151–173.

Gardner, H. (1983). *Frames of mind: The theory of multiple intelligences.* New York: Basic Books.

Garmezy, N. (1983). Stress-resistant children: The search for protective factors. In J. E. Stevenson (Ed.), *Recent research in developmental psychopathology* (pp. 23-59). *Journal of Child Psychology and Psychiatry* (Book Suppl. 4). Oxford: Pergamon Press.

Grotevant, H. D., Scarr, S., & Weinberg, R. A. (1977). Patterns of interest similarity in adoptive and biological families. *Journal of Personality and Social Psychology, 35,* 667–676.

Guilford, J. P. (1967). *The nature of human intelligence.* New York: McGraw-Hill.

Hogan, R. (1985, April). *Healthy personality.* Henry A. Murray Lecture, Michigan State University. Unpublished manuscript.

Humphreys, L. G. (1971). Theory of intelligence. In R. Cancro (Ed.), *Intelligence: Genetic and environmental influences* (pp. 31–55). New York: Grune & Stratton.

Humphreys, L. G. (1984). General intelligence. In C. R. Reynolds & R. T. Brown (Eds.), *Perspectives on bias in mental testing* (pp. 221–247). New York: Plenum Press.

Jensen, A. R. (1980). *Bias in mental testing.* New York: Free Press.

Juel-Nielsen, N. (1982). *Individual and environment: Monozygotic twins reared apart.* New York: International University Press.

Kamin, L. J. (1974). *The science and politics of IQ.* Hillsdale, NJ: Erlbaum.

Lytton, H. (1980). *Parent-child interaction: The socialization process observed in twin and single families.* New York: Plenum Press.

Maccoby, E. E. (1980). *Social development.* New York: Harcourt, Brace, Jovanovich.

Matheny, A. P., Jr., Wilson, R. S., Dolan, A. B., & Krantz, J. Z. (1981). Behavioral contrasts in twinships: Stability and patterns of differences in childhood. *Child Development, 52,* 579–598.

Newman, H. G., Freeman, F. N., & Holzinger, K. J. (1937). *Twins: A study of heredity and environment.* Chicago: University of Chicago Press.

Plomin, R., & Daniels, D. (1984). The interaction between temperament and environment: Methodological considerations. *Merrill-Palmer Quarterly, 30,* 2–13.

Plomin, R., & DeFries, J. C. (1980). Genetics and intelligence: Recent data. *Intelligence, 4,* 15–24.

Plomin, R., DeFries, J. C., & Loehlin, J. C. (1977). Genotype-environment interaction and correlation in the analysis of human behavior. *Psychological Bulletin, 84,* 309–322.

Ramey, C. T., Bryant, D., Sparling, J. J., & Wasik, B. H. (1986). Educational interventions to enhance intellectual development: Comprehensive day-care vs. family education. In S. Harel & N. Anastasiow (Eds.), *The at-risk infant: Psychological, social, and medical aspects* (pp. 212–231). Baltimore, MD: Paul H. Brooke.

Ramey, C. T., Sparling, J. J., Wasik, B. H., & Bryant, D. (1979, June). *A model for educating parents of high-risk infants.* Paper presented at the Ira J. Gordon Memorial Conference on Parent Education and Involvement, Chapel Hill, NC.

Rowe, D. C., & Plomin, R. (1981). The importance of nonshared (E1) environmental influences in behavioral development. *Developmental Psychology, 17,* 517–531.

Scarr, S. (1981a). *Race, social class and individual differences in IQ: New studies of old issues.* Hillsdale, NJ: Erlbaum.

Scarr, S. (1981b). Testing *for* children: Implications for assessment and intervention strategies. *American Psychologist, 36,* 1159–1166.

Scarr, S. (1982). On quantifying the intended effects of interventions: Or a theory of the environment. In L. A. Bond & J. M. Joffee (Eds.), *Facilitating infant and early childhood development* (pp. 466–484). Hanover, NH: University Press of New England.

Scarr, S. (1985a). An author's frame of mind [Review of *Frames of mind* by H. Gardner]. *New Ideas in Psychology, 3,* 95–100.

Scarr, S. (1985b). Constructing psychology: Facts and fables for our times. *American Psychologist, 40,* 499–512.

Scarr, S. (1986). Intelligence revisited. In R. J. Sternberg & D. Detterman, (Eds.), *Intelligence: Current conceptions* (pp. 101–109). Norwood, NJ: Ablex.

Scarr, S., & Carter-Saltzman, L. (1980). Twin method: Defense of a critical assumption. *Behavior Genetics, 9,* 527–542.

Scarr, S., & Grajek, S. (1982). Similarities and differences among siblings. In M. E. Lamb & B. Sutton-Smith (Eds.), *Sibling relationships* (pp. 357–381). Hillsdale, NJ: Erlbaum.

Scarr, S., & McCartney, K. (1983). How people make their own environments: A theory of genotype → environment effects. *Child Development, 54,* 424–435.

Scarr, S., Scarf, E., & Weinberg, R. A. (1980). Perceived and actual similarities in biological and adoptive families: Does perceived similarity bias genetic influence? *Behavior Genetics, 10,* 445–458.

Scarr, S., Webber, P. L., Weinberg, R. A., & Wittig, M. A. (1981). Personality resemblance among adolescents and their parents in biologically related and adoptive families. *Journal of Personality and Social Psychology, 40,* 885–898.

Scarr, S., & Weinberg, R. A. (1978). The influence of "family background" on intellectual attainment. *American Sociological Review, 43,* 674–692.

Scarr, S., & Weinberg, R. A. (1980). Calling all camps! The war is over! *American Sociological Review, 45,* 859–864.

Scarr, S., & Weinberg, R. A. (1983). The Minnesota adoption studies: Malleability and genetic differences. *Child Development, 54,* 260–267.

Shields, J. (1962). *Monozygotic twins brought up apart and brought up together.* London: Oxford University Press.

Sternberg, R. J., Conway, B. E., Ketron, J. L., & Bernstein, M. (1981). People's conceptions of intelligence. *Journal of Personality and Social Psychology, 41,* 37–55.

Teasdale, T. W., & Owen, D. R. (1984). Heredity and familial environment in intelligence and educational level: A sibling study. *Nature, 309,* 620–622.

Thomas, A., & Chess, S. (1977). *Temperament and development.* New York: Bruner/Mazel.

Wachs, T. D. (1983). The use and abuse of environment in behavior-genetic research. *Child Development, 54,* 396–407.

Wachs, T. D., & Gandour, M. J. (1983). Temperament, environment, and six-month cognitive-intellectual development: A test of the organismic specificity hypothesis. *International Journal of Behavioral Development, 6,* 135–152.

Wachs, T. D., & Gruen, G. (1982). *Early experience and human development.* New York: Plenum Press.

Watson, E. H., & Lowry, G. H. (1967). *Growth and development of children.* Chicago: Year Book Medical Publishers.

Wechsler, D. (1974). *Selected papers of David Wechsler.* New York: Academic Press.

Zajonc, R. B., & Markus, G. B. (1975). Birth order and intellectual development. *Psychological Review, 82,* 74–88.

Zajonc, R. B., Markus, H., & Markus, G. B. (1979). The birth order puzzle. *Journal of Personality and Social Psychology, 37,* 1325–1341.

4

Intelligence, Wisdom, and Creativity: Their Natures and Interrelationships

ROBERT J. STERNBERG

If we look to the great minds of history, we tend to respect them for one or more of three kinds of mental abilities: intelligence, wisdom, and creativity. Who would not respect the intelligence of Einstein, the wisdom of Solomon, or the creativity of Picasso? But what, exactly, are intelligence, wisdom, and creativity, and how, if at all, do they relate to each other? Are they truly differentiable, or merely different aspects of a single phenomenon? Are they all accessible to investigation, and if so, why has intelligence been so much more studied than creativity, and creativity so much more studied than wisdom? Can people actually judge the intelligence, wisdom, and creativity of others in a distinguishable way, or do these judgments merge into a single, all-encompassing evaluation? This chapter seeks to address and possibly even answer these questions. In particular, it is argued that wisdom and creativity deserve the attention in theory and research that heretofore has been reserved for intelligence.

Although in focusing our energies on understanding and measuring intelligence we have largely ignored the two other aspects of mental functioning that are at least as important as intelligence, namely, wisdom and creativity, the time is now at hand to reshape our priorities toward the understanding and measurement of wisdom and creativity, as well as of intelligence. To see why it has been so easy to ignore wisdom and creativity, one must first see why it has been so easy to focus our recent efforts in understanding mental functioning on intelligence.

Preparation of this chapter was supported by Contract N0001433K0013 from the Office of Naval Research and Army Research Institute.

119

Understanding Intelligence: Some Alternative Approaches

During the last two decades, we have made enormous strides in our quest to understand intelligence. However, these strides must be understood in terms of the psychometric theory and research that led up to them.

The Psychometric Approach

Just 20 years ago, our understanding of the nature of intelligence was based primarily upon the notion of IQ and the factors that underlie it. Using factor analysis and related techniques, investigators of intelligence would administer various kinds of psychometric tests to examinees, and then interpret what they believed to be the psychological bases of the psychometric test results. The inventor of factor analysis, Spearman (1927), suggested that intelligence could be understood primarily as comprising a general factor, which he suggested might be due to individual differences in mental energy as well as to a large number of test-specific factors. Thurstone (1938) suggested that intelligence was better understood not in terms of a single general factor, but rather in terms of a set of correlated primary mental abilities, namely, verbal comprehension, verbal fluency, number, spatial visualization, inductive reasoning, memory, perceptual speed, and possibly, deductive reasoning. More recently, most psychometric theorists have adopted hierarchical theories (e.g., Cattell, 1971; Vernon, 1971), according to which the factors of intelligence are arrayed at differing levels of generality. At the top of the hierarchy might be a general factor, followed by group factors such as fluid and crystallized abilities (measured by abstract reasoning tests and tests of knowledge base, respectively), followed by specific factors.

In recent years, two successive waves of theory and research have dramatically changed the landscape of the study of intelligence. The first wave of research, under the banner of the "information-processing" approach, was largely a response to the perception that the factor-analytic approach did not say enough about the mental processes underlying intelligence. The second wave of research was largely a response to the perception that the information-processing approach defined intelligence too narrowly.

Information-Processing Approaches

The first wave of theory and research, during the 1970s, increased the *depth* of our conceptualization of human intelligence. This wave of research sought to understand the mental processes underlying intelligence. Although earlier psychometric methods had been helpful in understanding global constellations of individual differences in intelligence, they had not been as helpful in elucidating the mental processes underlying many of these individual differences. The information-processing approaches of the 1970s specifically addressed the question of just what mental processes underlie intelligent performance. There were two main information-processing approaches, which Pellegrino and Glaser (1979) labeled the cognitive-correlates approach and the cognitive-components approach.

The cognitive-correlates approach. The cognitive-correlates approach, typified by the work of Hunt (1978; Hunt, Lunneborg, & Lewis, 1975), was used by others as well (e.g., Jensen, 1979; Keating & Bobbitt, 1978). Cognitive-correlates researchers sought to understand intelligence primarily in terms of lower level, or bottom-up processes. For example, Hunt et al. sought to understand verbal intelligence in terms of the speed with which individuals can retrieve lexical information (such as the name of the letter, *A*) from long-term memory. They measured this speed by presenting people with letter pairs such as "*A A*," "*A a*," and "*A b*," and asking them to indicate whether the two letters matched in name. The investigators were able to isolate speed of lexical retrieval by subtracting the time it took to recognize a physical match (*A A*) from the time it took to recognize a match in name only (*A a*).

The cognitive-components approach. The cognitive-components approach was typified by the work of Sternberg (1977, 1979), although it, too, was used by other investigators (e.g., Mulholland, Pellegrino, & Glaser, 1980; Whitely, 1977). Cognitive-components researchers sought to understand intelligence primarily in terms of higher level, or top-down processes. For example, Sternberg (1977) sought to identify the information-processing components of reasoning by analogy. By systematically varying attributes of various kinds of analogies, it was possible to estimate the amounts of time individuals were spending on each theorized component of solution, and to test whether the proposed model of analogical reasoning provided a good fit to the response times of individuals in solving the various kinds of analogies presented.

Diversified-Ability Approaches

The second wave of research, during the 1980s, increased the *breadth* of our conceptualization of intelligence. This wave of research has sought to understand the full range of mental abilities that constitute intelligence, broadly defined. Whereas the theories of the 1970s seemed to focus primarily on the mechanisms of intelligence, the theories of the 1980s seem to be focusing primarily on the extent of intelligence. Representative of this trend are the theory of multiple intelligences (Gardner, 1983) and the triarchic theory of intelligence (Sternberg, 1985).

The multiple-intelligences approach. According to Gardner's (1983) theory of multiple intelligences, intelligence is not one thing, but at least seven. Gardner has argued that it is necessary to distinguish the following types of intelligence from each other: (a) linguistic, (b) musical, (c) logical-mathematical, (d) spatial, (e) bodily-kinesthetic, (f) interpersonal, and (g) intrapersonal. Each of these intelligences, according to Gardner, is functionally and probably anatomically distinct, and can be identified separately in terms of different mental processes, developmental histories, and utilization of symbol systems. It is clearly not Gardner's goal to specify the nature of each of these intelligences in depth: the underlying processes, symbol systems, developmental histories, and the like are not clearly spelled out. Rather, it seems to be his purpose to expand the range of talents that, according to him, should be identified as "intelligences."

The triarchic approach. According to Sternberg's (1985a) triarchic theory, intelligence should be understood in terms of its relation to three, interrelated aspects: (a) the internal world of the individual (e.g., mental structures, mental processes, knowledge base), (b) the external world of the individual (e.g., the work environment, the home environment), and (c) the experience of the individual (e.g., the degree of novelty a given task or situation presents to the individual). Sternberg argues that intelligence is most aptly assessed by those tasks that measure the information-processing components as they are applied to ecologically representative tasks and situations that are either relatively novel or in the process of becoming automatized. Although Sternberg attempts to specify many of the details of information processing, his main goal, like Gardner's, is to expand the range of mental functioning that is identified as "intelligent."

These enlarged conceptions of intelligence serve the important function of encouraging psychologists and educators to broaden their vision of what intelligence is, and particularly, to broaden it beyond the fairly narrow spectrum of abilities tested by conventional intelligence tests. Those individuals who do indeed expand their notions of intelligence may feel somewhat secure in the knowledge that their conception of the range of human abilities is not confined by the boundaries of conventional psychometric intelligence tests.

This security may be illusory, and in some respects, pernicious, because it may lead individuals to focus upon particular kinds of thinking, and especially critical and analytic thinking, as it applies within a broad range of domains (e.g., the musical domain of Gardner or the practical domain of Sternberg). Indeed, the current emphasis in education upon the measurement and teaching of "critical thinking" would seem to represent this trend. At the same time, we may be led to ignore two other kinds of thinking that are at least as important as the kinds of thinking that underlie intelligence, namely, the kinds of thinking that underlie wisdom and creativity. Because these constructs are difficult to conceptualize and hence difficult to measure well, it is easy to put them aside, and concentrate on the constructs that have proven themselves more easily susceptible to conceptualization and measurement. But in putting these two constructs aside, we may be ignoring two kinds of thinking that are at least as important as intelligence, although possibly distinct from it. Perhaps the time has come, now that we are making great strides in understanding and measuring intelligence, to broaden the focus of our attention to include the two additional mental attributes of wisdom and creativity. And perhaps it is both unwise and uncreative not to do so, not to mention, unintelligent!

Understanding Wisdom: Some Alternative Approaches

Although wisdom is a topic that has been of interest to scholars through the ages, and one about which they have had a lot to say, the literature on wisdom derives largely from the humanities rather than from the social sciences (see review by Clayton & Birren, 1980). The social science literature is small and growing only slowly.

Those who have studied wisdom have borne the burden of demonstrating that this construct is even separable from that of intelligence. This burden is even greater for wisdom than it is for creativity, because our notions of what wisdom is are even fuzzier than our notions of what creativity is.

Clayton (1982) has argued that wisdom can be separated from intelligence in a number of ways. The first is simply definitional. She defines intelligence as the ability that allows the individual to think logically, to conceptualize, and to abstract from reality; she defines wisdom as the ability that allows the individual to grasp human nature, which operates on the principles of contradiction, paradox, and change. Whereas the knowledge that accrues as a result of intelligence is viewed as being nonsocial and impersonal, the knowledge that accrues as the result of wisdom is viewed as being both social and personal, including within its realm both the intrapersonal and the interpersonal spheres. Whether these spheres are wholly separable from the intellectual is a matter of debate. Gardner (1983) views intrapersonal and interpersonal competencies as separate intelligences, whereas Sternberg (1985a) and others classify them as aspects of social intelligence.

Whether or not wisdom is separate from social intelligence (including both intrapersonal and interpersonal aspects), it seems clear that whatever the construct is called, it differs in some respects from what we ordinarily think of as (cognitive) intelligence. It may be no coincidence that the two major psychological programs of research on wisdom—those of Clayton (1976) and of Dittmann-Kohli and Baltes (in press)—emanate from life-span psychologists: Wisdom seems to increase over the years, whereas intelligence in many of its aspects seems to decrease. Clayton further points out that the main skill in wisdom—application of paradoxical logic and dialectical operations to intrapersonal and interpersonal problems—is practically useless in the main operational measures of intelligence, such as inductive and deductive reasoning. Moreover, she argues that the knowledge accumulated by intelligence tends largely to be time-bound, whereas the knowledge accumulated by (or perhaps, *as*) wisdom tends to be timeless. Finally, she argues that whereas intelligence translates into questions of how to do things, wisdom translates into questions of what things should be done. For example, it is intelligence that has led to the development of nuclear weapons, but wisdom that might have led people to question whether they should be developed in the first place.

A Multidimensional Scaling Approach

Clayton was not content merely to speculate on the nature of wisdom. Rather, she conducted empirical investigations to determine that nature (Clayton, 1976; see also Clayton & Birren, 1980). In her 1976 study, 83 adult individuals representing three different age cohorts (young, median age 21; middle-aged, median age 49; and older-aged, median age 70), all of them having had at least 2 years of college, were asked to rate on a 1 (high degree of similarity) to 5 (low degree of similarity) scale the similarities of each of 105 possible pairs of 15 different stimuli. Twelve of these stimuli had been generated in an earlier study (Clayton, 1975) as descriptors of wise persons by younger, middle-aged, and older adults, and 3 of the stimuli were included for comparison purposes. The 12 main stimuli were: experienced, intuitive, introspective, pragmatic, understanding, gentle, empathetic, intelligent, peaceful, knowledgeable, sense of humor, observant. The three additional comparison stimuli were: wise, aged, myself.

The multidimensional scalings of the data for each of the three cohorts revealed both similarities and differences in their perceptions of wisdom, each of which will be considered here in turn.

Three interpretable dimensions appeared in each solution. The dimensions might better be referred to as "clusters," in that the points comprising them clustered together in the multidimensional space but did not seem to form a continuum from low to high values. This result may reflect restriction in the range of stimuli used in the study (all were associated with high degrees of wisdom) or may reflect an underlying property of the construct of wisdom. It is just not clear. Clayton found the interpretation of the first two clusters the most straightforward. The first cluster seemed to involve an *affective* component of wisdom. Included in the first cluster were terms such as "wise," "peaceful," and "empathetic." "Understanding" and "gentle" were also near this cluster. The second cluster seemed to involve a *reflective* component of wisdom. Included in this second cluster were terms such as "wise" and "introspective." Near to that cluster were "intuitive" and "myself." The third cluster, which Clayton considered to be less interpretable than the other two, was suggestive to her of a perceived, developmental, age-related component of wisdom. In my judgment, however, the data do not support Clayton's interpretation of the third cluster, and even the interpretations of the first two are, at best, weakly supported by her data.

According to Clayton, the most salient difference in the structure of the clusters with increasing age of the subjects was an increasing differentiation in the structure of wisdom. This increasing differentiation was in the stimuli that fell into neither the affective nor the reflective components of wisdom. Again, my inspection of the data did not yield strong confirmation of Clayton's interpretation of her data, but the idea of increasing differentiation is an interesting one, and might well have been better supported by data that yielded more clearly interpretable solutions.

A Neo-Functionalist Approach

Dittmann-Kohli and Baltes (in press) have taken what they refer to as a "functionalist" approach to the understanding of wisdom. These investigators view wisdom as an ability involving (a) an expertise in selected domains of knowledge; (b) contextual richness in the definition and solution of problems; (c) the pragmatics and metapragmatics of life; (d) uncertainty of problem definition; and (e) relativism in judgments and in recommendations involving action. Dittmann-Kohli and Baltes point out that their definition of wisdom results in measurements that are closely tied to the complexity, uncertainty, and pragmatics of everyday life, and not in measurements that are highly speeded, academic, and simple in the kinds of skills required. In this respect, the measurement of wisdom differs from the measurement of "fluid" intelligence, which tends to be highly speeded, academic, and simple in the structure of the requisite tasks.

Although Dittmann-Kohli and Baltes (in press) have not yet engaged in any formal data collection, they suggest that such data collection would be likely to take the form of studies such as one by Sternberg, Conway, Ketron, and Bernstein (1981), which sought to understand implicit theories of intelligence in various groups. Such implicit theories, or conceptions of a construct, can form a useful basis for defining at least the general boundaries of a construct under investigation. Moreover, by comparing implicit theories of closely related constructs—say, intelligence, creativity, and wisdom—one may be able to understand, at least to some extent, in what ways the constructs are similar and different.

Understanding Creativity: Some Alternative Approaches

Creativity has been studied by diverse means. Some of the main approaches to studying it have included the psychometric, the personality-correlates, the biographical, the historiometric, the social-psychological, and the cognitive-psychological.

The Psychometric Approach

The psychometric approach has generally involved use of creativity tests and the subsequent intercorrelating of these tests with each other, with intelligence tests, and with other psychometric tests believed to involve creative functioning in some way. Guilford (1959) used factor analysis to reveal what he believed to be some of the main aspects of creativity, namely, (a) word fluency (the ability to produce words, each of which contains a given letter or combination of letters), (b) associational fluency (the ability of an examinee to produce as many synonyms as possible for a given word in a given amount of time), (c) expressional fluency (production of phrases or sentences), and (d) ideational fluency (production of large numbers of not necessarily good ideas in a short amount of time). All of these factors reflect an emphasis in Guilford's tests on rapidity and quantity in production of ideas, rather than on either reflectivity or quality of the ideas. Guilford (1950) also proposed that creative thinkers are more flexible in their thinking. In particular, they produce a great variety of ideas (spontaneous flexibility) and are able to solve problems that require unusual kinds of solutions (adaptive flexibility).

Guilford's tests of creativity are largely based upon his structure-of-intellect model of intelligence (Guilford, 1956, 1967), according to which intelligence can be understood in terms of the operations, contents, and products involved in intellectual endeavor. Not all tests of creativity have been as theoretically based. For example, the Torrance (1966) tests of creativity provide separate measures for verbal and nonverbal creativity and measure skills similar to those in Guilford's theory, but are not based on a fully articulated or validated model of creative process.

Not all psychometricians have believed creativity to be subsumed within the realm of intelligence. Getzels and Jackson (1962), for example, found that tests of creativity seemed to tap mental skills that differ in kind from those tapped by intelligence tests. Wallach and Kogan (1965) argued that the evidence of Getzels and Jackson for a distinction between intelligence and creativity was weak, but then went on to propose a distinction of their own according to which creativity distinctively involves production of abundant and unique mental associations, and the presence, in the thinker who makes the associations, of a playful and permissive attitude toward task performance.

The Personality-Correlates Approach

This work, typified by the research of Barron (1955, 1963) and of MacKinnon (1975), seeks to understand creativity in part in terms of the personality dispositions that seem to underlie creative functioning. Barron, for example, believed that there is a "disposition toward originality," that creative individuals (a) prefer complexity and some degree of apparent imbalance in phenomena, (b) are more complex psychodynamically, (c) are more independent in their judgments, (d) are more self-assertive and dominant, and (e) reject suppression as a mechanism of impulse control. MacKinnon, whose particular sample happened to be of architects, found that creative individuals (a) are aesthetically more reactive than others, (b) have high aspiration levels, (c) value independence and autonomy, (d) are productive in their orientation, and (e) are concerned with their adequacy as persons. Other studies of the personality traits of creative individuals have been done as well, with related results. Cattell and Butcher (1968), for example, found that highly creative individuals tend to be more introverted than less creative individuals, and that they also tend to be high in both self-sufficiency and self-sentiment, or belief in themselves.

The Biographical Approach

In the biographical approach, one seeks to understand creativity in terms of the personal variables in people's lives that seem to be associated with, or even causal of, creative performance in childhood or adulthood. Perhaps the most famous example of the biographical approach is Roe's (1952) study of the lives of 64 eminent scientists. Looking back into their family lives, Roe found that they tended, on the average, to be the first-born child of a middle-class family in which the father was a professional of some sort. They were likely to have been somewhat sickly as children, and to have lost a parent at an early age. They started reading early, and read a great deal. They tended to feel lonely and different from their classmates, and to be shy in their social relations with their peers.

Cox (1926) also used a biographical approach in studying 300 "geniuses." She is most well known for her estimation of IQ scores based on accomplishments of these geniuses in childhood. She examined the age at which their biographies indicated they had started accomplishing certain things, relative to the age at which typical children would have started these accomplishments. Using this retrospective biographical approach, she estimated, for example, that John Stuart Mill, who began to learn Greek at 3 and who read Plato at 7, had an IQ of 190. She also measured degree of eminence, finding that Napoleon was the most eminent leader in her sample and Voltaire the most eminent creator.

Probably the most influential biographical study has been the ongoing one represented by the Terman study (e.g., Terman & Oden, 1947). This study examined the life histories of children, most of whom had IQs over 140, who grew up in California during the early 1900s. Terman found that when the members of his "genius" sample reached adulthood, their physical health was well above average. The number of individuals receiving advanced degrees, publishing articles, entering professions, and remaining married was well above the national average. Moreover, the incomes of the identified children as adults were well above average as well. Indeed, by almost any measure, the identified children fared much better in life than did mentally more typical individuals.

The Historiometric Approach

The historiometric approach has been tried by a number of individuals, but it is largely associated today with a single one, namely, Dean Simonton (e.g., Simonton, 1984). This approach examines the socio-

historical factors that influence creativity, as well as other mental characteristics. Simonton has found, for example, that particularly creative
individuals have tended to be first-borns, to have lost parents through
death (but not divorce) in childhood, to come disproportionately from
famous families, and to have been influenced by creative thinkers of
the past two generations. They tend to have had moderate amounts
of formal education, rather than very high or very low levels, and to
be very highly productive in their later careers. Their peak creativity
tends to be in their thirties, although this peak varies somewhat as a
function of field. Political instability has an adverse effect on certain
types of creativity, and wars have generally been detrimental to creative
expression.

The historiometric approach is obviously related to the biographical.
But there is one important difference.The biographical approach starts
with a list of creative individuals, and seeks to identify commonalities
in their backgrounds. The historiometric point of view starts with history, attempts to formulate certain laws of history and its influence,
and then looks at the effects of history and its laws upon creative
influence and production. Compared with the biographical approach,
the historiometric is less person-centered and more attuned to the
finding of generalizations about historical effects on creativity.

The Social-Psychological Approach

The social-psychological approach to creativity, like the historiometric, is today identified with one particular individual, Teresa Amabile
(see, e.g., Amabile, 1983), although there have been many others em-
ploying this approach. Amabile has examined and reviewed the effects
on creativity of such social-psychological variables as the educational,
work, and cultural environments. In reviewing the literature, including
her own work, she has found that creativity tends to be undermined
by extrinsic as opposed to intrinsic motivation, by evaluation and its
attendant anxiety, and by peer pressure. In contrast, creativity is en-
hanced by teachers who value autonomy in students and by a work
environment in which the individual is encouraged to assume responsibility for initiating new activities, enjoys a high degree of power to
hire research assistants, is free from interference by administrative
superiors, and experiences a highly stable environment. Thus, her review reveals that creativity is by no means totally traitlike, but rather
is at least partly situational: It responds to situational constraints in
major, and sometimes surprising, ways.

The Cognitive-Psychological Approach

This approach seeks to understand creativity in terms of the cognitive processes underlying it. Much of this work, which dates back especially to the Gestalt psychologists such as Wertheimer (1959), strives to understand the nature of creative insight.

There have been various points of view regarding the nature of such insights. The Gestalt psychologists never went very far in defining just what insight is, although they came up with some classical examples of it. Few introductory psychology students have failed to see a schematic picture of one of Kohler's (1927) apes putting together two parts of a rod so he could retrieve a banana. Views of insight associated with Gestalt psychology are that it represents a speeding up of mental processing, a leap in mental processing, or a short-circuiting altogether of normal mental processing.

A sharply contrasting view is that of Perkins (1981), who has held that insight is "nothing special," but rather represents only a significant product of fairly ordinary processing. To Perkins, insight is achieved by noticing things that others may not notice, but noticing them qualitatively in the same ways one would notice anything else.

Sternberg and Davidson (1983; Davidson & Sternberg, 1984) have argued that insight represents the extension of three mental processes to tasks and situations in which one has no or few prior rules to apply. These processes are selective encoding, which involves distinguishing relevant from irrelevant information; selective combination, which involves putting together relevant information; and selective comparison, which involves relating new to old information. These investigators have taken some of the major insights in history, and classified them as representing one or more of these three categories. For example, Darwin's formulation of the theory of evolution required selective combination of multiple pieces of diverse information. They have also shown how typical insight problems found in puzzle books and on tests can be categorized according to this process framework.

To summarize, creativity has been studied using a number of methods. There has not been a great deal of convergence among the methods, nor has the availability of a number of methods resulted in any particularly startling insights into the nature of creativity. The number of approaches probably reflects the lack of completeness and perhaps fruitfulness of any single approach in revealing the nature of creativity. One often hears complaints that for all our sophisticated tests and measures, we have attained little understanding of intelligence. Whatever the situation may be for intelligence, it is almost certainly worse for creativity. We still have relatively little idea of what it is.

The Interrelations of Intelligence, Wisdom, and Creativity: An Implicit-Theoretical Approach

A series of studies was carried out to understand intelligence, wisdom, creativity, and their interrelations better (see Sternberg, 1985b, for further detail). The series of studies was based on an implicit-theoretical approach. Before describing the studies and their results, it would be worthwhile to say something about this approach, and to contrast it to an explicit-theoretical approach.

Implicit Versus Explicit Theoretical Approaches

Explicit theories are constructions of psychologists or other scientists that are based upon or at least tested on data collected from people performing tasks presumed to measure psychological functioning. Although investigators working with explicit theories of psychological constructs might disagree as to the nature of the constructs (whether they should be factors, components, schemata, and so on), they would agree that the data base from which the proposed constructs are isolated should consist of performance on tasks requiring the kind or kinds of psychological functioning under investigation.

Implicit theories, whether by psychologists or laypersons, are constructions that reside in the minds of these individuals. Such theories need to be discovered rather than invented because they already exist, in some form, in people's minds. Discovering such theories can be useful in helping to formulate the common-cultural views that dominate thinking about a given psychological construct, whether the culture is one of people, in general, or of psychologists, in particular. Understanding implicit theories can also help us understand or provide bases for explicit theories, because explicit theories derive, in part, from scientists' implicit theories of the construct under investigation. The data of interest in the discovery of implicit theories are people's communications, in whatever form, regarding their notions as to the nature of the psychological construct under investigation.

An implicit-theoretical approach to studying a construct is particularly useful in the early stages of research on that construct, or when research using explicit-theoretical approaches is not advancing rapidly. Such conditions would appear to be met in the case of wisdom and creativity, which have not proved to be easily tractable for psychological investigation. Understanding implicit theories of these constructs, and of how they relate to intelligence, may provide a useful basis for subsequent explicit-theoretical investigations.

Prestudy

In a prestudy (Sternberg, 1985b), a brief questionnaire was filled out by 97 professors in the field of art (25), business (26), philosophy (20), and physics (26), at a variety of American universities (representing a return rate of 17% on questionnaires sent out). The questionnaire was also given to 17 laypersons (nonstudent adult residents of the New Haven area who answered a newspaper advertisement). The questionnaire asked respondents to spend a few minutes listing whatever behaviors they could think of that were characteristic of an ideally intelligent, wise, or creative person in their respective fields of endeavor (or, in the case of laypersons, in general). Those behaviors listed at least twice served as a basis for the subsequent investigations. The total numbers of behaviors obtained were 119 for art, 131 for business, 107 for philosophy, 138 for physics, and 156 for laypersons.

Experiment 1

Method. In Experiment 1, 800 professors, 200 in each of the fields of art, business, philosophy, and physics, were asked to rate the characteristicness of each of the behaviors obtained in the prestudy from the corresponding population with respect to their ideal conception of an ideally intelligent, wise, and creative individual in their occupation. Laypersons (nonstudent adult residents of the New Haven area) also provided these ratings, but for a hypothetical ideal individual without regard to occupation. Ratings were on a 1 (low) to 9 (high) scale, with a rating of 1 meaning "behavior extremely uncharacteristic" and a rating of 9 meaning "behavior extremely characteristic." For the art, business, philosophy, physics, and laypersons questionnaires, 65, 70, 65, 85, and 30 persons responded, respectively. Each participant provided all three ratings (of intelligence, wisdom, and creativity), but with the order of the three ratings counterbalanced across subjects.

Means. Mean ratings for all three psychological constructs from all four occupations ranged from 5.8 to 7.1 with a median of 6.4. Ratings were quite similar in value across constructs and fields. Reliabilities of the ratings were high, ranging from .88 to .97 with a median of .92.

Correlations. Correlations between pairs of ratings of attributes for the various groups of subjects revealed some interesting patterns.

First, the correlations between intelligence and wisdom (across subject groups) ranged from .42 to .78 with a median of .68. The correlations between intelligence and creativity ranged from .29 to .64 with a median of .55. The correlations between wisdom and creativity ranged from −.24 to .48 with a median of .27. Clearly, the rank ordering of the three possible relations between constructs is that intelligence and wisdom are most closely related, intelligence and creativity next most closely related, and wisdom and creativity least related. The only departure from this pattern was for philosophers, for whom intelligence and creativity were more highly related than were intelligence and wisdom (a correlation of .56 vs. .42).

Second, all correlations were positive and statistically significant except for the correlation between wisdom and creativity for the business professors, which was significantly negative. In other words, business professors saw greater amounts of wisdom as associated with lesser amounts of creativity.

Third, there were some interesting differences among magnitudes of correlations across groups. First, members of all groups saw intelligence and wisdom as fairly highly related. But for professors in the fields of art and physics, as well as for laypersons, the relations were very substantial ($r = .6$ to .8). For business professors, the relation was a bit weaker ($r = .5$), and for professors of philosophy, the relation was still weaker ($r = .4$). Second, the art, philosophy, and physics professors all saw intelligence and creativity as highly related ($r > .5$), but the business professors and laypersons saw them as only weakly to moderately related ($r = .3$). Third, the relation between creativity and wisdom reached moderate levels for the art professors ($r = .5$) and philosophy professors ($r = .4$), but was low for the other groups, and as mentioned earlier, actually negative for the business group.

Summary. Although the various groups do not differ substantially in the absolute magnitudes of their ratings, they do differ in the perceived relations between constructs rated. In general, intelligence and wisdom are seen as closest, and wisdom and creativity as farthest from each other, but there are differences in magnitudes of relations across fields.

These correlations tell us something about the interrelations of constructs, but not about the constructs themselves. The next experiment was designed to examine the internal structure of each construct.

Experiment 2

Method. In this experiment, 40 Yale College students were asked to sort three sets of 40 behaviors into as many or as few piles as they wished on the basis of which behaviors are "likely to be found together" in a person. These behaviors were from the listings for intelligence, wisdom, and creativity, respectively, from Experiment 1. Only the top

40 behaviors (in terms of laypersons' characteristicness ratings from Experiment 1) were used in each sorting task. Order of sortings for behaviors from the intelligence, wisdom, and creativity lists was counterbalanced in a Latin square arrangement. Subjects were not told in advance what the behaviors had in common (i.e., their being listed as characteristic of intelligence, wisdom, or creativity).

Nonmetric multidimensional scaling (ALSCAL) was used to analyze the ratings. (Stress was calculated via Stress Formula 1 and the primary method was used for resolving ties.) All scalings were principal-axis solutions. Hence, each dimension accounted for the maximum possible variance, controlling for earlier dimensions, with dimensions extracted in order of strength.

Intelligence. The solution for intelligence accounted for 82% of the data in three dimensions, with a Stress of .15. Because the scaling was a principal-axis solution, it tended to yield bipolar dimensions in which positive and negative polarities lent themselves to separate but related interpretations.

The first dimension yielded two interpretations: (a) *practical problem-solving ability* for the positive polarity (e.g., tends to see attainable goals and accomplish them; has the ability to change directions and use another procedure; able to apply knowledge to particular problems) and (b) *verbal ability* for the negative polarity (e.g., can converse on almost any topic; has demonstrated a good vocabulary; has a good command of language).

The second dimension also lent itself to two interpretations: (a) The positive polarity of this dimension was labeled *intellectual balance and integration* (e.g., has the ability to recognize similarities and differences; listens to all sides of an issue; is able to grasp abstract ideas and focus attention on those ideas) and (b) the negative polarity was labeled *goal orientation and attainment* (e.g., tends to obtain and use information for specific purposes; possesses ability for high achievement; is motivated by goals).

The third dimension yielded two interpretations: (a) *contextual intelligence* for the positive polarity (e.g., learns and remembers and gains information from past mistakes or successes; has the ability to understand and interpret the environment; knows what is going on in the world) and (b) *fluid thought* for the negative polarity (e.g., has a thorough grasp of mathematics and/or good spatial ability; has a high IQ level; thinks quickly).

Wisdom. The scaling for wisdom accounted for 87% of the variance in three dimensions, with a Stress of .14.

The first dimension yielded two interpretations: (a) *reasoning ability* for the positive polarity (e.g., has the unique ability to look at a problem or situation and solve it; has good problem-solving ability; has a logical mind) and (b) *sagacity* for the negative polarity (e.g., considers advice; understands people through dealing with a variety of individuals; feels can always learn from other people; is fair).

The second dimension also yielded two interpretations: (a) *learning from ideas and environment* for the positive polarity (e.g., attaches importance to ideas; is perceptive; learns from other people's mistakes) and (b) *judgment* for the negative polarity (e.g., acts within own physical and intellectual limitations; is sensible; has good judgment at all times; and thinks before acting or making decisions).

The third dimension yielded two interpretations: (a) *expeditious use of information* for the positive polarity (e.g., is experienced; seeks out information, especially details; learns and remembers and gains information from past mistakes or successes) and (b) *perspicacity* for the negative polarity (e.g., can offer solutions that are on the side of right and truth; is able to see through things—read between the lines; has the ability to understand and interpret the environment).

Creativity. The scaling for creativity accounted for 93% of the variance in the data in four dimensions, with a Stress of .08.

The first dimension yielded two interpretations: (a) *nonentrenchment* for the positive polarity (e.g., makes up rules as goes along; has a free spirit; is unorthodox) and (b) *integration and intellectuality* for the negative polarity (e.g., makes connections and distinctions between ideas and things; has the ability to recognize similarities and differences; is able to put old information, theories, etc., together in a new way).

The second dimension was also interpreted in terms of two polarities: *aesthetic taste and imagination* for the positive polarity (e.g., has an appreciation of art, music, etc.; can write, draw, compose music; has good taste) and (b) *decisional skill and flexibility* for the negative polarity (e.g., follows gut feelings in making decisions after weighing the pros and cons; has the ability to change directions and use another procedure).

The third dimension was interpreted in terms of (a) *perspicacity* for its positive polarity (e.g., questions societal norms, truisms, assumptions; is willing to take a stand) and of (b) *drive for accomplishment and recognition* for its negative polarity (e.g., is motivated by goals; likes to be complimented on work; is energetic).

The fourth and weakest dimension was interpreted in terms of (a) *inquisitiveness* (positive polarity) and (b) *intuition* (negative polarity). This dimension did not have many salient weights on either polarity.

Summary. Excellent fits to the nonmetric multidimensional scaling model were obtained for all three constructs—intelligence, wisdom, and creativity. Thus, one can have a reasonably high degree of confidence in the interpretation of the data, especially because the dimensions do, in fact, seem to capture people's intuitions about the respective natures of the three psychological constructs. Moreover, the substantive dimensions are consistent with the earlier correlational data (from Experiment 1), indicating that of the implicit theories for the three possible pairs of attributes, the greatest similarity is between the implicit theories for wisdom and creativity. Finally, the results for intelligence largely replicate those of Sternberg et al. (1981), who used a different methodology (factor analysis), a different set of subjects, and a different (but related) set of behaviors to study conceptions of intelligence. Thus, at least for the one psychological construct that has been subject to implicit-theoretical analysis before, the present results appear to be robust.

Experiment 3

Method. Thirty adult subjects from the New Haven area were given four psychometric tests: the Cattell and Cattell Test of *g*, the Group Embedded Figures Test, the George Washington Social Intelligence Test, and the Chapin Social Insight Test. These tests have been widely used in psychometric investigations of cognitive and social intelligence, and have been shown to have reasonable construct validity. Paper-and-pencil creativity tests were not employed because of the view of the investigator, as well as of many other investigators in the field (e.g., Amabile, 1983; Cronbach, 1984; Feldman, 1980; Simonton, 1984) that such tests capture, at best, only the most trivial aspects of creativity. In addition, subjects were asked to fill out all three of the questionnaires from Experiment 1—those for intelligence, wisdom, and creativity— as they pertained to themselves (rather than as they pertained to an ideal individual, as in Experiment 1). The same subjects filled out all three questionnaires in counterbalanced order. Only those questionnaire items were retained that had received principal-component loadings of .50 or greater in Experiment 1. Subjects used a 1–9 scale, where 1 indicated a behavior that was extremely uncharacteristic of the individual, and 9 indicated a behavior that was extremely characteristic. Subjects were given as long as they needed to complete the questionnaires.

Convergent-discriminant validation. Questionnaires were scored by correlating each subject's response pattern on the questionnaire he or she completed (intelligence, wisdom, or creativity) with the "prototype" questionnaire obtained from the laypersons in Experiment 1. The prototype contained the set of ratings for the hypothetical ideal individual, with respect to either intelligence, wisdom, or creativity. Thus, the correlation measured the degree of resemblance between the actual individual in this experiment and the hypothetical ideal individual emerging from Experiment 1. A higher correlation indicated greater correspondence to the hypothetical ideal, whereas a lower correlation indicated lesser correspondence to the ideal. A negative correlation indicated an inverse relationship.

The strongest correlations were obtained for intelligence. A correlation of .48 was obtained with the Cattell and Cattell Test of *g*, which is a nonverbal intelligence test. This result replicates the correlation with the verbal Henmon-Nelson Mental Ability Test obtained by Sternberg et al. (1981), which was also high (.52). The intelligence prototype correlation thus measures characteristics that overlap with those measured by intelligence tests, although the prototype also measures social-competence aspects of intelligence that are not measured by traditional psychometric intelligence tests. Significant correlations were also obtained with the Embedded Figures Test (.54), which is a measure of field independence that tends to correlate with spatial ability, and with the Chapin Social Insight Test (.43), a measure of social intelligence/competence. Meaningful correlations were obtained for the wisdom prototype scores and the George Washington Social Intelligence Test (.38) and the Chapin Social Insight Test (.46), both of which measure those aspects of intelligence that would seem to be most akin to wisdom. Finally, no significant correlations were obtained for creativity, but then, there were no creativity tests included in the battery for lack of adequate available tests.

Summary. The multidimensional scaling results of the previous experiment showed the high "internal validity" of the implicit theories described in the experimental results. But to be of psychological interest, implicit theories should also have external validity (i.e., relations to other theories), and measures based on implicit theories should have external validity as well (i.e., relations to measures based on other theories). The results of the present experiment show that the proposed implicit theories and the measures based upon them do indeed have external as well as internal validity. Prototype scores derived from the implicit theories were shown to have sensible correlations with measures based on external theories, with the correlations falling into a pattern suggesting both convergent and discriminant validity for the proposed measures. Thus, implicit theories of intelligence, wisdom, and creativity do not occur in a vacuum and are not isolated from explicit theories. Rather, implicit theories appear to be compatible with explicit theories, at least in the present results.

Experiment 4

Method. In this experiment, 40 New Haven area adults were presented with 54 simulated letters of recommendation.Two typical letters would contain the following descriptions:

Gerald

He possesses ability for high achievement.

He has the ability to grasp complex situations.

He has good problem-solving ability.

He attaches importance to well-presented ideas.

Doris

She is motivated by goals.

She questions societal norms, truisms, and assumptions.

She thinks quickly.

She is not materialistic.

She is totally absorbed in study.

Descriptions were generated so as to vary predicted levels of intelligence, wisdom, and creativity. Each description was either four, five, or six sentences in length, and was paired equally often with names of males and with names of females. A given subject saw a given description only once—either with a male name or with a female name. The subject's task was to rate the intelligence, wisdom, and creativity of each of the described individuals. The ratings were made in a Latin square order across subjects, so that each rating occurred equally often in each ordinal position. Ratings were made on a 9-point scale, where 1 indicated that the individual to be rated was not at all intelligent, wise, or creative, and 9 indicated that the individual was extremely intelligent, wise, or creative.

It was possible to obtain predicted ratings of intelligence, wisdom, and creativity by summing up the ratings of laypersons from Experiment 1 on each attribute for each subject and then dividing by the number of attributes given for the hypothetical individual. Averages rather than sums of ratings were used because the number of behaviors was not the same for each of the descriptions.

Suppose, for example, that five behaviors were given for Susan. The predicted intelligence rating would be the mean of the characteristicness ratings for intelligence in Experiment 1 (plus a constant); the predicted wisdom rating would be the mean of the Experiment 1 ratings for wisdom (plus a constant); and the predicted creativity rating would be the mean of the Experiment 1 ratings for creativity (plus a constant). Thus, the more closely the description of the hypothetical individual resembled the ideal (of Experiment 1) on each of the three attributes of intelligence, wisdom, and creativity, the higher should be the rating that hypothetical individual received in the present experiment.

Means. Mean ratings of hypothetical individuals were 5.8 for intelligence, 5.3 for wisdom, and 5.0 for creativity. The ratings were highly reliable, with split-half reliabilities of .84 for intelligence, .85 for wisdom, and .93 for creativity.

Intercorrelations of ratings. Intercorrelations of ratings were .94 between intelligence and wisdom, .69 between intelligence and creativity, and .62 between wisdom and creativity. Thus, the rank order of correlations was the same as that in past experiments, although in this experiment, intelligence and wisdom were almost indistinguishable. Use of male versus female names had no effect: The means were identical within .1 on the rating scale, and correlations of patterns of results for male versus female names were .97 for intelligence, .95 for wisdom, and .94 for creativity.

Simple correlations between predicted and observed ratings. The correlations between predicted and observed ratings generally showed the hoped-for fit of the model to the data. In each case, the correlation between the predicted and observed values of a given attribute was substantial: .89 for intelligence, .96 for wisdom, and .89 for creativity. Moreover, the correlation between predicted and observed values for a given attribute was always higher than the correlation between predicted and observed values across attributes (e.g., predicted values for creativity with observed values for wisdom). Thus, people not only seem to have implicit theories of intelligence, wisdom, and creativity, but to use these implicit theories in predictable ways to judge others.

Multiple regressions of observed on predicted ratings. How well could the observed ratings for each attribute be predicted if all three predicted ratings (intelligence, wisdom, and creativity) were allowed to enter into each regression equation? Multiple regressions were used to answer this question. The squared multiple correlations between observed ratings for intelligence, wisdom, and creativity, on the one hand, and the predicted values, on the other, were .85, .92, and .87, respectively. In other words, the observed ratings could be predicted very well from the combined predictions. In each regression, the highest standardized regression coefficient was for the attribute being predicted. Thus, for example, in predicting the wisdom rating, the highest weight was for the predicted wisdom rating, rather than for the predicted intelligence rating or the predicted creativity rating.

Summary. People not only have implicit theories, but also use their implicit theories in predictable ways. It is possible to predict their evaluations of others on the basis of knowledge about their implicit theories. Despite the seeming omnipresence of standardized tests in our society, most evaluations of people's abilities are still done informally—through informal conversations, interviews, letters of recommendation, secondhand comments, and the like. Psychometric tests tell us nothing about how these informal evaluations are made. But the results of implicit-theoretical evaluations do. It is possible to predict a person's evaluation of the intelligence, wisdom, or creativity of another by knowing the evaluator's implicit theory and the information available about the person to be evaluated.

Conclusions

Previous research has given us some sense of the nature of intelligence, wisdom, and creativity, but different methods, instruments, subjects, and experiments have made comparisons across these three constructs difficult. The research described here has made it possible to compare the natures of the three constructs more directly, at least as they are perceived by four groups of people. Consider each of the three constructs in turn, and what we have learned about it.

Intelligence

Laypersons. People's conceptions of intelligence overlap with, but go beyond, the skills measured by conventional intelligence tests. Thus, the problem-solving (fluid ability) and verbal comprehension (crystallized ability) skills measured by intelligence tests appear most prominently in the dimensions of the derived implicit theory of intelligence. The intelligent individual is perceived to solve problems well, reason clearly, think logically, use a good vocabulary, and draw upon a large store of information—just the kinds of things conventional intelligence tests measure. But also embedded within people's conceptions of intelligence are a person's ability to balance information, to be goal oriented and to aim for achievement of those goals, and to show one's intelligence in worldly, as opposed to strictly academic, contexts. People, in general, thus seem to be more concerned with the practical and worldly aspect of intelligence than are the creators of intelligence tests.

Specialists. Whereas the professors of art emphasized knowledge and the ability to use that knowledge in weighing alternative possibilities and in seeing analogies, the business professors emphasized the ability to think logically, to focus on essential aspects of a problem, and both to follow others' arguments easily and to see where these arguments lead. The emphasis on assessment of argumentation in the business professors' implicit theories is far weaker in the artists' implicit theories. The philosophy professors emphasized critical and logical abilities very heavily, and especially the ability to follow complex arguments, to find subtle mistakes in these arguments, and to generate counterexamples to invalid arguments. The philosophers' view very clearly emphasized those aspects of logic and rationality that are essential in analyzing and creating philosophical arguments. The physicists, in contrast, placed more emphasis on precise mathematical thinking, the ability to relate physical phenomena to the concepts of physics, and to grasp quickly the laws of nature.

Wisdom

Laypersons. The wise individual is perceived as having much the same analytical reasoning ability that is found in the intelligent individual. But the wise person has a certain sagacity that is not necessarily found in the intelligent person: He or she listens to others, knows how to weigh advice, and can deal with a variety of different kinds of people. In seeking as much information as possible for decision making, the wise individual makes use of the obviously available information but also reads between the lines. The wise individual is especially well able to make clear, sensible, and fair judgments, and in doing so, takes a long-term as well as a short-term view of the consequences of the judgments made. Wise individuals are perceived to profit from the experience of others, and to learn from others' mistakes, as well as from their own. Such individuals are not afraid to change their minds as experience dictates, and the solutions that are offered to complex problems tend to be the right ones.

Specialists. Implicit theories of wisdom show considerable overlap across fields of specialization. Nevertheless, there are some differences in implicit theories. Art professors emphasize insight, knowing how to balance logic and instinct, knowing how to transform creativity into concepts, and sensitivity. These aspects of wisdom would seem quite relevant in the mature appreciation and evaluation of art. Business professors emphasize maturity of judgment, understanding of the limitations of one's own actions and recommendations, knowing what one does and does not know, possession of a long-term perspective on things, knowing when not to act as well as when one should act, acceptance of reality, good decision making, the ability to distinguish substance from style, and appreciation of the ideologies of others. These aspects of wisdom would seem particularly relevant in making and evaluating business decisions. Philosophy professors emphasize balanced judgment, nonautomatic acceptance of the prevailing wisdom, concentration on fundamental questions, resistance to fads, looking for fundamental principles or intuitions behind a viewpoint, concern with large purposes, openness to ideas, ability to use facts correctly, avoidance of jargon, possession of a sense of where future progress is possible, unwillingness to become obsessed with a single theory, attention to both scope and detail, and a sense of justice. All of these talents would seem relevant to the construction and evaluation of philosophical arguments. Finally, physicists emphasize appreciation of the various factors that contribute to a situation, familiarization with previous work and techniques in the field, knowing if solving a problem is likely to produce important results, awareness of the significant problems in the field, knowledge of the human and political elements of scientific work, contemplation, and recognition of aspects of physical phenomena that underlie the concepts of physics. These skills would seem to be helpful in attaining a deep understanding of the nature of physics and of its place both in science and in the world.

Creativity

Laypersons. Conceptions of creativity overlap with those of intelligence, but there is much less emphasis in implicit theories of creativity on analytical abilities, whether they be directed toward abstract problems or toward verbal materials. For example, the very first dimension shows a greater emphasis on nonentrenchment, or the ability and willingness to go beyond ordinary limitations of self and environment and to think and act in unconventional and even dreamlike ways. The creative individual has a certain freedom of spirit and unwillingness to be bound by the unwritten canons of society, characteristics not necessarily found in the highly intelligent individuals. Implicit theories of creativity encompass a dimension of aesthetic taste and imagination that is absent in implicit theories of intelligence, and also encompass aspects of inquisitiveness and intuitiveness that do not seem to enter into the implicit theories of intelligence. Implicit theories of creativity go far beyond conventional psychometric creativity tests. A person's ability to think of unusual uses for a brick, or to form a picture based on a geometric outline, scarcely does justice to the kind of freedom of spirit and intellect captured in people's implicit theories of creativity.

Specialists. Implicit theories of creativity in the specialized fields were highly overlapping across fields and also overlapped highly with the implicit theories of laypersons; nevertheless, there were some differences worthy of note. Professors of art placed heavy emphasis upon imagination and originality, as well as upon an abundance of new ideas and a willingness to try them out. The creative visual artist is a risk-taker, and persists in following through on the consequences of risks. Such a person thinks metaphorically, and prefers forms of communication other than strictly verbal ones. Business professors also emphasize the ability to generate new ideas and to explore these ideas, especially as they relate to novel business services and products. The creative individual escapes traps of conventional thinking, and can imagine a possible state that is quite different from what exists. Philosophy professors emphasize the ability to toy imaginatively with notions and combinations of ideas, and to create classifications and systematizations of knowledge that differ from the conventional ones. Creative individuals never automatically accept the "accepted," and when they have novel hunches, these hunches pay off. The creative person is particularly well able to generate insights regarding connections between seemingly unrelated issues, and to form useful analogies and explanations. The physics professors share many of these same ideas about the creative individual, but show a particular concern with inventiveness, the ability to find order in chaos, and the ability to question basic principles. The physicists emphasize creative aspects of problem solving, such as the ability to approximate solutions, the ability to find shortcuts in problem solving, and the ability to go beyond standard methods of problem solving. Finally, the physicist seeks in a creative person the ability to make discoveries by looking for reasons why things happen the way they do. Such discoveries may result from the perception of physical and other patterns that most others simply do not perceive.

In conclusion, people have implicit theories of intelligence, wisdom, and creativity, and they use these theories both in conceptualizing the constructs, and in evaluating themselves and others. To understand these conceptions and their use, and to attain some appreciation of the psychological constructs themselves, it is useful to study people's implicit theories of the nature of their minds.

REFERENCES

Amabile, T. M. (1983). *The social psychology of creativity*. New York: Springer Press.

Barron, F. (1955). The disposition toward originality. *Journal of Abnormal and Social Psychology, 51*, 478–485.

Barron, F. (1963). The needs for order and disorder as motivation in creative activity. In C. W. Taylor & F. Barron (Eds.), *Scientific creativity: Its recognition and development* (pp. 153–160). New York: Wiley.

Cattell, R. B. (1971). *Abilities: Their structure, growth and action*. Boston: Houghton Mifflin.

Cattell, R. B., & Butcher, H. S. (1968). *The prediction of achievement and creativity*. New York: Bobbs-Merrill.

Clayton, V. (1975). Erikson's theory of human development as it applies to the aged: Wisdom as contradictory cognition. *Human Development, 18*, 119–128.

Clayton, V. (1976). *A multidimensional scaling analysis of the concept of wisdom.* Unpublished doctoral dissertation, University of Southern California.

Clayton, V. (1982). Wisdom and intelligence: The nature and function of knowledge in the later years. In S. Brent (Ed.), *Aging and wisdom: Individual development and social function*. New York: Springer.

Clayton, V., & Birren, J. E. (1980). The development of wisdom across the lifespan: A reexamination of an ancient topic. In P. B. Baltes & O. G. Brim (Eds.), *Life-span development and behavior* (Vol. 3). New York: Academic Press.

Cox, C. M. (1926). *Genetic studies of genius: Vol. 2. The early mental traits of three hundred geniuses*. Stanford, CA: Stanford University Press.

Cronbach, L. J. (1984). *Essentials of psychological testing* (4th ed.). New York: Harper & Row.

Davidson, J. E., & Sternberg, R. J. (1984). The role of insight in intellectual giftedness. *Gifted Child Quarterly, 28*, 58–64.

Dittman-Kohli, F., & Baltes, P. B. (in press). Toward a neofunctionalist conception of adult intellectual development: Wisdom as a prototypical case of intellectual growth. In C. Alexander & E. Langer (Eds.), *Beyond formal operations: Alternative endpoints to human development*. New York: Oxford University Press.

Feldman, D. H. (1980). *Beyond universals in cognitive development*. Norwood, NJ: Ablex.

Gardner, M. (1983). *Frames of mind: The theory of multiple intelligences*. New York: Basic Books.

Getzels, J. W., & Jackson, P. W. (1962). *Creativity and intelligence: Explorations with gifted students*. New York: Wiley.

Guilford, J. P. (1950). Creativity. *American Psychologist, 5*, 444–454.

Guilford, J. P. (1956). The structure of intellect. *Psychological Bulletin, 53*, 267–293.

Guilford, J. P. (1959). Three faces of intellect. *American Psychologist, 14*, 469–479.

Guilford, J. P. (1967). *The nature of human intelligence*. New York: McGraw-Hill.

Hunt, E. B. (1978). Mechanics of verbal ability. *Psychological Review, 85*, 109–130.

Hunt, E. B., Lunneborg, C., & Lewis, J. (1975). What does it mean to be high verbal? *Cognitive Psychology, 7*, 194–227.

Jensen, A. R. (1979). *g*: Outmoded theory or unconquered frontier? *Creative Science and Technology, 2,* 16–29.

Keating, D. P., & Bobbitt, B. L. (1978). Individual and developmental differences in cognitive processing components of mental ability. *Child Development, 49,* 155–167.

Kohler, W. (1927). *The mentality of apes.* New York: Harcourt, Brace.

MacKinnon, D. W. (1965). Personality and the realization of creative potential. *American Psychologist, 20,* 273–281.

MacKinnon, D. W. (1975). IPAR's contribution to the conceptualization and study of creativity. In I. A. Taylor & J. W. Getzels (Eds.), *Perspectives in creativity* (pp. 60–89). Chicago: Aldine.

Mulholland, T. M., Pellegrino, J. W., & Glaser, R. (1980). Components of geometric analogy solution. *Cognitive Psychology, 12,* 252–284.

Pellegrino, J. W., & Glaser, R. (1979). Cognitive correlates and components in the analysis of individual differences. In R. J. Sternberg & D. K. Detterman (Eds.), *Human intelligence: Perspectives on its theory and measurement* (pp. 61–88). Norwood, NJ: Ablex.

Perkins, D. (1981). *The mind's best work.* Cambridge, MA: Harvard University Press.

Roe, A. (1952). *The making of a scientist.* New York: Dodd, Mead.

Simonton, D. K. (1984). *Genius, creativity and leadership.* Cambridge, MA: Harvard University Press.

Spearman, C. (1927). *The abilities of man.* New York: Macmillan.

Sternberg, R. J. (1977). *Intelligence, information processing, and analogical reasoning: The componential analysis of human abilities.* Hillsdale, NJ: Erlbaum.

Sternberg, R. J. (1979). The nature of mental abilities. *American Psychologist, 34,* 214–230.

Sternberg, R. J. (1985a). *Beyond IQ: A triarchic theory of human intelligence.* New York: Cambridge University Press.

Sternberg, R. J. (1985b). Implicit theories of intelligence, creativity, and wisdom. *Journal of Personality and Social Psychology, 49,* 607–627.

Sternberg, R. J., Conway, B. E., Ketron, J. L., & Bernstein, M. (1981). People's conceptions of intelligence. *Journal of Personality and Social Psychology, 41,* 37–55.

Sternberg, R. J., & Davidson, J. E. (1983). Insight in the gifted. *Educational Psychologist, 18,* 52–58.

Terman, L. M., & Oden, M. (1947). *The gifted child grows up.* Stanford, CA: Stanford University Press.

Thurstone, L. L. (1938). *Primary mental abilities.* Chicago: University of Chicago.

Torrance, E. P. (1966). *Tests of creative thinking.* Lexington, MA: Personnel Press.

Vernon, P. E. (1971). *The structure of human abilities.* London: Methuen.

Wallach, M. A., & Kogan, N. (1965). *Modes of thinking in young children.* New York: Holt, Rinehart and Winston.

Wertheimer, M. (1959). *Productive thinking* (rev. ed.). New York: Harper & Row.

Whitely, S. E. (1977). Information-processing on intelligence test items: Some response components. *Applied Psychological Measurement, 1,* 465–476.

5

Construct Validation
After Thirty Years

LEE J. CRONBACH

This chapter happily recalls the team effort of 1950–54 in which Lloyd Humphreys and I took part, from which came the first professional standards for tests (American Psychological Association, 1954) and the formal recognition of construct validation (CV).[1] In adopting the fourth edition of its *Standards for Educational and Psychological Testing*, the profession has just this year renewed its commitment to that line of thought (American Educational Research Association, American Psychological Association, and National Council on Measurement in Education, 1985). It is therefore timely to review why construct validation was introduced and how it has worked out so far.

My evaluation, though positive, will not be relentlessly upbeat. The formal statement of the idea harmonized with the philosophy of science of 1950, whereas recent philosophy voices such ideas in a much lower key. Beyond that is the sad fact that almost every psychologist writing about CV applies to it the word "confusing." The conception has been hard to translate into actions, and the literature on CV wavers across the range from utopian doctrine to vapid permissiveness. So I am speaking of unfinished business.

Perinatal Events

The currents of professional politics brought CV into psychology. Prior to 1940, when the American Psychological Association was dominated by academics, psychologists with clinical, educational, industrial, and counseling responsibilities had been sufficiently unhappy to form their own Association for Applied Psychology. Around 1945, a merger created a "new APA" committed to scientific *and* service ideals. One of its first activities was to prepare a code of ethics.

Practitioners and academics differed about propriety in testing. Practitioners were optimistically expanding the variety and use of tests while academics expressed skepticism and advised restraint. In those days many tests, being by-products of work having other objectives, were inadequately supported by rationale or by evidence. Enthusiasts for some tests (mostly tests of personality) made dubitable claims, and discredited tests were being exploited in some personnel selection. As a part of professional self-governance, the Association intended to impose sanctions on violators of the ethics code, but to achieve that goal the bounds of acceptable practice had to be defined.

A team of specialists in measurement was asked in 1950 to spell out the marks of adequacy in a psychological test. Those who established our committee saw the task as forthright, I think. Did not specialists agree as to how accurate a group mental test for schools should be? as to the predictive power necessary in a test for salespersons?—and so on. Our committee refused to draw a line between good and bad tests, because a test unsuitable in one setting can serve well in another. Moreover, to impose on all testing the standards appropriate in traditional applications would inhibit investigation of elusive variables like creativity and motivation to achieve. We concluded that developers meet their obligations by providing a potential purchaser with the information needed to choose a test and use it appropriately.

Statistical test theory was pertinent, but questions beyond its scope quickly arose. Measures of vocational interests became the proving ground for the first draft of trial standards. Expert counselors, we learned, were treating the test neither as a direct predictor nor as an inventory based on logical content rubrics; the counselor was seeking to extend the client's understanding, relying on the test scales for a conceptual framework. Scales of Strong's interest blank could distinguish persons in a given occupation from persons in general, but the meaning of scores was not transparent. To summarize in terms of "Physician interests," for example, underplays the fact that medical specialties differ in the interest patterns they appeal to. Furthermore, the Physician scores should advance the self-understanding of young persons *not* going into medicine.

The committee asked two members—Paul Meehl and Robert Challman—to consider what evidence would justify the *psychological* interpretation that was the stock-in-trade of counselors and clinicians. From responses to an anxiety scale, for example, the clinician may make inferences about a client's level of chronic distress, willingness to attempt difficult problems, or risk of underachievement. To validate a type of inference (said the subcommittee) is to determine whether other lines of evidence are congruent with the inference, in suitable samples of subjects. Our final report recognized this as "construct validation," as one way to justify use of a test. The committee requested preparation of an unofficial supplement to spell out the logic and methods of CV. Challman being busy with his private practice, Meehl developed the article with my help as committee chairman and generalist in testing (Cronbach & Meehl, 1955).

We were not radical innovators, but tellers of a tale already known in fragmentary form. Thus Humphreys (1952) had written on the requirements for measuring a trait and on the limits of criteria. In educational testing, the Thorndikean emphasis on matching tests to lesson content was giving way to Tyler's emphasis on generalized educational outcomes such as understanding the nature of mathematical proof. But in a doctoral dissertation that investigated the "Nature of Proof" test of the Tyler group, Damrin (1952) had found that pupils' response processes were inconsistent with the interpretation offered by those authors. Another inspiration for us was the many excellent research programs whose instruments did not admit of conventional validation. Honesty (Hartshorne & May, 1928–1930) is inferred from actions and words, but is not identified by any one indicator. This is also the case with authoritarianism (Adorno, Frenkel-Brunswik, Levinson, & Sanford, 1950). Such variables, then, are constructs and the classic investigations of them were steps toward validation.

What CV Is

In a study of premature infants, a key construct is "gestational age at birth." Nothing is "hypothetical" in that notion—but date of conception does have to be inferred, either from the mother's report or from a test on the fetus or neonate. The mother's report has notorious faults. A test such as Ballard's signs of physical development (Ballard, Novak, & Driver, 1979) has other limitations. Even apart from measurement error, identical twins need not have the same Ballard score. How much to trust the test, and in which cases, is a classic CV problem.

A test interpretation says something about the examinee's physiology or feelings or behavior outside the test setting. Construct validation employs various probes to check on interpretations, then assesses and reports the strengths and limits of the interpretive principles. No one was discontented with the call of our committee for clear statement of the proposed principles, empirical checking, and candor. Many psychologists, however, worried that legitimating CV would encourage insubstantial, jawboning defenses of clinical inferences.

An Illustrative CV Argument

Humphreys's 1979 paper, "The Construct of General Intelligence," illustrates the shape of a CV argument.[2] You should note how diversified his approach was.

Test-criterion correlations gave one conclusion. In almost any military specialty, *general* ability accounts for the power of a comprehensive aptitude battery to predict success; only in a few lines of work do narrower abilities contribute to aptitude. From correlations across tests, Humphreys was able to argue that Piaget's tasks measure general ability plus, secondarily, command of so-called "conservation" principles. This suggested to Humphreys that much research on children's thinking is better interpreted in terms of general ability than in complex Piagetian terms. It also suggested that introducing conservation tasks would improve general tests. Experimental manipulation can check on focused hypotheses about process. Humphreys experimented with scoring rules. When the rule put a premium on quick response, the score did not behave as expected of a measure of general ability. In contrast, scoring rules that emphasized careful discrimination brought scores into line with the construct. Retests over a span of years were compared, to look into the proposition that superior intelligence is a precursor of superior learning. Among young school children, a measure of listening comprehension gave the best forecast of academic development, so in this respect listening is a sounder indicator of general ability than other early performances. Humphreys went on to use twin data, data on educational selection, and much else; I pass over these empirical strands to take up a strand of logical argument.

Items in a mental test should be diverse, Humphreys said, because any redundant component in a set of test items cumulates, whereas a contaminant present in only a few items does not. (In 1960, Humphreys had developed this principle into a criticism of the multitrait-multimethod doctrine, which I shall come to shortly.) The more similar the items, the more the total score is weighted with any shared element. The homogeneous items of the Peabody Picture Vocabulary Test (PPVT) probably have several common elements; *most* items call upon the child's verbal experience, judgment, and adeptness at test taking. All such elements cumulate, and load into the final score. With respect to a construct of intelligence, some of these components are contaminants. If a homogeneous test points at precisely the locus in the ability space that matches a proposed interpretation, it is uncontaminated. But how is an investigator to know that the common demand of the items in a given test matches that ideal locus, having no pervasive contaminant?

But then, how is *Humphreys* to know that the redundant core of his heterogeneous test points toward the desired spot? His "general ability" is to some extent a cultural artifact, the central tendency of the ability tests American psychologists have worked with (Jensen, 1984, p. 573). Has the historical process located that center where it should be? The Kaufmans (1983) would say not. In their new "intelligence test," closure and memory tasks receive unprecedented emphasis, while emphasis is withdrawn from verbal comprehension. I understand their working hypothesis to be (in part) that intelligence does not correlate with ethnicity; if a task correlates with ethnicity, that is evidence of invalidity for them but not for Humphreys. In the long run, the community will judge which conceptualization provides the most satisfying explanation for the many phenomena in which general ability plays a part.

Developments After 1955

Generalizing Beyond Science

The conception of CV has evolved. CV came in as an alternative style of validation—almost, as a last resort where analysis of content or predictive power could not support a validity claim. Today, CV is seen as the base on which the other approaches rest (e.g., Messick, 1975).

In criterion-related validation we generally should inspect the criterion for contaminants and missing ingredients. That is, CV of the criterion is wanted (Cronbach, 1971; Dunnette, 1976). Content validation stops with a demonstration that the test conforms to a specification; however, the claim that the *specification* is well chosen embodies a CV claim (Cronbach, 1971, pp. 460–464). Frederiksen's (1984) phrase "the real test bias" reminds us that a test certifying possession (or lack) of job skills is probably invalid if it calls mostly for verbal answers, no matter how relevant the topics are to the job. Moreover, measures of "competence" are used as forecasts of learners' ability to cope in various future situations. These inferences are construct mediated (Linn, 1979). Any interpretation invokes constructs if it reaches beyond the specific, local, concrete situation that was observed. Then it is a proper subject for CV.

To call Test A valid or Test B invalid is illogical. Particular interpretations are what we validate. To say "The evidence to date is consistent with the interpretation" makes far better sense than saying, "The test has construct validity." Validation is a lengthy, even endless process. A test interpretation almost never has a consolidated theory as its armature; mostly, we rely on crude theory-sketches. The loose assembly of concepts and implications used in typical test interpretations I shall call "a construction" rather than "a theory."

Interpretation must rest partly on common sense. A rule used in law-school admissions, for example, is not justified merely by establishing a formula that predicts grades from aptitude. The selection rule embodies judgments. To note just one: The school might select top-down on the basis of predicted grade average, or might rule out truly inadequate students at the bottom and then select among the survivors in a way that maximizes diversity. This choice rests on value assumptions, or, you might say, on beliefs about the long-run empirical consequences for society. Such assumptions or beliefs require diligent scrutiny.

As House (1980) points out, social decisions cannot be based solely on facts and logic. Knowledge is incomplete, and members of the community fill in the gray areas on the basis of their world views. In the face of this, a persuasive defense of an interpretation will have to combine evidence, logic, and rhetoric. What is persuasive depends on the beliefs in the community. Even in science, rationality is now identified with collective judgments that allegiances and prior beliefs influence (Toulmin, 1972, esp. p. 485).

A major source on validity is the writings of Donald Campbell and his colleagues (Campbell, 1957, 1960; Campbell & Fiske, 1959; Campbell & Stanley, 1963; Cook & Campbell, 1976, 1979). It was Cook and Campbell who gave proper breadth to the notion of constructs. In 1955 Cronbach and Meehl (to be referred to as CM; see Note 1), preoccupied with tests of personality and ability, identified constructs solely with characteristics of persons. Cook and Campbell (1976, p. 276) advanced the larger view that constructs enter whenever one pins labels on causes or outcomes.[3] Social and behavioral scientists label kinds of work, lessons, clinical treatments, perceptual tasks, practice conditions, etc., as well as variables describing the person or community. Constructs, then, are ubiquitous.

Falsification

Meehl and I wrote as if validation consists not so much in questioning the proposed interpretation as in accumulating results consistent with it, and the same "confirmationist" bias has colored the *Standards*. Writers of the first *Standards* (then designated "technical recommendations") were calling on soft psychology to present hard evidence. Perhaps it was a desire not to be perceived as blue-nosed persecutors that led us to accent the positive, to talk mostly about how to *support* an interpretation.

According to Popper, however, serious validation gives a construction a hard time by searching out conditions under which it breaks down and by looking into plausible alternative interpretations. In a 1953 lecture, Popper had said: "Every genuine *test* of a theory is an attempt . . . to refute it. . . . Confirming evidence should not count *except when* it . . . can be presented as a serious but unsuccessful attempt to falsify the theory" (1962, p. 36). CM did mention the special virtue of daring predictions, but it remained for Campbell (1957) to stress "plausible rival hypotheses." Of rival hypotheses there is no end; the one that hearers find credible is the one that has impact. The advocate can offset that impact—or profit from the criticism—only by carrying out the checks the counterargument suggests.

Despite many statements calling for focus on rival hypotheses, most of those who undertake CV have remained confirmationist. Falsification, obviously, is something we prefer to do unto the constructions of others. Besides, as Kuhn (1962) taught us, falsification does not quite work. Theorists have a wonderful power to shake off lethal doses of it (Serlin & Lapsley, 1985). I find appealing a substitute for the language of falsification that McGuire (1983, esp. pp. 7, 43) has recently offered. For him, empirical confrontation is a constructive search for hidden assumptions, and an effort to distinguish contexts that the hypothesis fits from those where it is misleading.

Convergence and Discrimination

The Campbell-Fiske paper (1959) has been enormously popular because it offered a recipe for investigating CV. The *Standards* and the CM paper, calling for diversified inquiry, had dismissed the thought of any off-the-shelf procedure. Campbell and Fiske, however, produced a software package—the multitrait-multimethod (MM) matrix—to help beginners make a start toward CV. Unfortunately, users of their package rarely go beyond it, to match inquiry specifically to the construction under test.

Two notions about good constructs are embedded in the MM package. The first, a call for convergence, is that a construct gains power as we devise more ways to measure it. Instruments supposedly measuring the same variable should correlate. If the measures do not concur, they cannot properly be given the same interpretation.

The second notion, a call for divergence, is that constructs should not be redundant. If constructs are distinct, their measures ought to rank persons differently, or in some other way to give distinctive reports.

For example, persons' rankings on certain measures of "social intelligence" nearly duplicated their rankings on measures of scholastic aptitude. This seemed to warrant rejecting social intelligence, as a superfluous construct.

The Campbell-Fiske correlational check is not subtle. A substantial correlation of Trait 1 with Trait 2 does not make the 1–2 distinction untenable; rather, the correlation puts the advocate under pressure to create conditions under which the variables pull apart. (Sternberg and Weil, 1980, did this with subtypes of syllogistic reasoning.) Person variables that correlate highly can have distinct meanings. Ability to compute accurately is so consistent from one kind of problem to another that computation satisfies all the usual statistical criteria for an indivisible trait. Nonetheless, investigators who dig deeper can divide the trait. Less able pupils have particular faulty techniques ("buggy algorithms") that cause failure on one subcategory of arithmetic tasks and not on another (Birenbaum & Tatsuoka, 1982).

Pluralism and Process

Science is pluralistic. Subgroups in a discipline adopt distinct research programs, resting on different interpretive schemes and different strategies. New findings do not lead to a quick choice of "the sounder theory," in part because a theory tells its adherents what facts to take seriously (Boyd, 1981; Glymour, 1980).

Weltanschauungen such as preference for simplicity or for complexity also make for pluralism. Compare Fiedler's audacious strategy (e.g., Fiedler & Leister, 1977) with the conservatism of Schmidt, Hunter, and Pearlman (1981), strategies widely separated on the bandwidth-fidelity continuum. The validity-generalization thesis of Schmidt et al. appropriately warns against interpreting variation among correlations whenever it might be statistical noise. At times this goes too far—for example, when in the occupational context Hunter (1982) rejects the distinction between numerical and verbal aptitudes (see Cronbach, 1984, pp. 305f.). Still, these authors do make a case that ability tests have much the same validity for all jobs in a broad category, regardless of the situation. For Fiedler, situations matter; the intelligence of a group leader predicts productivity in some situations and not others—and this can be explained. The correlation seems to be appreciable when the leader is motivated, experienced, and at ease with his boss, and not otherwise. Fiedler, tracing multiple contingencies in smallish samples, develops an illuminating construction by accepting the very risk that Schmidt et al. warn against.

The CM paper and many of its successors oversimplify, by underplaying processes and situations. We have the habit of speaking as if a test can be matched to a single trait-construct or, at worst, to a fixed composite of factors. Yet, in an important sense, a performance is not explained until someone identifies the processes that generated it—as the research on arithmetic is doing. In 1965 John French exposed the Achilles' heel of factor analysis: The explanation of a test performance depends on the respondent's process or style. Therefore, no one explanation for a test score is adequate. We will have to accept the viability of alternative explanations, and then will need to explain why the person uses one process rather than another. Now that cognitive psychology is aggressively probing into styles and strategies (Cooper & Regan, 1982; Kyllonen, Lohman, & Woltz, 1984), it becomes more and more evident that the proper rule for interpretation of the test score is not the same for every subject or for the same subject on all occasions. We can hope that integration of information-processing analyses with older research designs will produce more informative CV of real-world tests. (But don't hold your breath; I published that same forecast in 1971!)

CV in Applied Testing

The best examples of CV come from the scientific literature rather than from test manuals or articles concerned with test use. That is no coincidence; CV was drawn from scientific norms. Programs of CV are more recognizable in review articles than in single empirical studies. Wylie's two volumes (1974–1979) on the self-concept and its measurement illustrate the scale of effort required to do justice to a construct that has been studied by investigators from several schools of thought.

Test Manuals

As for the sections labeled CV in test manuals, the good news is that today's manuals rarely flood users with jawboning speculative defenses. The bad news is that they rarely report incisive checks into rival hypotheses, followed by an integrative argument. Rather, they rake together miscellaneous correlations.

The manual for the Peabody Picture Vocabulary Test (PPVT-R; Robertson & Eisenberg, 1981) is a suitable example—in part because I can discuss the ostensible validation without finding fault with the test per se. The CV section says that the construct to be evaluated is "vocabulary," but it does nothing to translate that term into hypotheses; in particular, it says nothing about how this ability differs from general intelligence. Under the CV heading, the Peabody manual tabulates 227 correlations of PPVT with other vocabulary or intelligence scores, followed by 55 pages of abstracts of the sources. In addition, it gives correlations with readiness tests and with two utterly arbitrary variables, Embedded Figures and Bender Gestalt. The correlations for readiness tests range from a discouraging low of .23 to a value of .80—too high to be trusted. The manual does not digest such results or use them to sharpen interpretation. Its conclusion is a feeble evasion: "PPVT and these readiness tests seem to be measuring a common attribute, although the relationship . . . is far from perfect." The manual hands readers a do-it-yourself kit of disjoint facts.

A CV study in a journal most frequently consists of cross-trait and cross-method correlations laid out à la Campbell and Fiske. Although the MM matrix originally rested on subtle reasoning, in most applications the meaning of MM degenerates to "mindless and mechanical." Conclusions are pumped out with no thought to the construction being tested (e.g., Kavanagh, MacKinney, & Wolins, 1971; Phillips, 1981). Here, as with the Peabody test, CV is claimed when no construction has been examined.

A major fault is the presumption that method variance is contamination. Campbell and Fiske (1959) were willing to take as a validity coefficient, as evidence of convergence, the correlation of self-report anxiety with peer ratings of that trait. Their justification could only be that *their* construction viewed self and others as interchangeable perceivers, equally willing to report what they see. For me, self-concept and reputation are distinct constructs, so I would find a high correlation troublesome rather than assuring.

Assessing convergence and divergence is only a first step toward CV; any method variance is a phenomenon to be explained. To illustrate sensible attention to method variance, I mention another study of peer ratings. Some investigators, as Schofield and Whitley (1983) point out, ask pupils to list names of a few classmates they prefer to work with, or play with. Asking the pupil to rate every name on the class roster is usually regarded as a cumbersome way to get the same information. No doubt the two methods satisfy the convergence standard, as the persons nominated will also be rated high. Nonetheless, the two measures require distinct interpretations. Consider the important question: When schools are desegregated, do pupils accept classmates of a different race? Same-race pairings predominate in nomination data, but in full-roster ratings preferences do not follow racial lines. Schofield and Whitley explain the disparity: Race is implicated in *close* companionship. Thus, imperfectly converging measures with the same name may both have validity, when more fully interpreted.

CV and the Law

In politics and law, the CV label has been used to dignify partisan arguments. Psychologists cheered when the Supreme Court began to call for evidence of validity on any selection test that disproportionately rejects minority applicants. We were pleased when the *Standards* were cited as one of the Court's authorities (*Albemarle Paper Co. v. Moody*, 442 U.S. at 435, 1975) and again when the Court was persuaded to give content and construct validation a status comparable to criterion-related validation (*Washington v. Davis*; 426 U.S. at 229, 1976). All three approaches were endorsed in the "Uniform Guidelines" issued shortly thereafter by the major regulatory agencies (Equal Employment Opportunity Commission [EEOC] et al., 1978). By this time, however, CV in the employment context was being hotly contested.

Earlier guidelines issued by the EEOC alone had not sanctioned CV, and EEOC tried to keep it out of the multiagency guidelines. Those of us who saw CV as a particularly toughminded check on test interpretations were bemused by the suspicion of CV arguments as tenderminded and likely to shelter bad tests. EEOC, then committed to increasing minority employment, wanted to discourage testing — "intelligence testing" in particular. One psychologist so felt the heat that he said the EEOC was equating CV with racism (Gorham, 1980, p. 3).

CV made it into the "Uniform Guidelines" because personnel psychologists, including those responsible for government hiring and promotion, wanted to defend tests without collecting criterion data (which is often impracticable). One can sympathize with their problem. Common sense says that nuclear-power operators should be screened for emotional stability, but lapse of self-control on the job is too rare to be taken as the criterion in a statistical study. I fear, though, that an attempt at genuine CV for personality screening would remain a bald and unconvincing narrative, given the sorry state of constructions related to traits like self-control.

As described in the "Uniform Guidelines," CV has two parts: a job analysis identifying a characteristic needed to perform the job, and presentation of evidence that the test measures the characteristic. The only evidence specifically acknowledged as acceptable is the power of the test to predict success on jobs having the same analysis, at other sites. Again, the label CV is attached to an inquiry that essentially ignores construct meanings. Moreover, no thought is given to the validity of job analysis. In contrast, the quasiofficial statement developed by personnel psychologists (American Psychological Association, 1980,

p. 16) was aligned with the *Standards* of that date and made clear that CV is never a quick fix.

CV and "Bias"

A self-critical study of scores used for hiring would have to investigate whether a test contains illegitimate race-related variance, so CV could serve the cause of equal opportunity. Most recently, however, some of those devoted to that cause have overreached. They assert that a test lacks CV unless the statistical relationships it has with other variables among white-majority subjects reappear in every minority group (Mercer, 1984, p. 350; Reynolds & Brown, 1984, pp. 26–28).

For mathematical reasons, correlations and regressions must vary over populations with different score ranges (Linn, 1983). Moreover, it is logically impossible to calculate what the relationships—numerical or causal—would be if, counterfactually, the score ranges became similar (Meehl, 1971). More fundamental than that, interactions are inescapable. The variables engineers use to describe automobile performance are functionally related to the octane rating of the fuel. What the functions will be depends upon the engine design, the cleanness of the engine, and the driving speed. These complications are matters for the engineer to understand, but the variation of the parameters does not per se call the validity of octane measurement into question. So also with ability measures. In principle, every test that correlates with other variables or that changes nonrandomly with conditions can be given a supportable construct interpretation.

Possible Sources of Confusion

I return now to the mainstream of CV discussion. Some of the "confusion" so often mentioned by sympathetic colleagues originated in what CM did and did not say in 1955.

The Nomological Ideal

Many minds have been boggled by the philosophical rationale CM offered. Rather than quote CM, I draw on a recent phrasing by Meehl and Golden (1982). From several pages of metatheory, I have pasted together just enough phrases and sentences to outline the argument.

> Theoretical concepts are defined conceptually or implicitly by their role in a network of nomological or statistical "laws." The meaning is partially given by the theoretical network, however tentative and impoverished that network may be. You know what you mean by an entity to the extent that statements about it in the theoretical language are linked to

statements in the observational language. These statements are about where it's found, what brings it about, what it does, what it's made of. Only a few of those properties are directly tied to observables (p. 136). In [an early] theory sketch, based upon some experience and data, everything said is conjectural. We have tentative notions about some fallible indicators [of the construct] with unknown validities (p. 144). [When we check up empirically on predictions from the model] we are testing the crude theory sketch, we are tightening the network psychometrically, and we are validating the indicators. All of these are done simultaneously (p. 149).

Some of this language harks back to the positivists' ideal of "reconstruction" of scientific knowledge as a formal deductive system. A generalization was to count as lawlike only if it was embedded in "an established scientific deductive system" (Braithwaite, 1953, p. 301), and only if it stated what occurs whenever and wherever certain specified conditions arise (Kaplan, 1964, pp. 91ff.).[4] Even in the 1950s, the philosophers were careful to say that such systems are achieved only approximately and only in a mature branch of science, and that in psychology such strong theory is at best a hope for the distant future (Hempel, 1965, pp. 111, 150; Scriven, 1956). Though the 1955 CM paper did emphasize that constructs are initially crude and even speculative, it may have been a tactical error to tie CV to the deductive ideal.

Paragraphs on the network and on links between theoretical notions and observables added dignity to the CM paper. They bolstered a virtuous claim that CV was in line with philosophy of science, and not a nostrum brewed up hastily to relieve psychology's pains. Still, it was pretentious to dress up our immature science in positivist language; and it was self-defeating to say (CM, p. 290) that a construct not part of a nomological network is not scientifically admissible. On the most encouraging reading, this distinguishes established constructs from candidate constructs, and holds out hope that the testers' candidates will someday be admissible. A construct such as "encoding" or "self-concept" or "social status" points to a conjectural explanation. These interim understandings are the crude ore the scientific method intends to turn into gold.

In his 1960 paper, Campbell both endorsed the CM rationale and demurred. He evidently feared that CV would price itself out of the market by calling for a deductive power that psychologists' constructions lack—but so do those of physics (Putnam, 1978, p. 72). He advised test psychologists to set aside the standard of ideal nomological argument, and to concentrate on establishing what he called "trait validity." Psychologists are working with "folk constructs," not theoretical terms (Campbell, personal communication, 1985; see also Cook & Campbell, 1979, p. 38). Simple tactics, including the MM matrix, could check out the main notions in what I am calling a "construction." Unfortunately, Campbell's 1960 paper did not fix attention on the role of rival hypotheses, and most of his would-be followers lost sight of the substantive aspect of trait validity (as I have already illustrated).

The Operationalist Orthodoxy

Norris (1983, p. 71) has a certain justification for saying that "the foundations of CV theory rest heavily on an outmoded and largely discredited theory of science—that is, logical positivism." Philosophers now avoid Hempel's term "deductive-nomological," and they distrust the distinction between constructs and observables (Glymour, 1980; Suppé, 1977). The new cliché, "Observations are theory-laden," recognizes how a scientist has to work. A particular conceptualization determines what a scientist tries to observe; in describing procedures, the investigator omits to mention whatever details or conditions lack a place in that network. What was "discredited" was an attempt by philosophers to distinguish the empirical work of scientists from their intellectual work (Achinstein & Barker, 1969; Shapere, 1984, chap. 8). Richard Boyd, a contemporary philosopher who has no kind word for positivists, not only states principles of validation for "theoretical entities" that coincide with the concepts of Meehl and Golden in all save wording, but refers to those principles as "commonplace" in philosophy (Boyd, 1981, p. 619).

In the history of CV, the only sustained attack came from associates of the philosopher Gustav Bergmann at the University of Iowa (Bechtoldt, 1959; Brodbeck, 1957; Ebel, 1961). These critics undertook a last-ditch defense of the doctrine of "operationalism," which nearly all the philosophers were rejecting in the 1950s. Bergmann (1953) himself had called the contrast between complexly defined "intervening" (operational) variables and constructs a pseudodistinction. Scriven was to say later (1969, p. 198) that operationalism never made good sense as philosophy, and that psychology was the only science that had espoused it. The constructs defined by CM as relationships in an abstract network puzzled and troubled the psychologists who espoused operationalism.

When our committee set to work, words such as the following were much in the air: "To claim that a test measures anything over and above its criterion is pure speculation of the type that is not amenable to verification and hence falls outside the realm of experimental science" (Anastasi, 1950, p. 67). Psychologists were told not to pursue the "will-o'-the-wisp" of processes distinct from observed performance (Anastasi, p. 77). If we took that bygone language seriously, we could not discuss whether a poor ability score reflects lack of motivation, lack of competence, or emotional upset. Anastasi did not in fact hobble herself as the doctrine suggested. The validation procedures she recommended were included in the program of CV (CM, p. 286), and she in turn incorporated CV into her later writings.

Operationalism lingers on in the hearts of some specialists in achievement testing (see Ebel, 1984, p. 144; Norris, 1983). For them, interpretation begins and ends with a highly specific definition of the kinds of tasks the examinee should be faced with; a test sampling from the defined domain is valid by fiat. This program is coherent but short-sighted. For understanding poor performance, for remedial purposes, for improving teaching methods, and for carving out more functional domains, process constructs are needed.

Realism

The remarks of Meehl and Golden (1982) about an "entity" are realist in flavor; their research is pursuing a hypothetical "schizotype" that is presumed to be as real as a blood type. Another interpreter, however, may adopt a construct he or she finds useful without asking that it cut Nature at a joint God put there. In the fields where I have worked, the terms entering conclusions are closer to common sense than to some presumed structure of Nature. I would not claim entity status for "Intelligence B," "physician interests," "inductive teaching," or the like; I rather doubt that even God perceives such aspects of behavior as segmented (Cronbach, 1986). If this is "instrumentalism," it stops short of antirealism. When realism fits the research program of a Meehl or a Ballard, I feel no need to protest.

As I read the philosophers (e.g., Hesse, 1981; Hochberg, 1961; Morgenbesser, 1969; Shapere, 1984, esp. pp. 398ff.), the choice among the various forms of realism and instrumentalism has negligible significance for investigators. Validation follows the same path in both perspectives. Some critics (e.g., Loevinger, 1957; Norris, 1983) have complained because CM declined (p. 284) to choose between realism and instrumentalism. This complaint is inappropriate, because our committee's function was not to dictate a style of interpretation. The *Standards* were and are deliberately eclectic, so as to facilitate the work of psychologists of all persuasions.

Philosophers, I think, can accept our position because even the realists expect truthlike, close-to-the-joint constructs only in a "mature" science, not in a field whose constructions are mostly in flux (Boyd, 1981).

Popper (1962, pp. 111–114), Toulmin (1972, pp. 489–493), Putnam (1981), and van Fraassen (1981) suggest to me a further reason for evading the issue of realism. For the community of pure scientists, progress consists in better understanding of the world; for technologists, in alleviation of everyday problems; and for the legal discipline, in increased equity and justice. The realist aspiration is suited to the very long-run enterprise of pure science. The instrumentalist stance is suited to technological or practical activity. Neither stance faces toward the value concepts that go into policy making. Testing serves all three kinds of activity, and different challenges arise in each context.

The Strong and Weak Programs of CV

Only as I prepared this paper did a fundamental inconsistency[5] in our original presentations become salient for me. Two concepts of CV were intermingled in the 1954 *Standards:* a strong program of hypothesis-dominated research, and a weak program of *Dragnet* empiricism: "Just give us the facts, ma'am . . . *any* facts." The CM paper unequivocally sets forth the strong program: a construction made explicit, hypotheses deduced from it, and pointedly relevant evidence brought in. This is also the stance of the 1985 *Standards.*

Some sentences in the *Standards* of 1954 to 1974 had this strong tone, but in other passages wishy-washy language gave up all sense of validation as a critical process. (I confess that I must have written my share of the sentences I now complain about.) Some standards listed under CV amount to no more than "test users want all the information they can get." Thus one standard called for correlations of the test with "other tests that are better understood." This is a call for empirical miscellany, whereas a developer's hypotheses can be checked only with measures of constructs present in his network. In the 1950s the Rorschach test was a conspicuous candidate for CV; yet I cannot think of a "better understood" test whose correlations with Rorschach scores would have provided evidence highly relevant to the main theses of Rorschachers.

The weak program, not being centered on a construction, is only remotely connected to CV. The strong program asks the proponent to state and test one particular construction. As CM noted, when a second network is developed around a similarly named construct by another psychologist, the original validity argument is beside the point; to justify the new interpretation, this psychologist will organize the evidence differently. Because this argument is likely to bring in variables omitted from the first construction, some of the miscellaneous facts produced by the weak program can conceivably help in this validation. Although unfocused empiricism only haphazardly serves validation, I do not disparage it. Pretheoretical, unsystematized knowledge enables us to identify sensible alternatives in practical affairs and in planning of research; it is essential in comprehending even physics (Putnam, 1978, p. 72).

Validation as a Community Process

In my remaining pages I shall bring latter-day ideas about the development of knowledge to bear on testing, and suggest a realistic strategy for CV efforts. The idealized strong program is most appropriate to a scientific perspective that reaches centuries into the future (Cronbach, 1986). No science can live only for the day when truth becomes crystal clear. Social and behavioral scientists in particular are obligated to help contemporaries think through their problems and evaluate proposed solutions. We have to do this using present constructions.

For even one construct, developing a sturdy interpretation takes a long time. Nearly a century has elapsed between Binet's first efforts to characterize intelligence and our present modest understanding. As, slowly, a construction becomes more precise, elaborate and refined probes into validity tend to repay the extra investment they require.

Any of our measures is open to plural interpretations. Constructions can be "mutually supplementary" (McGuire, 1983, p. 35), and a proper review need not—generally should not—be contentious. Justification is seriously incomplete when the proponent of an interpretation does not show respect, however reluctantly, for the rival interpretations some peers in the discipline are likely to favor.

The more explicit the chain of argument and the more self-critical the theorist, the more plausible can this view of matters be made; but a theorist is *not* his or her own best critic. Colleagues are especially able to refine the interpretation, as they compensate for blind spots and capitalize on their own distinctive experience. Typically, in scientific history, an investigator and later other members of the same school of thought have committed themselves to one construction and left to others the task of confronting it with alternative theses. Not even a book-length presentation by the proponent, then, is the natural locus for serious and comprehensive CV.

Indeed, there rarely is a definable locus. Validation is pursued mostly in the cut-and-thrust tactical exchanges of journal articles. Each alternative construction is likely to retain a significant number of adherents for many years. In time, one view comes to predominate, usually without there having been a coherent, dispassionate review of the competing theories. Current philosophers, attuned to the history of science as much as to logic, are telling us that construct validation is mostly implicit in the continuing discussions of scientists, not a task performed at a certain time by any one thinker. Students of politics are saying almost precisely the same thing about choices among social policies, including those influenced by social research (Cronbach et al., 1980).

Philosophers no longer visualize scientific change as a straightforward ascent from fallacy to first approximate truths to sound propositional networks of increasing scope, and ultimately to a God's eye view of the universe (Hesse, 1981; Putnam, 1978, p. 77). In science, technology, and policy alike, a theory succeeds by commanding widespread support in the relevant community, and the process is social as much as rational. Acceptance of constructions is inherently a community process (McGrath & Brinberg, 1983; Suppé, 1977). This dilution of the rationalist ideal does not dissolve away the recommendations for research in the CM paper.

Advice to the Test Evaluator

Responsibility for CV is necessarily diffuse, but allow me the rhetorical device of concentrating that responsibility in a new profession, test evaluation. Unlike the test developer, the evaluator holds no brief for or against the test, but rather is committed to serve all the persons having stakes in affairs the test might influence. Unlike the writer of test reviews, the evaluator undertakes independent research. Unlike the investigators who accumulate background knowledge while satisfying motives of their own, but like the program evaluator, the test evaluator is expected to produce a report in a limited time. Perhaps no one will ever be charged with precisely the job thus defined, but my comments should be useful for an investigator who takes up even a fraction of the burden.

Evaluations of compensatory education and other social interventions have been much discussed. The recommendations made for program evaluation (Cronbach, 1982; Cronbach et al., 1980) seem to translate readily into recommendations for test evaluators. Here, I make a start on the translation.

Evaluation planning starts with a divergent phase. Evaluators collect questions that concern members of the relevant community, and add questions on the basis of their own expertise. They try to grasp the interpretations offered by the test developer and the skeptical views of others (Boyd, 1981, p. 620). They look for circumstances that can render the test interpretation or the construction invalid. They ask, What data about a particular case or setting would imply that interpretation *A* fits better than alternative *B*, or that neither fits? Such probes produce a long list of possibly significant lines of inquiry, far more than can be pursued.

Question seeking gradually gives way to deciding which investigations to pursue. The priority assigned to a line of inquiry depends on four features:

1. Prior uncertainty. Is the issue genuinely in doubt?
2. Information yield. How much uncertainty will remain at the end of a feasible study?
3. Cost. How expensive is the investigation, in time and dollars?
4. Leverage. How critical is the information for achieving consensus in the relevant audience? (Consensus regarding appropriate use of the test, or consensus that it should not be used.)

After weighing these criteria, the evaluator will probably choose a few questions for intensive research, with other questions covered incidentally by inexpensive side-studies, or not at all.

This prioritizing steers the test evaluator away from *Dragnet* empiricism. Background knowledge probably should be left without regulation or special standards, to accumulate from basic research and from incidental observations by practitioners. Standards do have a function when evaluators undertake CV as agents of the community.

This strategy generates a short-term program of investigation that is feasible and does not aspire to produce definitive answers. In an occasional instance, the test or construct will be found totally devoid of merit, but the usual report will not come out unequivocally for or against the test interpretation. More likely, it will suggest modifications in the technique or the interpretation. A given report will be received differently by persons having different intellectual and value commitments. The investigation should aim to illuminate the test and the related construction so that persons making decisions see more clearly how to use the test, and so that those pursuing research know where the greatest perplexities lie. Already, in that uncertainty, the next wave in the endless summer of construct validation is starting its move.

NOTES

1. The terse "CV" will serve hereafter for either "construct validation" or "construct validity." Also, "CM" will stand for the Cronbach and Meehl (1955) paper on the subject.

2. This view is amplified by Humphreys (1984) and by Hulin and Humphreys (1980), and again in the present volume.

3. Campbell referred to the validity of extrapolations as "external validity" in 1957, and I have used his term that way, as a synonym for CV (Cronbach, 1982). Later, Campbell (Cook & Campbell, 1976) identified "external validity" with simple generalization to new sites or populations, and CV with explanation. I, however, consider the two inseparable. For example, the class of sites to which one generalizes is described in terms of constructs, and the indicated boundaries of the class are hypotheses to be evaluated. Campbell (1986) acknowledges that his distinction is problematic.

4. Requirements for "statistical laws" were as stringent as those for nomologicals. Such laws amounted to point estimates of parameters of a distribution that is invariant with time and place, as in the probabilistic decay of radon (Hempel, 1965, pp. 175, 302, 381).

5. John Campbell (1976, p. 202) discussed this as a mingling of deductive and inductive strategies.

REFERENCES

Achinstein, R., & Barker, S. F. (1969). *The legacy of logical positivism.* Baltimore: Johns Hopkins University Press.

Adorno, T. W., Frenkel-Brunswik, E., Levinson, D. J., & Sanford, R. N. (1950). *The authoritarian personality.* New York: Harper.

Albemarle Paper Co. v. Moody, 422 U.S. 405 (1975).

American Educational Research Association, American Psychological Association, and National Council on Measurement in Education. (1985). *Standards for educational and psychological testing.* Washington, DC: American Psychological Association.

American Psychological Association. (1954). Technical recommendations for psychological tests and diagnostic techniques. *Psychological Bulletin, 51* (Suppl.).

American Psychological Association, Division of Industrial-Organizational Psychology. (1980). *Principles for the validation and use of personnel selection procedures* (2d ed.). Berkeley, CA: Author.

Anastasi, A. (1950). The concept of validity in the interpretation of test scores. *Educational and Psychological Measurement, 10,* 67–78.

Ballard, J. L., Novak, K. K., & Driver, M. (1979). A simplified score for assessment of fetal maturation of newly born infants. *Journal of Pediatrics, 95,* 769–774.

Bechtoldt, H. (1959). Construct validity: A critique. *American Psychologist, 14,* 619–629.

Bergmann, G. (1953). Theoretical psychology. *Annual Review of Psychology, 4,* 435–458.

Birenbaum, M., & Tatsuoka, K. K. (1982). On the dimensionality of achievement test data. *Journal of Educational Measurement, 19,* 259–266.

Boyd, R. (1981). Scientific realism and naturalistic epistemology. In P. D. Asquith & R. N. Giere (Eds.), *PSA 1980* (Vol. 2, pp. 613–662). East Lansing, MI: Philosophy of Science Association.

Braithwaite, R. (1953). *Scientific explanation.*Cambridge: Cambridge University Press.

Brodbeck, M. (1957). The philosophy of science and educational research. *Review of Educational Research, 27,* 427–440.

Brodbeck, M. (1963). Logic and scientific method in research on teaching. In N. L. Gage (Ed.), *Handbook of research on teaching* (pp. 44–94). Chicago: Rand McNally.

Campbell, D. T. (1957). Factors relevant to the validity of experiments in social settings. *Psychological Bulletin, 54,* 297–213.

Campbell, D. T. (1960). Recommendations for APA test standards regarding construct, trait, and discriminant validity. *American Psychologist, 15,* 546–553.

Campbell, D. T. (1986). Relabeling internal and external validity for applied social scientists. In W. M. K. Trochim (Ed.), *Advances in quasi-experimental design and analysis. New directions in program evaluation* (No. 31, pp. 67–77). San Francisco: Jossey-Bass.

Campbell, D. T., & Fiske, D. W. (1959). Convergent and discriminant validity in the multitrait-multimethod matrix. *Psychological Bulletin, 56,* 81–105.

Campbell, D. T., & Stanley, J. C. (1963). Experimental and quasi-experimental designs for research on teaching. In N. L. Gage (Ed.), *Handbook of research on teaching* (pp. 171–246). Chicago: Rand McNally.

Campbell, J. P. (1976). Psychometric theory. In M. D. Dunnette (Ed.), *Handbook of industrial and organizational psychology* (pp. 185–222). New York: Wiley.

Cook, T. D., & Campbell, D. T. (1976). The design and analysis of quasi-experiments and true experiments in field settings. In M. D. Dunnette (Ed.), *Handbook of industrial and organizational psychology* (pp. 223–326). Chicago: Rand McNally.

Cook, T. D., & Campbell, D. T. (1979). *Quasi-experimentation: Design and analysis issues for field settings.* Chicago: Rand McNally.

Cooper, L. A., & Regan, D. T. (1982). Intelligence, attention, and perception. In R. J. Sternberg (Ed.), *Handbook of human intelligence* (pp. 123–169). Cambridge: Cambridge University Press.

Cronbach, L. J. (1971). Test validation. In R. L. Thorndike (Ed.), *Educational measurement* (pp. 443–507). Washington, DC: American Council on Education.

Cronbach, L. J. (1982). *Designing evaluations of educational and social programs.* San Francisco: Jossey-Bass.

Cronbach, L. J. (1984). *Essentials of psychological testing* (4th ed.). New York: Harper & Row.

Cronbach, L. J. (1986). Social inquiry for Earthlings. In D. W. Fiske & R. A. Shweder (Eds.), *Metatheory in social science: Pluralisms and subjectivities* (pp. 83–107). Chicago: University of Chicago Press.

Cronbach, L. J., & Meehl, P. E. (1955). Construct validity in psychological tests. *Psychological Bulletin, 52,* 281–302.

Cronbach, L. J., Ambron, S. R., Dornbusch, S. M., Hess, R. D., Hornik, R. C., Phillips, D. C., Walker, D. F., & Weiner, S. S. (1980). *Toward reform in program evaluation.* San Francisco: Jossey-Bass.

Damrin, D. E. (1952). *A comparative study of information derived from a diagnostic problem-solving test by logical and factorial methods of scoring.* Unpublished doctoral dissertation, University of Illinois, Urbana-Champaign.

Ebel, R. E. (1961). Must all tests be valid? *American Psychologist, 16,* 640–647.

Ebel, R. E. (1984). Achievement test items: Current issues. In B. S. Plake (Ed.), *Social and technical issues in testing: Implications for test construction and usage* (pp. 141–154). Hillsdale, NJ: Erlbaum.

Equal Employment Opportunity Commission [EEOC] et al. (1978, August 25). Adoption by four agencies of uniform guidelines on employee selection procedures. *Federal Register, 34,* 38290–38315.

Fiedler, F. E., & Leister, A. (1977). Intelligence and group performance: A multiple screen model. *Organizational Behavior and Human Performance, 20,* 1–14.

Frederiksen, N. (1984). The real test bias: Influences of testing on teaching and learning. *American Psychologist, 39,* 193–202.

French, J. W. (1965). The relationship of problem-solving styles to the factor composition of tests. *Educational and Psychological Measurement, 25,* 9–28.

Glymour, C. (1980). The good theories do. In A. P. Maslow, R. H. McKillip, & M. Thatcher (Eds.), *Construct validity in psychological measurement* (pp. 13–21). Princeton, NJ: Educational Testing Service.

Gorham, W. A. (1980). The setting for this colloquium. In A. P. Maslow, R. H. McKillip, & M. Thatcher (Eds.), *Construct validity in psychological measurement* (pp. 1–4). Princeton, NJ: Educational Testing Service.

Hartshorne, H., & May, M. A. (1928–1930). *Studies in the nature of character.* New York: Macmillan.

Hempel, C. G. (1965). *Aspects of scientific explanation.* New York: Free Press.

Hesse, M. (1981). The hunt for scientific reason. In P. D. Asquith & R. N. Giere (Eds.), *PSA 1980* (Vol. 2, pp. 3–24). East Lansing, MI: Philosophy of Science Association.

Hochberg, H. E. (1961). Intervening variables, hypothetical constructs, and metaphysics. In H. Feigl & G. Maxwell (Eds.), *Current issues in philosophy of science* (pp. 448–457). New York: Holt, Rinehart & Winston.

House, E. R. (1980). *Evaluating with validity.* Beverly Hills, CA: Sage.

Hulin, C. L., & Humphreys, L. G. (1980). Foundations of test theory. In A. P. Maslow, R. H. McKillip, & M. Thatcher (Eds.), *Construct validity in psychological measurement* (pp. 5–12). Princeton, NJ: Educational Testing Service.

Humphreys, L. G. (1952). Individual differences. *Annual Review of Psychology, 3,* 5–15.

Humphreys, L. G. (1960). Note on the multitrait-multimethod matrix. *Psychological Bulletin, 57*, 86–88.

Humphreys, L. G. (1979). The construct of general intelligence. *Intelligence, 3*, 105–120.

Humphreys, L. G. (1984). General intelligence. In C. R. Reynolds & R. T. Brown (Eds.), *Perspectives on bias in mental testing* (pp. 221–248). New York: Plenum Press.

Hunter, J. E. (1982, August). *The dimensionality of the General Aptitude Test Battery.* Paper presented at the meeting of the American Psychological Association, Washington, DC.

Jensen, A. R. (1984). Test bias: Concepts and criticisms. In C. R. Reynolds & R. T. Brown (Eds.), *Perspectives on bias in mental testing* (pp. 507–586). New York: Plenum Press.

Kaplan, A. (1964). *The conduct of inquiry.* San Francisco: Chandler.

Kaufman, A. S., & Kaufman, N. L. (1983). *Kaufman Assessment Battery for Children: Interpretive manual.* Circle Pines, MN: American Guidance Service.

Kavanagh, M. J., MacKinney, A. C., & Wolins, L. (1971). Issues in managerial performance: Multitrait-multimethod analysis of ratings. *Psychological Bulletin, 75*, 34–49.

Kuhn, T. (1962). *The structure of scientific revolutions.* Chicago: University of Chicago Press.

Kyllonen, P. C., Lohman, D. F., & Woltz, D. (1984). Componential modeling of alternative strategies for performing spatial tasks. *Journal of Educational Psychology, 76*, 1325–1345.

Linn, R. L. (1979). Issues of validity in measurement for competency-based programs. In M. Bunda & J. Sanders (Eds.), *Practices and problems in competency-based measurement* (pp. 108–126). Washington, DC: National Council on Measurement in Education.

Linn, R. L. (1983). Predictive bias as an artifact of selection procedures. In H. Wainer & S. Messick (Eds.), *Principals of modern psychological measurement* (pp. 27–40). Hillsdale, NJ: Erlbaum.

Loevinger, J. (1957). Objective tests as instruments of psychological theory. *Psychological Reports, 3*, 635–694.

McGrath, J. E., & Brinberg, D. B. (1983). External validity and the research process. *Journal of Consumer Research, 10*, 115–124.

McGuire, W. J. (1983). A contextualist theory of knowledge. In L. Berkowitz (Eds.), *Advances in experimental social psychology* (Vol. 16, pp. 2–47). Orlando, FL: Academic Press.

Meehl, P. E. (1971). High school yearbooks: A reply to Schwartz. *Journal of Abnormal Psychology, 77*, 143–148.

Meehl, P. E., & Golden, R. R. (1982). Taxometric methods. In P. C. Kendall & J. N. Butcher (Eds.), *Handbook of research methods in clinical psychology* (pp. 127–182). New York: Wiley.

Mercer, J. A. (1984). What is a racially and culturally nondiscriminatory test?

A sociological and pluralistic perspective. In C. R. Reynolds & R. T. Brown (Eds.), *Perspectives on bias in mental testing* (pp. 293–356). New York: Plenum Press.

Messick, S. (1975). The standard problem: Meaning and values in measurement and evaluation. *American Psychologist, 30,* 955–966.

Morgenbesser, S. (1969). The realist-instrumentalist controversy. In S. Morgenbesser, P. Suppes, & M. White (Eds.), *Philosophy, science, and method: Essays in honor of Nagel* (pp. 200–218). New York: St. Martin's Press.

Norris, S. P. (1983). The inconsistencies at the foundation of construct validation theory. In E. R. House (Ed.), *Philosophy of evaluation. New directions in program evaluation* (No. 19, pp. 53–74). San Francisco: Jossey-Bass.

Phillips, L. W. (1981). Assessing measurement error in lay informant reports: A methodological note on organizational analysis in marketing. *Journal of Marketing Research, 18,* 395–415.

Popper, K. R. (1962). *Conjectures and refutations: The growth of scientific knowledge.* New York: Harper & Row.

Putnam, H. (1978). *Meaning and the moral sciences.* London: Routledge and Kegan Paul.

Putnam, H. (1981). *Reason, truth, and history.* Cambridge: Cambridge University Press.

Reynolds, C. R., & Brown, R. T. (1984). Bias in mental testing: An introduction to the issues. In C. R. Reynolds & R. T. Brown (Eds.), *Perspectives on bias in mental testing* (pp. 1–40). New York: Plenum Press.

Robertson, G. J., & Eisenberg, J. L. (1981). *Peabody Picture Vocabulary Test— Revised* (Tech. Suppl.). Circle Pines, MN: American Guidance Service.

Schmidt, F. L., Hunter, J. E., & Pearlman, K. (1981). The validity and fairness of employment tests in selection: A red herring. *Journal of Applied Psychology, 66,* 166–185.

Schofield, J. W., & Whitley, B. E., Jr. (1983). Peer nomination vs. rating scale measurement of children's peer preferences. *Social Psychology Quarterly, 46,* 242–251.

Scriven, M. (1956). A possible distinction between traditional scientific disciplines and the study of human behavior. In H. Feigl & M. Scriven (Eds.), *Minnesota studies in the philosophy of science* (Vol. 1, pp. 330–339). Minneapolis: University of Minnesota Press.

Scriven, M. (1969). Logical positivism and the behavioral sciences. In P. Achinstein & S. Barker (Eds.), *The legacy of logical positivism* (pp. 195–209). Baltimore: Johns Hopkins Press.

Serlin, R. C., & Lapsley, D. K. (1985). Rationality in psychological research: The good-enough principle. *American Psychologist, 40,* 73–83.

Shapere, D. (1984). *Reason and the search for knowledge. Boston studies in the philosophy of science* (Vol. 78). Dordrecht, Netherlands: Reidel.

Sternberg, R. J., & Weil, E. M. (1980). An aptitude-strategy interaction in linear syllogistic reasoning. *Journal of Educational Psychology, 72,* 226–234.

Suppé, F. (Ed.). (1977). *The structure of scientific theories* (2d ed.). Urbana: University of Illinois Press.

Toulmin, S. E. (1972). *Human understanding.* Chicago: University of Chicago Press.

van Fraassen, B. (1981). Theory construction and experiment: An empiricist view. In P. D. Asquith & R. N. Giere (Eds.), *PSA 1980* (Vol. 2, pp. 663–678). East Lansing, MI: Philosophy of Science Association.

Washington v. Davis, 426 U.S. 229 (1976).

Wylie, R. C. (1974–1979) *The self-concept: Theory and research on selected topics* (Vols. 1, 2). Lincoln: University of Nebraska Press.

6

Intelligence and Law

BARBARA LERNER

Intelligence—like excellence—had been out of fashion for about a decade before Judge Peckham ruled its measurement unconstitutional in *Larry P. v. Riles* in 1979.[1]

General intelligence, as Lloyd Humphreys, the scientist we honor today defines it, is abstract and symbolic problem-solving ability.[2] That, as he points out, is the common thread that ties together the great variety of tasks that a long succession of psychologists have included on their various tests of intelligence for nearly a century now. Why was this venerable tradition so vehemently rejected in the 1970s, first by psychologists themselves, and, ultimately, by a federal court? It was not for want of empirical validity, or social utility either. The evidence for both—as any scientist conversant with Lloyd Humphreys' work over the last half-century knows—is overwhelming.

There is no scientific explanation for the rejection of intelligence in the 1970s. To begin to understand it, we must turn away from the Humphreys definition and from the great masses of empirical data he has so rigorously analyzed, and focus instead on a totally different definition, one that is part strawman, part ideological bogyman. I call it the "straw-bogy" definition of intelligence.

Paper presented at the Symposium on Intelligence sponsored by the University of Illinois in honor of Professor Lloyd G. Humphreys, Urbana, Illinois, May 2, 1985.

1. 495 F. Supp. 926. *Contra*, PASE v. Hannon, 506 F. Supp. 831 (1980). See generally: Hebb, *Open Letter to a Friend Who Thinks the I.Q. is a Social Evil*, 33 AM. PSYCH. 1143 (1978); Lambert, *Psychological Evidence in Larry P. v. Riles*, 36 AM. PSYCH. 937 (1981); Scarr, *From Evolution to Larry P., or What Shall We Do About I.Q. Tests?* 2 INTELLIGENCE 325 (1978).

2. See, *e.g.*, Humphreys, *Individual Differences*, 3 ANN. REV. PSYCH. 131 (1952); Humphreys, *The Organization of Human Abilities*, 17 AM. PSYCH. 475 (1962); Humphreys, *Theory of Intelligence*, in CANCRO (ed.), INTELLIGENCE: GENETIC AND

The Straw-Bogy Definition of Intelligence

The straw-bogy definition starts out with the fact that human intelligence is partly a function of genetic inheritance and goes on from there to insist that *if* this is true, then two false and frightening nonfacts must also be true.

False and frightening nonfact number one is the *unalterable fate* idea—the notion that each individual's intelligence is fixed at birth, rather like sex is, or used to be, and remains the same at every point from birth to death, no matter what the individual does, or what is done to or for him.

False and frightening nonfact number two is the *permanent caste* idea—the notion that children's intelligence is a mirror image of their parents; therefore, all high-scoring parents always produce high-scoring children; average parents, average children; and below-average parents, below-average children, generation after generation marching in hopeless hereditary lockstep with its progenitors.

Intelligence, thus defined, is a fundamentally unAmerican concept, in the sense that it is incompatible with the idea of an open society with opportunity and possibilities for mobility for all. It conjures up a vision of doomed individuals in a closed society, a grim vision that Americans have always rejected, and no wonder; our history is its refutation.[3]

This straw-bogy definition of intelligence is just as incompatible with the empirical data on intelligence and its vicissitudes as it is with the facts of American history. The unalterable fate part of the definition is refuted by empirical data on changes in intelligence over time, mas-

---

ENVIRONMENTAL INFLUENCES (1971); Humphreys, *The Misleading Distinction Between Aptitude and Achievement Tests*, in GREEN (ed.), THE APTITUDE-ACHIEVEMENT DISTINCTION (1974); Humphreys, *Theory of Intelligence and the Management of Classroom Learning*, 7 INTERCHANGE 45 (1976–77); Humphreys, *The Construct of General Intelligence*, 3 INTELLIGENCE 105 (1979); Humphreys & Parsons, *Piagetian Tasks Measure Intelligence and Intelligence Tests Assess Cognitive Development*, 3 INTELLIGENCE 369 (1979); Humphreys, *A Conceptualization of Intellectual Giftedness*, in HOROWITZ & O'BRIEN (eds.), THE GIFTED AND TALENTED: DEVELOPMENTAL PERSPECTIVES, (1985); Humphreys, *General Intelligence: An Integration of Factor, Test, and Simplex Theory*, in WOLMAN (ed.).

3. See, *e.g.*, GLAZER & MOYNIHAN, BEYOND THE MELTING POT (2d ed.) 1970; SOWELL, ETHNIC AMERICA (1981); THERNSTROM, THE OTHER BOSTONIANS (1973); THERNSTROM (ed.), HARVARD ENCYCLOPEDIA OF AMERICAN ETHNIC GROUPS (1980).

sive data showing that major changes can and do take place, in individuals, in groups, and in whole nations.[4]

There is no fundamental mystery about why this should be so. Abstract and symbolic problem-solving ability has a genetic base, but it is also a developed ability in much the same sense that skill in basketball is. It is developed in much the same way, too, through hard, disciplined work in self-critical pursuit of high standards. When discipline and standards are absent, skills and abilities deteriorate, or fail to develop in the first place. When they are restored or initiated, scores improve, on the court and off.

Standards and discipline improve all scores; they do not make them all the same. Midgets do not grow up to threaten Dr. J. on the basketball court, no matter how hard they work or how rigorously self-critical they are; youngsters with Downs Syndrome do not mature into Nobel Prize winners.

That is fundamentally unfair, but it is nature's unfairness, not man's, following her rules and riding roughshod over our social distinctions, in whatever form they are enshrined. Small groups of men sometimes monopolize power and pass it on to their descendants for a time; they cannot do the same with intelligence. We are not our parents' clones, much as some might wish it, and have no built-in class or caste marks carved into our brains. Rather, we and they, together with all mankind, are participants in a great genetic lottery that relies heavily on random recombination, insuring enormous variability within as well as between families, at every level of society, from top to bottom.

Children are not psychosocial clones, any more than they are biological ones. Highly disciplined upper class parents can and do produce grossly undisciplined children, children who fare poorly in competition with better disciplined youngsters, from their own families as well as from other, poorer families. Arthur Jensen reports that about one family in 20 has a pair of siblings who differ from each other by more than two standard deviations on intelligence tests.[5] Christopher Jencks found that the difference in occupational status between grown-up brothers

---

4. Humphreys has made this point repeatedly, throughout his career. See note 2 *supra*. See also: JONES, BAYLEY, MAC FARLANE & HONZIK, THE COURSE OF HUMAN DEVELOPMENT (1971); Lynn, *I.Q. in Japan and the United States Shows a Growing Disparity*, 297 NATURE 222 (1982); Sowell, *Assumptions versus History in Ethnic Education*, TCHRS. C. REC. 37 (Fall, 1981); Tuddenham, *Soldier Intelligence in World Wars I and II*, 3 AM. PSYCH. 54 (1948).

5. JENSEN, STRAIGHT TALK ABOUT MENTAL TESTS 243 (1981).

was nearly as great as that between unrelated males[6] in this amazingly mobile country of ours, a land of genuine opportunity and genuine risk for all.

The permanent caste part of the straw-bogy definition of intelligence then, fits the empirical data no better than the unalterable fate idea. Both are false. They do not follow from the fact that human intelligence is partly a function of genetic inheritance. They are nonsequiturs, as much at odds with the empirical data on intelligence as they are with the realities of American society and the values that sustain it.

All these strikes against it notwithstanding, the straw-bogy definition of intelligence not only survived but triumphed in the 1970s, crowding out competing definitions, not only in the law courts and in the media, but in academic and professional circles too. The result was that the study of intelligence and its development became, to many, a suspect activity, fit only for denunciation, much of it retroactive, since precious few *living* scientists—most of them here today—had the courage to persevere in so hostile a climate.

The denouncers were not deterred. When they ran out of live targets, as they quickly did, they enthusiastically attacked the dead. Witness the sudden proliferation of straw-bogy histories of the study of intelligence, and of the lives and times of scientists who studied it in earlier eras.[7] Note, too, that these revisionist histories are not the works of misguided laymen, overtly hostile to academia or science. The opposite is the case. The men who insured the triumph of the straw-bogy definition in the 1970s by insisting, against all the evidence, that it is and always was what scientists "really" meant when they used the word "intelligence," and that the only righteous course was to reject its study entirely, were not laymen at all, for the most part. They were scientists themselves—usually social scientists—often eminent ones.

The critical questions about intelligence and law, then, are these: Why did social scientists themselves promote the straw-bogy definition of intelligence in the 1970s, along with a number of other false doc-

6. JENCKS, INEQUALITY: A REASSESSMENT OF THE EFFECT OF FAMILY AND SCHOOLING IN AMERICA 179 (1972).

7. See, *e.g.*, GOULD, THE MISMEASURE OF MAN (1981); KAMIN, THE SCIENCE AND POLITICS OF I.Q. (1974); LEWONTIN, ROSE, & KAMIN, NOT IN OUR GENES (1984).

For a nontendentious account of some of the major historical experiences and forces that shaped the xenophobic reaction of the first three decades of this century, see HANDLIN, THE UPROOTED (1951); HANDLIN, RACE AND NATIONALITY IN AMERICAN LIFE (1957).

trines? How and why did the federal judiciary come to incorporate
these false doctrines into the very fabric of constitutional law?

To answer these questions, we must begin by going back three decades to examine the special relationship between social science and
constitutional law established in *Brown v. Board of Education* in 1954.[8]
I was an undergraduate at this University (Illinois) in that fateful year,
and I well remember the joy and exhilaration that I and all my friends
and teachers felt. We did not really understand the precise legal position
of the *Brown* Court or the peculiar nature of the bargain it had struck
with social science, and we did not care. Like most of our fellow
Americans in the 1950s, we knew that discrimination on the basis of
race was a great moral evil, and it was enough for us that the Supreme
Court of the United States was on our side at last. It had held segregation
unconstitutional, hadn't it? And social scientists had contributed to that
happy outcome, hadn't they? The rest was detail, I thought, arcane
technical matters of concern only to specialists in law and social science,
and at the time, I was neither.

Shortly afterwards, I, too, became a specialist, first in social science,
later in law, but my basic understanding of *Brown* did not change for
a long time. I was vaguely aware, before the 1950s ended, that a few
legal scholars who fully supported the *result* of the *Brown* decision felt
that the Court had reached it in a technically shoddy and unprincipled
way that boded ill for the future,[9] but my own optimism was enormous,
and much more widely shared than the forebodings of a handful of
constitutional lawyers. I cannot recall any social scientists who were
comparably critical, in those days, of the technical adequacy of the
social science research the Court relied on to reach its decisions. If they
existed, their voices were drowned out by those of us who celebrated
that reliance, seeing it as a great victory for social science in general,
and because the Clarks' study[10] was the legally critical one, for psychology in particular. How could something so immediately good for
us and for society be bad for law, bad for science, and ultimately, for
the nation?

Thirty years later, after a decade's worth of educational policy decisions as senseless as the one in *Larry P.*, it is painfully clear that it

8. 347 U.S. 483.
9. See especially HAND, THE BILL OF RIGHTS 54–55 (1958); Wechsler, *Toward
Neutral Principles of Constitutional Law*, 73 HARV. L. REV. 1, 22, 31–35 (1959). See also
Kurland, *Brown v. Board of Education was the Beginning:The School Desegregation Cases
in the United States Supreme Court, 1954–1979*, 2 WASH. UNIV. L. Q. 309 (1979).
10. See, *e.g.*, Clark & Clark, *Racial Identification and Preference in Negro Children*, in
NEWCOMB & HARTLEY (eds.), READINGS IN SOCIAL PSYCHOLOGY 169 (1947).

could be and it was, because the special relationship between the courts and the social sciences established in the *Brown* case was based on a bad bargain, one that allowed the federal judiciary to do less than the Constitution required, while simultaneously requiring social scientists to do more than their science allowed. Ultimately, that bargain played a major role in defeating the high hopes that I and my activist friends, along with most of our countrymen, entertained on that deceptively bright May morning, 31 years ago.

Let us look critically, then, at the bargain in *Brown* and at its consequences, first from the perspective of law, then from that of social science, and finally and most importantly, from the perspective of American society as a whole, focusing on its impact on education and on the development of intelligence in students of all races.

The Legal Bargain in *Brown*

To understand the legal side of the bargain the Court made with social science in *Brown*, you have to understand that there were *two* great questions in the case: First, shall state-imposed segregation be abolished? Second, shall the interpretation of the Fourteenth Amendment that permitted it be overruled? The *Brown* Court answered the first question, at long last, with an overdue "yes," but it evaded the second question, and it used social science to do it. That evasion, that substitution of social science for legal principle, is the source of many of our subsequent troubles with the Fourteenth Amendment. It is the reason why the law in this area is the confused and inconsistent morass it now is, and it is responsible for the existence of cases like *Larry P. v. Riles* and a host of similarly disastrous educational policy cases before and after *Larry P.*

To understand the second question and the effects of the Court's failure to answer it, you have to start with the Fourteenth Amendment itself. The Fourteenth Amendment was added to the Constitution of the United States in 1868, three years after the end of the Civil War. Here is the full text of the critical section, Section 1:

All persons born or naturalized in the United States, and subject to the jurisdiction thereof, are citizens of the United States and of the State wherein they reside. No State shall make or enforce any law which shall abridge the privileges or immunities of citizens of the United States; nor shall any State deprive *any person* of life, liberty, or property, without due process of law; nor deny to *any person* within its jurisdiction the equal protection of the laws. (emphasis supplied)

How should those sweeping words be interpreted? What did the war-weary Congressmen who proposed them and the conflict-weary state legislators who ratified them intend? The *Brown* Court was clear and candid when it told us that "The most avid proponents of the post-War Amendments undoubtedly intended them to remove all legal distinctions among 'all persons born or naturalized in the United States.'"[11] The Court was equally clear and candid in telling us that "Their opponents, just as certainly, were antagonistic to both the letter and the spirit of the Amendments and wished them to have [only] the most limited effect."[12]

The *Brown* Court was neither clear nor candid in telling us which side the Supreme Court came down on the very first time it had a chance to decide the question, in the *Slaughter House* cases in 1873.[13] It tells us only that "In the first cases in this Court construing the Fourteenth Amendment, decided shortly after its adoption, the Court interpreted it as proscribing all state-imposed discrimination against the Negro race."[14]

Legal innocents assume this means that the *Slaughter House* Court came down on the side of the Amendment's proponents. It did not. It rejected their expansive neutral law interpretation and adopted in its stead the limited special benefit interpretation favored by those who opposed it. It was not an easy course to take legally, because the language of the Amendment indicated that the proponents had prevailed: The word "person," used repeatedly throughout the Amendment as in "All persons" and "any person" indicates—as clearly as any words can—that its coverage was intended to be all-inclusive, giving every American a stake in the protection against discrimination that it provided.

Nonetheless, the *Slaughter House* Court, by a vote of 5 to 4, announced that the Amendment was intended to be essentially exclusive in its coverage, designed to be of special benefit to black Americans. Was that, still, a victory for black plaintiffs, albeit a limited one? Hardly. There were no black plaintiffs in the *Slaughter House* cases. The plaintiffs were white men, suing other white men whom they believed had discriminated against them. They sued under the Fourteenth Amendment because they thought it protected their rights, too. The *Slaughter*

11. 347 U.S. at 489.
12. *Id.*
13. 16 Wall 36.
14. 347 U.S. at 490.

House Court told them that they were mistaken; it protected only blacks.[15]

Just how much protection the limited special benefit interpretation provided for blacks was quickly made apparent in subsequent cases in which blacks *were* the plaintiffs, challenging actions which singled them out for special treatment different from that accorded whites. They lost, repeatedly. Special treatment for blacks alone was automatically unconstitutional only under the expansive neutral law interpretation of the Fourteenth Amendment. Under the restricted special benefit interpretation, it was all a matter of effects, and it was up to the courts — not the black plaintiffs — to decide which actions had harmful effects on them and which had good effects, or none at all.

Hall v. deCuir[16] is an especially interesting case in point because it was decided just 4 years after *Slaughter House*. Mrs. deCuir, the black plaintiff, had sued the owner of a steamship for ejecting her from the whites-only cabin he had established on his ship. She sued under an 1869 Louisiana statute that implemented the neutral law interpretation of the Fourteenth Amendment, and she won, in the state courts, all the way up the line, but lost in the Supreme Court of the United States. The High Court's membership, with a single exception,[17] had not changed since the *Slaughter House* decision, but it was no longer divided. The vote against Mrs. deCuir was 9–0.

The Court's holding was that the Louisiana statute which prohibited race-based distinctions between passengers on common carriers was itself unconstitutional—only Congress could pass such a law. The Fourteenth Amendment was not even mentioned in the Court's opinion. It did receive attention, though, in a separate, concurring opinion issued by Mr. Justice Clifford, who makes explicit the argument that separate-but-equal facilities for the two races do no violence to the Fourteenth Amendment—as he and his colleagues had interpreted it in *Slaughter House*—because the facilities that were provided were only special, not harmful, foreshadowing, from the start, the nefarious holding in *Plessy v. Ferguson*[18] in 1896, the holding that made segregation the law of the land for half a century.

15. "We doubt very much whether any action of a State not directed by way of discrimination against the negroes as a class, or on account of their race, will ever be held to come within the purview of this provision. It is so clearly a provision for that race and that emergency, that a strong case would be necessary for its application to any other." 16 Wall at 81

16. 95 U.S. 485 (1877).

17. Morrison Waite replaced Salmon Chase as Chief Justice.

18. 163 U.S. 537.

The only really bright page in this dark judicial history is the one written by Justice John Marshall Harlan, the elder, a strong proponent of the neutral law position, who was appointed to the Court a few months after the decision against Mrs. deCuir. Always eloquent but increasingly isolated, his was the sole dissenting voice in 1883[19] when the Court invalidated congressional legislation implementing the same neutral law conception of the Fourteenth Amendment that was struck down in Mrs. deCuir's case. In the *Plessy* case, his was, again, the sole dissenting voice. He argued, forcefully, that the question of effects should not even reach the Court; special treatment per se was unconstitutional under a proper reading of the Fourteenth Amendment. "Our Constitution is color-blind," he wrote, "and neither knows nor tolerates classes among citizens."[20]

Fifty painful years later, the *Brown* Court finally said so, but gave him only half a victory. *Brown* partially overruled *Plessy*; it did not overrule *Slaughter House* at all. Instead of holding that discrimination per se is unconstitutional under the Fourteenth Amendment, it let the effects test stand, and used social science research to reach a different conclusion from that reached by the *Plessy* Court on the nature of those effects. Segregation was not held to be unconstitutional per se; it was unconstitutional "in the field of public education"[21] because it was thought to have harmful effects on the self-esteem of black school children and, as a consequence, on their educational development.

That momentous choice—to look to social science to decide what is good or bad for children, and to determine what will advance their educational development and what will retard it—had an enormous shaping impact on American law, on social science, and on American society as a whole. Its impact on its intended beneficiaries—a whole generation of black Americans—was and is enormous too.

What might have been, had the *Brown* Court gone the other way? What might have been, had the Court affirmed Justice Harlan's neutral principle instead of relying on social science to give new life to the old special benefit interpretation? To begin to grasp the impact of that choice on American constitutional law, it is essential to have a clear sense of the alternative, a vision of what Fourteenth Amendment law would have looked like. Let us, then, go back to 1954 and proceed to the present, tracing out the contrasting legal implications of the two alternatives, focusing on three crucial differences.

19. Civil Rights Cases, 109 U.S. 3 (1883).
20. 163 U.S. at 559.
21. 347 U.S. at 495.

First, under the neutral principle, it would have been clear immediately that segregation was unconstitutional in all state facilities, not just in schools. It would have been clear why, too: because "Our Constitution is color-blind and neither knows nor tolerates classes among citizens." Under the alternative chosen in *Brown*, there was great confusion, initially, about the scope of the decision. A rationale focused on the special importance of education and the special effects of school segregation on black students had no obvious applicability to segregation in settings that had nothing to do with schools. Parks, beaches, golf courses, and other state facilities with no apparent educational purpose did not seem to be covered.

Happily, the Court said that they were, not long after *Brown*. It didn't say why, though. It gave no reasons. It simply declared, by judicial fiat, in a series of per curiam decisions, that *Brown* had made it so.[22] It was a victory for desegregation, a rout for legal logic. Justice Harlan's neutral principle would have given us both: across-the-board desegregation and a clear and consistent legal rationale for it. *Brown* gave us the former; it made a shambles of the latter.

Second, under the neutral law principle, it would have been clear, in 1954, that the Court had a compelling constitutional duty not only to abolish segregation across-the-board, but to do it forthwith, via a straightforward legal order: desegregate *now*. Opposition would certainly have been intense, as it was anyway, but it would have expressed itself over a much briefer period of time. The battle would almost certainly have been over by decade's end, and there is no reason to doubt the outcome. Public opinion poll data from 1950 on show that a majority of Americans were convinced that segregation was a great wrong, and that its abolition was overdue.[23]

The more limited rationale adopted in *Brown* carried no such urgency. Under it, segregation was not an obvious constitutional wrong from the start; it had become so only in recent years as a result of new evidence about its effects, evidence produced by social scientists. As a result, desegregation was due, but not overdue, and immediate redress was not constitutionally mandated. Benefits were the issue, and if opposition was intense, it could, conceivably, dilute them. A "desegregate now" order was certain to provoke such opposition in at least some parts of the country. Hence, a slower and more gradual approach, giving the federal district courts maximal discretionary leeway to take

22. Muir v. Louisville Park Theatrical Ass'n., 347 U.S. 971 (1954); Mayor of Baltimore v. Dawson, 350 U.S. 877 (1955); Holmes v. City of Atlanta, 350 U.S. 879 (1955).

23. See, *e.g.*, JANOWITZ, THE LAST HALF-CENTURY: SOCIETAL CHANGE AND POLITICS IN AMERICA 381 (1978).

local circumstances into account in each case seemed, to the *Brown* Court, the wiser course.

Wise or not, it was the approach the Court adopted, mandating, in *Brown II*,[24] only "deliberate speed," and leaving the working out of the meaning of that ambiguous term to the open-ended equitable jurisdiction of the federal trial courts. The result was that school desegregation proceeded at a painfully, often maddeningly, slow pace in much of the South and in some other parts of the country, too, not only in the 1950s but throughout most of the 1960s as well.

Angered at last by the decade and a half of foot-dragging that followed its failure to order immediate and total desegregation in 1954, the Court, in effect, ordered immediate and total integration beginning with *Green* and its companion cases in 1968.[25] Immediate and total desegregation was and is an achievable goal; immediate and total integration proved to be a much more elusive one. The federal courts, in collaboration with social scientists and educators, have been pursuing it aggressively for 15 years now, and no honest and informed observer can call their efforts a success. Justice Harlan's neutral principle would have given us the reality of immediate and total desegregation in the 1950s; it would not have promised immediate and total integration, and it would not have disrupted the public schools of America for a decade and a half in an unsuccessful effort to achieve it.

The third and last "might have been" in this sad series has to do with the legal status of educational policy choices. Under neutral law, responsibility for those choices would have remained where it always had been in America, from our constitutional beginnings in 1787 and 1791 until the *Brown* decision in 1954: in the hands of state and local citizens, and of educators responsive to their concerns. The federal judiciary would have had no power to make or unmake those choices. Its role would have been limited to insuring that they were translated into practice in an evenhanded, nondiscriminatory fashion in every part of the country.

Under the special benefit interpretation, the legal imperatives were quite different. Nondiscrimination was not enough. Educational benefit was the issue, and if social scientists testified in court that particular educational policy choices would be harmful to black students, no matter how evenhandedly they were applied, federal judges were obliged to hear their arguments, and to decide the questions that they raised.

24. 349 U.S. 294 (1955).

25. Green v. County School Board of New Kent County, Virginia, 391 U.S. 430 (1968); Raney v. Board of Education of the Gould School District, 391 U.S. 443 (1968); Monroe v. Board of Commissioners of the City of Jackson, Tennessee, 391 U.S. 450 (1968).

That is how educational policy questions got transformed into questions of constitutional law, to be decided by federal judges, and imposed on the nation, under the aegis of the Fourteenth Amendment.

Courts of the *Plessy* era could have intervened in black educational affairs, or in other areas of black life to a comparable extent, if they had been sincere in their desire to benefit black citizens, but they were not. The *Brown* Court and its successor Courts were sincere, and they did intervene, massively, beginning with the *Green* case in 1968, and increasingly, throughout the 1970s. They genuinely meant to bestow benefits on their black wards, and educational development was the main benefit they intended to bestow.

Social scientists wanted the same thing, and thought they knew how to provide it. They sincerely believed, at the outset, that the psycho-educational theories they espoused could, if implemented, erase the gaps between black and white students, and transform American education for the better in the process. Federal judges came, increasingly, to accept their arguments, and to impose their educational theories on the nation.

The results of those years of unprecedented collaborative effort were apparent in the empirical data from the late 1970s on.[26] The National Commission on Excellence in Education confirmed them, and announced them to the American public in its climactic 1983 report, *A Nation at Risk.*[27] American education had not been transformed for the better in the late 1960s and in the 1970s. It had been transformed for the worse. Scores on all major norm-referenced tests of intellectual development from grade 5 on showed striking declines—the largest in our recorded history—and the gap in intellectual achievement between black and white students had not been closed or even appreciably narrowed.

Our black-robed school board had been a great failure, and it left our priceless heritage of constitutional law in pitiful shape, burdened and distorted as it now is with the discredited psychoeducational theories of the three decades just past. Let us turn, then, to an examination of those theories, and of their development and application over time.

26. Lerner, *The Minimum Competence Testing Movement: Social, Scientific, and Legal Implications*, 36 AM. PSYCH. 1057 (1981); Lerner, *American Education: How Are We Doing?* 69 PUBLIC INTEREST 59 (1982); Lerner, *Facing the Unpleasant Facts About Achievement*, 72 PUBLIC INTEREST 129 (1983); Lerner, *Our Black-Robed School Board: A Report Card*, in BUNZEL (ed.), CHALLENGE TO AMERICAN SCHOOLS: THE CASE FOR STANDARDS AND VALUES (1985).

27. NATIONAL COMMISSION ON EXCELLENCE IN EDUCATION, A NATION AT RISK: THE IMPERATIVE FOR EDUCATIONAL REFORM (1983).

The Social Science Bargain and the
Self-Esteem Theory of Education

The basic postulates of the psychoeducational theory that began it all, the one the Court wove into the fabric of constitutional law in 1954, are stated quite explicitly in *Brown*. The Court told us that school segregation damaged the self-esteem of black children, giving them what the Court called "a sense of inferiority."[28] That was not only a painful thing, in and of itself; it was also a matter of profound educational importance, the Court said, because low self-esteem "affects the motivation of a child to learn," and has a "tendency to retard" children's "educational and mental development."[29] That is the essence of what I will hereafter refer to as the self-esteem theory of educational development.

The self-esteem theory of educational development has enormous intuitive appeal. It sounds right and righteous, and simple and comforting besides. And, its initial application by the *Brown* Court brought about a wonderful result: the beginning of the end of segregation. It is understandable, then, that social scientists did not subject this theory to vigorous critical analysis, in the beginning. Understandable, but unfortunate, because the self-esteem theory of education was not as simple as it looked. It carried in its train a whole host of questionable assumptions with complex and far-reaching implications for educational policies and practices, matters too important to be decided without careful critical scrutiny, and serious consideration of the merits and implications of alternative hypotheses.

That kind of critical scrutiny is now 30 years overdue. Let us attempt it here, and because it is a social science theory, let us do it in the time-honored scientific way. The first step is to make the theory's implicit assumptions explicit. The second step is to spell out their main implications for educational policies and practices. The third step is to examine the accumulated empirical evidence of the last 30 years. The fourth and final step, and the point of the other three, is to allow us to answer the questions we are obliged to answer, as scientists. Did the self-esteem theory of education fare as well in empirical testing as it did in the law courts? Did it turn out to be true, or false? And were its effects on the education of black students constructive or destructive?

Here, for starters, are the theory's three main assumptions. Assumption one is that low self-esteem is a major cause of low academic achievement. Assumption two is that black students have lower self-

28. 347 U.S. at 494.
29. *Id.*

esteem than white students; that is why their achievement levels are lower. Assumption three is that the self-esteem of black children is not determined by their interactions with their parents or other intimates but is, in major part, a function of the way members of their group are perceived and treated by the larger society around them.

If those three major assumptions are correct, then a number of implications would logically follow. Implication one is that efforts to improve black education should give priority to measures designed to raise self-esteem. After all, if low self-esteem is the major cause of low academic achievement, then raising self-esteem would be the most effective way to raise achievement. Implication two is that efforts to raise black achievement by raising black self-esteem should be largely directed towards changing the attitudes and behaviors of members of white society. After all, if black self-esteem is mainly a function of white attitudes and behaviors, then efforts by black students and their parents to make use of the new opportunities made available to them by the ending of segregation could not, realistically, be expected to have much impact.

Any small effects such intragroup efforts might have would be easily swamped by residual signs and symbols of the depreciation of black students by white society. Racially homogenous schools would be the most potent symbols of that depreciation and would, as a result, have a profoundly negative impact on black self-esteem and achievement, irrespective of whether those schools were a product of segregation or not. From this, it follows that integration would be an especially effective method of raising black self-esteem and achievement. Desegregation would be a grossly inadequate strategy; immediate and total integration would be needed to achieve maximal educational benefits.

Vigilant monitoring of educational policies and practices within newly integrated schools would also be needed, to make sure that no policies and practices with potentially harmful effects on black students' self-esteem were permitted to exist in those schools, or in any others. Arguments about the educational utility of such policies and practices would be given short shrift, no matter how evenhandedly those policies and practices were applied. After all, if high self-esteem is the essential ingredient in superior intellectual performance, then anything and everything that could damage a student's self-esteem, however slight and transient the injury, would be educationally counterproductive, and would, accordingly, be seen in a new and negative light, viewed as threats to the educational development of black students, rather than as essential pedagogical tools with which to help them grow and develop and make maximal use of the new opportunities opened up to them by the decision in *Brown*.

All of these implications follow, *if* the three major assumptions on which they are based are true. In the 1950s, most social scientists believed that they were true, and the very limited empirical evidence available then seemed confirmatory. The most dramatic single piece of evidence was the Clark study, cited by the *Brown* Court in its famous footnote 11.[30] Kenneth and Mamie Clark had presented black pre- and primary school pupils with two dolls, identical in every respect save one, color, and asked them a series of questions about positive and negative attributes. They found that black students had a strong tendency to pick the black doll whenever the attribute in question was a negative one, and to opt for the white doll whenever it was positive. These dramatic findings seemed, initially, to provide powerful evidence that the self-esteem of black children was dangerously low, and that large numbers of them did, indeed, suffer from what the *Brown* Court called "a feeling of inferiority."[31]

It didn't, and they don't. When the self-esteem of black students was measured directly, by asking them about themselves instead of about dolls, as researchers did many times in the thirty years since *Brown*, it turned out that the self-esteem of black students was actually quite high — as high or higher than that of white students.[32] It tended to be highest of all in the youngest age groups, often unrealistically so, and that was true for white youngsters, too. What the Clark's research had picked up was the nascent awareness very young black children have of negative stereotypes about black people. Their research, and many subsequent studies, demonstrated that this sort of awareness is pervasive, even among black children as young as three. Fortunately for the children, subsequent research also showed that their self-esteem is not determined by their awareness of these stereotypes, or of any other negative attitudes and behaviors manifest in the larger society around them. It is determined, in major part, by the way their parents or parent surrogates treat them, just as it is among white children.

Worst of all for the theory, black youngsters in all-black schools do

30. *Id.*

31. *Id.*

32. See especially BACHMAN, YOUTH IN TRANSITION, Vol. 2 (1970); Drury, *Black Self-Esteem and Segregated Schools*, 53 SOCIOL. ED. 88 (1980); Rosenberg & Simmons, *Black and White Self-Esteem: The Urban School Child*, ROSE MONOGRAPH SERIES, AM. SOCIOL. ASS'N. (1971); ST. JOHN, SCHOOL DESEGREGATION: OUTCOMES FOR CHILDREN, Chart A-6, 165–174 (1975).

not have lower self-esteem than black youngsters in integrated schools.[33] The difference, when there is one, tends to be in the reverse direction, a finding that showed up first in the original Clark study, ironically enough, and one that has reappeared many times since. Given these findings, it is hardly surprising that racial integration, in and of itself, proved to have no significant impact at all on the educational achievement of black students, a finding that was manifest in the data from the massive Coleman Report in 1966,[34] and one that has been reconfirmed with depressing regularity in a host of subsequent studies.[35]

What of self-esteem itself and its alleged centrality to educational development? The accumulated empirical data indicate that this, too, is a false notion. Integration was not effective as a self-esteem raiser, but the widespread trashing of academic and disciplinary standards seen as harmful to it was. It helped to raise the already high self-esteem of American students of all races to new and dizzying heights in the 1970s, and greatly increased the prevalence of narcissism and grandiosity too.[36] If high self-esteem really did play a major causal role in promoting educational achievement, the test scores of American students would have risen too, and the gap between black and white students would have closed during that extraordinary decade. It did not happen. Instead, scores declined, steeply, and the gap remained wide.

Evidence notwithstanding, most social scientists continued to believe in the self-esteem theory of educational development, or, worse yet, to simply take its validity for granted. The bargain we had made with the Court in *Brown* required an untested theory to be treated like an established scientific fact, and it was kept. Thus, when the bad news about the effects of the theory's implementation began to accumulate, social scientists responded, initially, by attacking the researchers who produced it and the measuring instruments that recorded it as racist and wrong. James Coleman and his co-workers were early targets; tests in general and intelligence tests in particular were later ones, and there were many others.

Attacks notwithstanding, most social scientists and some education experts finally came to accept the fact that black students had not made

---

33. See notes 10 and 32, *supra.*

34. COLEMAN ET AL., EQUALITY OF EDUCATIONAL OPPORTUNITY (1966).

35. MOSTELLER & MOYNIHAN (eds.), ON EQUALITY OF EDUCATIONAL OPPORTUNITY (1972); ST. JOHN, Op. cit. at n32, *supra;* U.S. DEPT. OF EDUC., SCHOOL DESEGREGATION AND BLACK ACHIEVEMENT (1984).

36. See note 32 *supra,* and see Wynne, *Behind the Discipline Problem: Youth Suicide as a Measure of Alienation,* 59 PHI DELTA KAPPAN 307 (1978).

the rapid educational progress we all expected them to make, back in the optimistic days of the 1950s and the early 1960s. Still, they did not lose faith in the theory; they lost faith in the ability of black students to make rapid educational progress instead. Committed to the belief that American education had been at least partially reshaped in ways that were beneficial to black students in the 1960s and 70s, many social scientists, lawyers, and judges could imagine only two basic alternative explanations for their lack of progress. Either American society and all its tests and standards were hopelessly racist, or else something was wrong with the genetic equipment black students brought to school with them. The second alternative was unthinkable, the straw-bogy come to life. It scared the hell out of social scientists, and out of judges and lawyers, too, and they rejected it with vigor. The problem was that they had no real explanation to offer in its place.

The Effects of the Bargain on the Nation

Let me, in closing, offer that alternate explanation and, in the process, give just a hint of what might have been if desegregation had been carried out with dispatch on the basis of a strictly legal rationale, and the self-esteem theory of educational development had not been imposed on the nation. The alternative explanation is that black students did not make substantial intellectual progress in the 1960s and 1970s because American education was reshaped in those years in ways that were harmful to them. Social scientists, professional educators, and federal judges did the reshaping, and they did it with the best will in the world, but what they did undercut discipline and standards and retarded the intellectual development of all students, black ones especially.

In hinting at what might have been if this had not happened, I want to focus on a single, stunning example. It comes from the state of Florida, and has to do with the effects of the institution of minimum competence standards for high school graduation on that state's black students. Social scientists and education experts all across the nation were convinced that its effects would be bad, and the early results were terrible indeed: 80 to 90% of the state's black high school students failed to meet the standard on the first few tries.

Social scientists and their educational and legal allies fought to stop the implementation of this standard in the federal courts. They succeeded only in delaying it, and that turned out to be a great blessing for Florida's black high school students.[37] By the fifth try, more than 90% of them met the standard. These were, by and large, the same students who had failed the test initially. Their genes had not changed; neither had American racism, whatever its extent, and their self-esteem had not been raised, initially: It never feels good to fail a test. Academic standards had been raised, and Florida's black students responded by making rapid educational progress.

Consider, then, what might have been if the academic and disciplinary standards that were in force in most American schools in the 1950s had been kept in force and extended to encompass all public school pupils equally. The sort of minimum competence standards that Florida and some 37 other states decided, finally, in the late 1970s, to require of their high school graduates are the sorts of standards that used to be required for grade school graduates, and why not? They require only that the graduates have the basic skills: literacy and numeracy.

If those standards had been in force for grade school graduation throughout the 1960s and 70s, I believe that black grade school students would have done exactly what black high school students did when confronted with that same standard. They would have met it, developing their capacity for disciplined self-critical intellectual work in the process. Then, in high school, they would have had the tools and time to learn something substantial about mathematics, science, history and literature. That would, inevitably, have served to hone and develop their abstract and symbolic problem-solving abilities, and they and the nation would have benefited enormously, because, as Lloyd Humphreys' work so clearly shows, those are the most broadly and generally useful intellectual skills a human being can have.[38]

High self-esteem, based on a rejection of standards and discipline, proved to be a poor substitute for those skills, but that, alas, is the special benefit that black students, and American students generally, got out of the peculiar bargain between law and social science in the *Brown* case.

It is a sad history that I have abbreviated for you here today, but a number of converging trends in the 1980s make me more optimistic about the future than I have been for some time. Standards and discipline are coming back, in law and education both, and excellence is

37. Debra P. v. Turlington, 474 F. Supp. 244 (M.D. Fla. 1979); *aff'd in part, remanded in part,* 644 F. 2d 397 (5th Cir. 1981); *rehearing denied,* 654 F. 2d 1079 (5th Cir. 1981); 564 F. Supp. 177 (M.D. Fla. 1983); aff'd 730 F. 2d 1405 (11th Cir. 1984).

38. See note 2 *supra,* and see Lerner, *Test Scores as Measures of Human Capital and Forecasting Tools,* 8 J. SOC., POL. & ECON. STUD. 131 (1983).

back in fashion. General intelligence is likely to make a comeback too. After all, it makes no sense to be for excellence and against intelligence.

TABLE OF CASES

REFERENCES

Bachman, J. G. *Youth in transition,* Vol. 2. Ann Arbor: University of Michigan Institute for Social Research, 1970.

Clark, K. E., & Clark, M. P. Racial identification and preference in Negro children. In T. M. Newcomb & E. L. Hartley (Eds.), *Readings in social psychology.* New York: Holt, 1947.

Coleman, J. et al. *Equality of educational opportunity.* Washington, D.C.: Government Printing Office, 1966.

Drury, D. W. Black self-esteem and segregated schools. *Sociology of Education,* 1980, *53,* 88–103.

Glazer, N., & Moynihan, D. P. *Beyond the melting pot* (2d ed.). Cambridge, Mass.: MIT Press, 1970.

Gould, S. J. *The mismeasure of man.* New York: Norton, 1981.

Hand, L. *The Bill of Rights.* Cambridge, Mass.: Harvard University Press, 1958.

Handlin, O. *Race and nationality in American life.* New York: Doubleday Anchor, 1957.

Handlin, O. *The uprooted.* New York: Gosset & Dunlap, 1951.

Hebb, D. O. Open letter to a friend who thinks the I.Q. is a social evil. *American Psychologist,* 1978, 1143–1144.

Humphreys, L. G. A conceptualization of intellectual giftedness. In F. D. Horowitz

& M. O'Brien (Eds.), *The gifted and talented: Developmental perspectives.* Washington, D.C.: American Psychological Association, 1985 (a).

Humphreys, L. G. General intelligence: An integration of factor, test, and simplex theory. In B. Wolman (Ed.), *Handbook of intelligence.* New York: Wiley, 1985 (b).

Humphreys, L. G. The construct of general intelligence. *Intelligence,* 1979, *3,* 105–120.

Humphreys, L. G., & Parsons, C. K. Piagetian tasks measure intelligence and intelligence tests assess cognitive development. *Intelligence,* 1979, *3,* 369–382.

Humphreys, L. G. Theory of intelligence and the management of classroom learning. *Interchange* 1976–77, *7,* 45–50.

Humphreys, L. G. The misleading distinction between aptitude and achievement tests. In D. R. Green (Ed.), *The aptitude-achievement distinction.* Monterey, Calif.: CTB/McGraw-Hill, 1974.

Humphreys, L. G. Theory of intelligence. In R. Cancro (Ed.), *Intelligence: Genetic and environmental influences.* New York: Grune & Stratton, 1971.

Humphreys, L. G. The organization of human abilities. *American Psychologist,* 1962, *17,* 475–483.

Humphreys, L. G. Individual differences. *Annual Review of Psychology,* 1952, *3,* 131–150.

Janowitz, M. *The last half-century: Societal change and politics in America.* Chicago: University of Chicago Press, 1978.

Jencks, C. *Inequality: A reassessment of the effect of family and schooling in America.* New York: Basic Books, 1972.

Jensen, A. R. *Straight talk about mental tests.* New York: Free Press, 1981.

Jones, M. C., Bayley, N., MacFarlane, J. W., & Honzik, M. P. *The course of human development.* Waltham, Mass.: Xerox College Publishing, 1971.

Kamin, L. J. *The science and politics of I.Q.* Hillsdale, N.J.: Erlbaum, 1974.

Kurland, P. K. Brown v. Board of Education was the beginning: The school desegregation cases in the U.S. Supreme Court, 1954–1979. *Washington University Law Quarterly,* 1979, *2,* 309–405.

Lambert, N. M. Psychological evidence in Larry P. v. Riles: An evaluation by a witness for the defense. *American Psychologist,* 1981, *36,* 937–952.

Lerner, B. Our black-robed school board: A report card. In J. H. Bunzel (Ed.), *Challenge to American schools: The case for standards and values.* New York: Oxford University Press, 1985.

Lerner, B. Test scores as measures of human capital and forecasting tools. *Journal of Social, Political and Economic Studies,* 1983, *8,* 131–160(a).

Lerner, B. Facing the unpleasant facts about achievement. *Public Interest,* 1983, *72,* 129–132(b).

Lerner, B. American education: How are we doing? *Public Interest,* 1982, *69,* 59–82.

Lerner, B. The minimum competence testing movement: Social, scientific and legal implications. *American Psychologist,* 1981, *36,* 1057–1066.

Lewontin, R. C., Rose, S., & Kamin, L. J. *Not in our genes*. New York: Pantheon, 1984.

Lynn, R. I.Q. in Japan and the United States shows a growing disparity. *Nature, 1982, 297,* 222–223.

Mosteller, F., & Moynihan, D. P. (Eds.). *On equality of educational opportunity.* New York: Random-Vintage, 1972.

National Commission on Excellence in Education. *A nation at risk: The imperative for educational reform.* Washington, D.C.: U.S. Government Printing Office, 1983.

Rosenberg, M., & Simmons, R. G. *Black and white self-esteem: The urban school child.* Washington, D.C.: American Sociological Association, Rose Monograph Series, 1971.

St. John, N. *School desegregation: Outcomes for children.* New York: Wiley, 1975.

Scarr, S. From evolution to Larry P., or what shall we do about I.Q. tests? *Intelligence,* 1978, *2,* 325–342.

Sowell, T. Assumptions versus history in ethnic education. *Teachers College Record,* 1981, *83,* 37–71(a).

Sowell, T. *Ethnic America.* New York: Basic Books, 1981 (b).

Thernstrom, S. (Ed.). *Harvard encyclopedia of American ethnic groups.* Cambridge, Mass.: Harvard University Press, 1980.

Thernstrom, S. *The other Bostonians: Poverty and progress in the American metropolis.* Cambridge, Mass.: Harvard University Press, 1973.

Tuddenham, R. D. Soldier intelligence in World Wars I and II. *American Psychologist,* 1948, *3,* 54–56.

U.S. Department of Education. *School desegregation and black achievement.* Washington, D.C.: Government Printing Office, 1984.

Wechsler, H. Toward neutral principles of constitutional law. *Harvard Law Review,* 1959, *73,* 1–35.

Wynne, E. A. Behind the discipline problem: Youth suicide as a measure of alienation. *Phi Delta Kappan,* 1978, *59,* 307–315.

7

Intelligence: Three Kinds of Instability and Their Consequences for Policy

LLOYD G. HUMPHREYS

At the outset it is desirable to state my position concerning the relationship of scientific data to the development of social policy. Policy formation is basically directed by values, not by evidence. Values can and should at times override evidence that suggests a contrary course of action. One's values, however, may direct action in different directions. Hence data concerning consequences become highly relevant to a decision. Courses of action are also frequently buttressed by mythical or completely inadequate data. Such data should be criticized, and dependable data, when available, should be made known. In a democracy the electorate and their representatives should be well informed, and they have a right not to be sold a bill of goods on the basis of mythical evidence.

A Definition of Intelligence

A discussion of intelligence and social policy requires a definition of the former as well as an explanation of the preceding statement concerning the latter. Critics say that no one knows what intelligence is, least of all psychologists. Psychologists certainly do not agree with each other. Among laymen there is broad agreement at the behavioral level, as Sternberg, Conway, Kutrin, and Bernstein (1981) have documented, and there is probably substantial consensus concerning an abstract definition as well. This consensus is not far removed from the definition offered by a standard modern dictionary. Capacity or power of the mind to solve problems is prominent. My dictionary says nothing about genetic causation when it defines intelligence as "the capacity to acquire and apply knowledge," but the concept "fixed" is associated with that of capacity. Many would add that the capacity is fixed by the genes.

I proposed a more or less formal definition of intelligence in a symposium held on this campus in 1970 that was sharply at variance with the lay conception, which, incidentally, is held by a good many psychologists (Humphreys, 1971). The definition is not widely known or even widely shared by those who are familiar with it, so I shall repeat with only a few additions the definition offered at that symposium.

Intelligence as Repertoire

Intelligence is the acquired repertoire of intellectual (or cognitive) skills available to the person at a particular point in time. The circularity is broken by defining intellectual by the consensus of those working in the field. It is illustrated by the similarities among the tasks (items) that appear in standard tests of intelligence. The consensus has extended now for 80 years. Items similar to those found in the first Binet-Simon scale are typical of those used today. Experimental cognitive psychologists, who represent quite a different tradition, would also agree with psychometricians doing research with intelligence tests.

The repertoire is acquired by a biological organism in a social environment. The repertoire has both a genetic and an environmental substrate, but I do not try to analyze total variance into genetic, environmental, correlated, and interactive components. The attempts to do this are based on observations not under experimental control. The resulting debate is little more than a " 'tis and 'taint" exchange. The debate itself has been counterproductive because it has deflected attention from important problems for which precise knowledge of the heritability of the trait is not required.

This definition of intelligence may be similar to Boring's "Intelligence is what intelligence tests measure," but it is not identical. Intelligence is the repertoire; the repertoire is sampled by the test. Some tests sample the repertoire more adequately than others. The conditions of measurement must also be such that the repertoire can be sampled reliably and validly. A repertoire in Spanish must be sampled in Spanish. The examinee must also be motivated to respond, either to test items or to life situations, in a way that accurately reflects the repertoire.

Intelligence as Phenotype

Intelligence defined in this way is as much a phenotypic trait as height or weight. It differs from traits of physique in that it is behavioral, and it is not exhibited as consistently from one situation to another; nevertheless, persons who know an individual well can make judgments of intelligence that are substantially correlated with scores on a standard test. As a function of the consensus that has developed concerning intellectual behavior, judgments made by teachers undoubtedly agree more with those made by other teachers and with scores on tests than they do with judgments made by athletic coaches and playground supervisors. The latter judgments would also not agree as highly with the rankings furnished by the test.

The repertoire grows as children learn and mature. The widely known and widely used intelligence quotient or IQ, however, is *not* an estimate of anyone's repertoire. The mental age metric was a reasonable way of measuring the growth of the phenotypic trait in children, but a change in the computation of an IQ has led to the disuse of mental age. For use in both practice and research it is as important to measure both phenotypic intelligence and relative phenotypic intelligence as it is to measure height in millimeters and height relative to an age group. The technology is available to develop a scale for intelligence that would have an arbitrary zero but approximately equal intervals that would allow one to measure growth and decline throughout the life span. Psychometricians should apply themselves to the problem. One of the factors that attenuates the correlation between teachers' ratings and measured intelligence is the difficulty that raters have in distinguishing phenotypic intelligence from relative intelligence. The youngest children in a classroom tend to have the highest IQs, the oldest children the lowest, but children perform in class in accordance with their mental ages.

Tasks Central to the Repertoire

It is possible to characterize individual intellectual tasks in terms of the degree to which they represent the repertoire. Some tasks are highly related to others and can be considered geometrically to be close to the centroid or the center of gravity of the domain. Test items that measure the ability to reason, to draw valid inferences from information and to manipulate symbolic materials, are close to the centroid. Measures of both fluid and crystallized intelligence in the Cattell-Horn theory are close to the centroid. Reading and aural comprehension of language are central to the domain.

In the periphery of the repertoire are measures of short-term memory, ability to repeat strings of digits forward and backward, and many relatively simple but speeded tasks. Such tasks belong in the repertoire but are not highly correlated with other intellectual tasks. A recently developed and actively marketed test has been arbitrarily labeled an intelligence test by its authors, but it is based on items that are peripheral to the intellectual repertoire and that are too few in number and variety to compensate for their lack of centrality.

Some persons are critical of the central importance given to language in intelligence tests. Language is acquired, and "real" intelligence is said by these critics to be a fixed capacity of the organism independent of variation in environmental opportunities. Supposedly, an intelligence test assumes that opportunity to learn has been equal for all examinees. My definition avoids this absurdity, whereas a construct that cannot be measured or inferred from measurements has no place in science. There are no prospects for devising an instrument that is immune to environmental influences. It hardly seems surprising, incidentally, that the use of language is central in the intellectual repertoire. Our species, after all, differs from our primate relatives most sharply in our highly developed use of language.

Ramifications of Intelligence

Intelligence defined in this way has ramifications throughout our society. It is more highly correlated with the progress of students up the educational ladder than is any other variable, although this correlation is attenuated by the child's degree of privilege or deprivation associated with the socioeconomic status of the family. Intelligence is highly correlated with occupational placement in our society, including the status of chronic unemployment and marginal employment, although these correlations are also attenuated by privilege or deprivation.

Intelligence is broadly based from the measurement point of view as well. For children who have been exposed to several years of primary schooling in a common language, scores on a composite of academic achievement tests are as highly correlated with intelligence as scores on one intelligence test are with another. A composite of a wide range of information, including information that would be considered nonacademic, has a centroid very close to the centroid of the intellectual repertoire. It is also possible to measure intelligence with a composite of the reasoning items used by Piagetians in their studies of cognitive development (Humphreys, Rich, & Davey, 1985). One does not need an intelligence test to sample the repertoire in a manner that allows the same inferences about future performance of the individual as one would make from the intelligence test. Intelligence is truly general.

Although it is possible to develop a theory of intelligence with this definition as a starting point by the addition of principles derived from the research literature of genetics, development, attention, motivation, and learning, I shall concentrate on the empirical correlates of intelligence defined in this way. I shall briefly refer to theory in advancing explanations of these correlates. The empirical research that I shall discuss is related to three kinds of instability of intelligence. The definition that I use, and that you must use if you are to understand me, makes no assumptions concerning the stability or instability of the trait, or the relative amounts of genetic and environmental variance in the distribution of the trait.

Instability of Population Means

Between 1917 and 1942 the mean intelligence of army draftees and enlistees increased by approximately one standard deviation (Tuddenham, 1948).The median soldier in 1942 would have been above the 80th percentile in 1917. Such data are lacking in experimental control, but the gain cannot be explained by differences in manpower policies. There is obviously no control over the population gene pool, but there is a wide consensus that the important factor in this gain was the increase in the number of years of schooling that took place in this country during those 25 years. These data are summarized in Table 1.

The birth dates in Table 1 were not selected to make it easy to determine the educational levels of young men of military age in 1917 and 1942, but a gain of 3 years of schooling during that time span is about right. Although there are no similar data on gains in intelligence by women, it can safely be assumed from test standardization comparisons of the sexes that their performance was at about the same level. Women did fall a little behind the men in years of schooling during this period.

Many people react to this evidence of instability of the population mean by declaring that "real" intelligence surely did not increase be-

TABLE 1
Mean Number of Years of Educational Attainment
by Birth Cohort and Sex

Birth date	Males	Females
1866–1875	6.77	7.25
1876–1885	7.17	7.60
1886–1895	7.65	7.99
1896–1905	8.59	8.89
1906–1915	9.67	9.91
1916–1925	10.76	10.73
1926–1935	11.53	11.30
1936–1940	12.01	11.67

tween the two world wars. This is not unlike expressing a belief in a soul. By definition, no form of sensorimotor contact is possible. I do know that a highly functional intelligence did increase. The average 18-year-old in 1942 was able to learn general military and specialty skills more quickly than his counterpart in 1917. A well-documented increase in intelligence and in educational attainment occurred in Scotland from the midthirties to shortly after World War II (Scottish Council for Research in Education, 1949). A second carefully documented increase in intelligence and in years of schooling occurred in this country between 1942 and 1960 (Tupes & Shaycoft, 1964).

Costs of the Gains

These gains were not quickly or cheaply accomplished, even though it seemingly was by an environmental manipulation. Twenty-five years is long by the standards of psychological research or by the lifetime of an individual. Furthermore, the increase required a massive national effort. Consider the number of school buildings built and maintained, teachers trained, and books published. Look at the man-years of students, teachers, and school administrators who were diverted from the production of goods and provision of other services. I have not tried to develop a cost estimate. It would be huge, but the ultimate economic and social gains were well worth the cost. One policy implication is that we could probably produce future gains, by making qualitative changes, but we should not underestimate the cost in time and money. If we have a problem of this sort, furthermore, hoping that it will disappear with little effort is, to say the least, an inadequate response.

Gains Turn to Losses

A second implication of this example of instability of intelligence is that what goes up can come down. We have heard a great deal about decreases in scores on college entrance tests. These tests, incidentally, sample the intellectual repertoire in important areas, but are not as general as standard tests of intelligence. It is interesting that in the last few years it has become popular to call them measures of developed abilities. I am quite comfortable with this designation, but it should be made clear that we do not measure any other kind. General intelligence is itself a developed ability.

The decrease in college entrance scores has been real and now seems to have leveled off. There are also data that suggest the decrease has not occurred at all levels of schooling. Lerner (1982) has reported that grade-school children did not show a decrease at the appropriate lead time for the college entrance decrease. The problem started in the junior high years. These data are not as firm as one would like and as their importance would justify, but they are not improbable for the intelligence that I have defined. If there is a widespread decline in the quality of learning opportunities starting at a particular point in development and extending over a considerable period of time, one would expect the growth of intelligence to be retarded.

Part of the decrease at the time of college entrance is due to a marked decrease in the number of students scoring at the very highest levels of intelligence. Learning opportunities can decline more in one portion of the distribution of intelligence than in another. Expectations for excellence did decline, and egalitarian values gained a substantial following. *Pygmalion in the Classroom* (Rosenthal & Jacobsen, 1968) was based on inadequate data, and the study was also designed with a weak experimental manipulation of teacher expectations for their students. In contrast, expectations that take the form of textbooks, classroom materials, presentations, examinations, and grading standards operating over several years would be expected to have measurable effects.

Participants in the Decline

It is incorrect to place the blame for the decline entirely or even largely on teachers and administrators in our primary and secondary schools. They are products of the society and embody their society's attitudes and values. During the period of the decline they were also representative of the ages and attitudes of the parents of the children they were trying to educate. The generation of students entering college during the period of decline was relatively undisciplined socially and intellectually. The social Zeitgeist infected university faculties as well. Look at the way we gave in to the irrational demands of our students in the late sixties and early seventies.

Instability of Individual Differences

The conventional wisdom among many theorists and most users of intelligence tests is that intelligence is not stable during infancy and the early preschool years, but that IQs become highly stable during the early school years and remain stable thereafter. The reason given for the early instability is that the child's behavioral repertoire does not allow one to measure real intelligence. The later assumed stability provides the basis for predictions of long-term performance that have important consequences. A description of a child as either mentally retarded or gifted places that child in a fixed diagnostic category. The

British program, which placed children at age 11 in university preparatory study leading to university entrance, was based on the assumed stability.

The evidence does show that the stability of intelligence from year to year is quite moderate in the early preschool years and becomes high after school entrance. Unless one looks closely at the data, it is easy to conclude that the absence of a perfect relationship over the one-year period in the later years is due to the error present in all measurement operations. When one looks beyond one year, however, the stability observed is reduced. The degree of instability is a monotonic function of the amount of time between the original score and the score at retest. The correlations in Table 2 illustrate the phenomenon.

Early Research on Instability

The instability of individual differences in intelligence becomes more dramatic when analyzed in the way first used by Anderson (1939). He correlated the gain in mental age from one year to another with the mental age (base) at the beginning of the year. The result was a series of near-zero correlations. This research was later extended and confirmed by Roff (1941). Because I was following a different research literature at the time, I was not one of the individual-differences theorists who ignored these findings that rejected so completely intelligence as a fixed capacity. I did discover these articles shortly before 1960 and, one way or another, I have been working on problems concerned with individual instability for the past 25 years.

TABLE 2
*Intercorrelations of Intelligence
Over Ages 2 to 15 Years*

Age	2	3	4	5	6	7	8	9	15
2	—	74	68	63	61	54	58	56	47
3	74	—	76	72	73	68	67	65	58
4	68	76	—	80	79	72	72	71	60
5	63	72	80	—	87	81	79	79	67
6	61	73	79	87	—	86	84	84	69
7	54	68	72	81	86	—	87	87	69
8	58	67	72	79	84	87	—	90	78
9	56	65	71	79	84	87	90	—	80
15	47	58	60	67	69	69	78	80	—

Note. Adapted from Wilson (1983), decimal points omitted.

A Model for Instability

A possible model for the instability of individual differences in intelligence was developed by Guttman (1955) for a different purpose. He suggested the simplex model for the description of differences in the complexity of performance required by different tests administered at a single point in time. In the longitudinal, developmental application of this model, one assumes that gains in true scores are uncorrelated with true scores on the first of the two occasions. When this model was applied in a sample of more than 1,400 persons to the intercorrelations of a composite serving as an excellent surrogate for an intelligence test in Grades 5, 7, 9, and 11, the fit was excellent (Humphreys & Parsons, 1979). An acceptable fit statistically, but with slightly larger residuals, was obtained for a measure of aural comprehension of English discourse. Humphreys, Park, and Parsons (1979) created four subsamples defined by sex and race (black/white) and studied the fit of the model to the 16 individual components of the intellectual composite. In only two instances the fit of the model could be rejected with a probability of less than .01, but even these residuals were small. During the age range represented by the four grades, the phenomenon appeared to be quite general.

More recently the same model has been applied by Humphreys and Davey (1988) to the intercorrelations of tests of infant development and standard intelligence extending from 3 months to 15 years. A selection of these correlations is presented in Table 2. The total time period had to be divided into two overlapping segments because of missing data. The first period extended from 3 months to 9 years; the second extended from 18 months to 15 years, although there were no observations from 10 to 14 years. The model can be rejected unequivocally in the first matrix when the age of first test is 3 months, but an acceptable fit is obtained for 9 months to 9 years. In the second matrix, perhaps because of the missing test occasions, the fit is not quite as close. The largest residual is between 9 and 15 years.

This research provides an alternative interpretation of the stability and instability of intelligence from infancy through the 11th grade in school. One cannot reject the hypothesis that infant tests as early as 9 months are measuring the same general ability as standard intelligence tests at 15 years and as an intellectual composite at approximately 17 years. Individual differences in this interpretation change more rapidly in the early years because the intellectual repertoire is smaller than it becomes during the school years.

The Degree of Instability

I submit, tentatively to be sure, the following formula for estimating the stability of observed intelligence over any given number of years for children in primary and secondary schools. Based on present data, the stability of true scores over one year is about .96 to .97, perhaps a bit lower in the first one or two grades. Raise the estimated one-year stability to the power of the number of years between the first test and the retest. Then, to return to fallible observed scores, multiply the true score stability by the square root of the product of the separate reliabilities.

If I assume reliabilities of .95, surely on the high side, the stability of observed scores over 10 years would be represented by a correlation of between .63 and .70. A child with an IQ of 140 on the first test is expected to have an IQ of about 125 ten years later. The variability about this expected value is almost as great as the variability among unselected children. An appreciable number of such children will be below average on retest.

After High School

There are no data that allow an estimate of the amount of change in individual differences for individuals who leave high school for a job. There are no adequate data that allow the same estimate for undergraduate college students. Retesting of graduating seniors at the University of Minnesota was reported by Laughlin (1940), but only two points in time were represented and odd-even estimates of reliabilities were probably spuriously high. In this restricted range of talent and with the somewhat inflated reliabilities, the correlations between true scores for the 4-year interval were about .85. This suggests that the stability of general intelligence is no higher than in earlier development. Whether the instability present is about the college student mean or about the unselected student mean represents an important unsolved problem.

There are also data indicating that individual differences in narrow achievement, a portion of the total repertoire, are changing at a more rapid rate (Humphreys, 1968; Humphreys & Taber, 1973; Lin & Humphreys, 1977). It is not surprising that the college experience allows students to specialize, but the amount of change in individual differences in narrow areas while general intelligence remains relatively stable was surprising to me. There is, however, one loose end. The systematic evaluations of rate of change in college are based on academic grades. The instability of grades does, of course, contain other sources of variance than change in a narrow repertoire.

To obtain information concerning the stability of narrow achievement, it is necessary to look at precollege data. Estimated stabilities of true scores on narrow information tests between Grades 5 and 11 are consistently lower than those for aural and reading comprehension (Humphreys et al., 1979). A broadly based composite of eight information tests, on the other hand, has estimated true score stabilities at about the same level as the tests measuring comprehension (Humphreys & Davey, 1983). When interests change, narrow information changes more rapidly than general information or general intelligence.

Important components of the broad intellectual repertoire appear to be highly resistant to change after the completion of primary and secondary schooling. Native English-speaking students, including those using so-called black English, who have completed 12 years of schooling and are still reading and writing English and using arithmetic at the 6th-grade level or below, are presently showing little evidence of compensation for their deficits in remedial programs. I know of no evidence that human intelligence is a power or force, presumably measured inaccurately in environmentally deprived persons by standard intelligence tests, that is released once an opportunity is provided. Instead, intelligence is slowly acquired over many years and change is slow.

Stability of Other Traits

Can one reduce the regression to the mean and the variability about the regressed score by measuring different or additional attributes? Standards for the diagnosis of mental retardation include an evaluation of adjustment to the individual's environment. The diagnosis of giftedness may include academic grades or desirable personality traits. To the best of my knowledge there are no data concerning the stabilities of these other attributes over extended periods of time on samples of adequate size, but I am willing to conclude that there are no fixed behavioral traits. The substitution for or the addition to intelligence of measures of other attributes in the description of a child as mentally retarded or gifted might change the degree of stability observed, either up or down, but would not abolish instability.

Educational Policy Implications

There are several policy issues that are affected by the instability of individual differences in intelligence. In the first place, an educational system should be forgiving of early performance that is less than illustrious and should not give undue weight to early illustrious performance. By and large we do have a forgiving system in our variety of primary, secondary, and postsecondary schools. Individual school policies might become more forgiving as well. Academic probation requirements can be geared to a reasonable rate of recovery from a disastrous start. Adults returning to college after a long absence should be evaluated in terms of how they currently perform, not on the basis of grades obtained immediately after high school. These recommendations are not based on sentiment, but on the expectation of obtaining more accurate long-term predictions.

The problem with the English system that determined university entrance at age 11 was that it assumed too much stability in performance. It was not a forgiving system. It did qualify a larger proportion of children of working-class families for university entrance than did the system that preceded or followed it. Considering the rigidity of English social classes, this was a substantial achievement. The examination was abolished by a labor government that accepted the rhetoric claiming that it discriminated against working-class children.

Implication for Diagnosis

A second implication is that no child should be labeled mentally retarded on behavioral evidence alone. That diagnosis should be restricted to low IQ, low adjustment, and a known biological etiology. When the educable mentally retarded are followed up later in life, they are found to be doing much better than the original label would suggest. There is no need to resort to the hypothetical presence of compensating personality traits. In the absence of organic etiology, the expectation is for improvement even in the absence of planned intervention. In contrast, a Down's syndrome child today will still be a Down's syndrome child 10 years hence. Although special training will help Down's children to perform more effectively in society, the expectation concerning their instability is that they will regress toward the Down's syndrome mean, not toward the population mean.

In the absence of planned intervention, gifted children will regress toward the population mean. A diagnostic category is as misleading here as it is at the other end of the distribution of intelligence. It is possible that an effective planned intervention would reduce the expected regression. It is also possible that a planned intervention would reduce the expected regression of a behaviorally retarded child, but in this case ineffective is a more valid adjective to apply. The planned interventions for the retarded that have been used may, as many critics have claimed, reduce the regression toward the mean that would take place without formal intervention. Such programs are planned to provide training for children with a supposedly permanent handicap.

Implications for Remediation

Available evidence points strongly to the importance of early remediation for environmental deficits. In Jones's (1984) analysis of black/white differences on the reading and arithmetic items in the National Assessment of Educational Progress (NAEP) over the first three cycles of that program, the gap between the races was almost imperceptibly narrowed for 17-year-olds. In contrast, the gap for 9-year-olds was almost halved, and that for 13-year-olds was intermediate. The search for causes for the black gains would be narrowed if we had data on possible changes in black performance before school entrance.

Jones (1984) also showed that black gains were not made at the expense of the whites, but there is one disquieting outcome from these assessments. Without regard to race, gains were made predominantly in the lowest quartile of the distributions and losses occurred in the highest quartile. The NAEP data are in keeping with the losses occurring at the high end of the Scholastic Aptitude Test (SAT) at the time of high school graduation.

There is no evidence that the black/white gap in intelligence narrows as a result of undergraduate special admissions programs. Although there are measurement problems in comparing SAT and American College Test (ACT) scores for entering freshmen with the scores on admissions tests used in the selection of graduate and professional school students, mean differences of seemingly the same magnitude persist over the 4 intervening years. The test score differences are also accompanied by professional school performance differences in the same direction. First-year grades for blacks in law schools are lower than those for whites at each level of test score (Powers, 1977). Furthermore, at each level of undergraduate grade point average (GPA), the race difference in law school GPA is greater than it is for the entrance test. Compensation for early deficits may be possible after the age of 18, but it is not now occurring for black students. Proportionate representation in higher education and in occupations cannot be accompanied by equivalent levels of performance of the two races as long as we are unable to correct the deficits in basic intellectual skills.

All organisms live in and adapt to their environments with their complement of phenotypic traits. The heritability of a particular trait is immaterial. The extent to which a trait can be modified, by what mechanisms, in what amount of time, and at what point in development is material.

Instability from Generation to Generation

A variety of degrees of relationship are reported for the intelligence of one parent and a child. Sex of parent and child seems to be unimportant, but whether the child develops in the home of a biological or foster parent is important. It is also necessary to control the nature of the test used, its reliability, and the range of talent in which the correlation is computed. For a standard test administered carefully in a wide range of talent, the correlation between parent and child is about .50. There is also assortative mating for intelligence, and again, a variety of degrees of relationship are reported, but a correlation of .50 based on a good test in a wide range of talent is a reasonably accurate estimate. On statistical grounds alone these figures provide an estimate of the correlation between midparent intelligence and child's intelligence of .58.

Regression in Intelligence

If one knows the intelligence quotient of one of the two parents and the child has lived with the parent during development, the expected value for the child's relative intelligence is half-way back toward the mean of the child's generation from the amount by which parental intelligence differs from the parental mean. Superior parents tend to have superior children and inferior parents inferior children, but on average the children are less extreme than the parents. The expected variability about the expected value of the child's intelligence is almost as great as for children in general. The predicted intelligence for an individual child, knowing the intelligence of a parent, is subject to a great deal of error in either direction about the expected value.

If one knows the midparent intelligence quotient, the expected regression toward the children's mean of any given child is about one-third of the distance that the average parent deviates from the parental mean. The variability about the expected value is somewhat reduced in comparison to the one-parent situation, but there is still a substantial amount of error in either direction. Careful selection of a spouse will reduce somewhat the expected regression of a child, but will not abolish it.

Regression is not unidirectional. Finding a very bright child in a classroom does not lead to an expectation that a parent or the parents are themselves extremely bright. For a single parent the expectation is an intelligence quotient half-way back to the parental mean. For midparent it is also half-way back toward the midparent mean. (Note that the distribution for midparent IQs is less variable than the one for single parents.) Because there are many more parents close to the mean than at superior levels, a larger number of superior children have average parents than superior parents.

Family Status and Regression

If one substitutes a traditional measure of socioeconomic status (SES) of the family for parental intelligence, the correlation between good measures of both status and child's intelligence in a wide range of talent is about .40. High-status families pass on high intelligence to their offspring less effectively than highly intelligent parents do. Furthermore, it helps at most a trivial amount to have measures of both status and intelligence in estimating an expected IQ for a child. The largest pool of intellectual talent is located more heavily in the middle of the distribution of status than of parental intelligence.

Quite recently, students and I have developed a measure that we are, perhaps unwisely, calling intellectual privilege/deprivation. We know full well that our measure does not control possible genetic variance, though the name may suggest otherwise. (A traditional measure of SES has the same fault.) The new measure has a correlation with children's intelligence of quite close to .65. Thus we can estimate a child's intelligence more accurately with this measure than by knowing the IQs of both parents. The family background information utilized was from Project Talent (Flanagan et al., 1962). We excluded information about race and ethnicity and developed measures separately for each sex, but these turned out to be highly similar. We also excluded information about background that was directly related to the child's ability. Thus we did not key information about courses taken or liked.

The new measure has some interesting correlates even though we are not yet ready to draw conclusions about their meaning. It is more highly related to the verbal component of general intelligence than to the short-term memory or spatial visualization components. It is also more highly related to academic information than to nonacademic information. It covers the variance of the measure of SES in the child's intelligence, but includes something more. Vernon (1950), on the one hand, and Horn and Cattell (1966), on the other, have divided the general intelligence that I have defined into correlated major group factors. Our measure of privilege/deprivation discriminates more sharply between Vernon's verbal-numerical-educational and his mechanical-spatial-practical factors than between the fluid and crystallized group factors of Cattell and Horn.

To the best of my knowledge there are no correlations in the literature between grandparents and grandchildren, but the available correlations of aunts and uncles with nieces and nephews, or those with first cousins, indicate strongly that regression to the mean in both directions over three generations would be approximately three-quarters of the distance. High ability may persist over several generations in selected families, but this might be as much a matter of chance as of choice of child-rearing and educational practices. For several possible reasons, high status and large fortunes may be passed on over several generations more effectively than high intelligence. These reasons include the social inventions of trust funds and financial advisers. Irving Kristol, the so-called neoconservative who is actually as much an old liberal, wrote an essay (1978) recommending the breakup of large fortunes. He suggests a mechanism other than confiscatory taxation, a limitation of the amount that an individual can bequeath to a given person, that I find attractive.

Intelligence is not unique with respect to regression phenomena. Physical, biochemical, athletic, temperamental, and attitudinal traits exhibit regression. Attitudes toward God and toward communism show somewhat less regression than intelligence. Intelligence shows less regression than occupational interests or personality as defined by our measurement devices. Obviously there are many possible causes for the similarities and differences between parents and offspring that produce correlations greater than zero but less than one. Also, unless the measure of a hypothetical trait shows some moderate degree of similarity across generations, the measure is inadequate or the trait is not important psychologically. Both heredity and environment are expected to produce similarity but not identity.

Implications for Education

The emphasis placed on education by this country was revealed clearly by the data presented earlier concerning the growth in years of education provided to successive birth cohorts. The provision of educational facilities for the children of all of the people has been an important tenet of our democratic philosophy for a good many years. Public education was a basic institution in support of the "melting pot," and it played an important role in providing for a good deal of fluidity of the class structure. By virtue of providing educational facilities for all children, public education served to discover and nurture talent wherever it was to be found.

On a priori grounds it seems inescapable that public education serves the function of finding talent more effectively than private education. For example, the 10th-grade children in Project Talent who were enrolled in private nonparochial schools in 1960 were substantially higher in the SES index of their families than in their own intelligence. Boys were almost a full standard deviation above the mean in SES, half a standard deviation in intelligence. The difference between the differences for girls was a little less. Financial support for public education should not depend solely on unselfish motives of doing good for the children of the less privileged. Our society needs to support the education of all of our children on purely selfish grounds because in doing so we support the general welfare.

I realize that the melting-pot concept has come under attack in recent years by persons who think of themselves as liberals. This is unfortunate. It was a liberal doctrine in our earlier days, and it still is. This country accepted persons representing all races, religions, and ethnic groups, and they became Americans. America changed in the process as well. Our culture became enriched from many cultural sources, but our citizens acquired a core culture, language, and values.

An alternative model has developed in education in recent years. It is said that an important objective for public education is to maintain a child's cultural heritage. This objective is frequently stated in the negative: "We should not deprive a child of his cultural heritage." This is one of the fuzziest-minded and short-sighted ideas that I have read and heard in many years of association with educators. I grew up using poorly educated white English, but fortunately my teachers had not heard of this philosophy. They worked hard to deprive me of my cultural heritage. They were more successful in developing my written English than in changing my speech. Oral language is difficult to change, with habits of pronunciation being most difficult of all.

A good deal of data on language usage and academic achievement suggests that we are not interfering enough with the cultural heritages of black and Hispanic children.

College Attendance and Social Class

Positions of leadership are associated with one or more college degrees. Rates of college attendance as functions of intelligence and SES reflect the degree to which we are getting our ablest young people into college and starting them toward future leadership positions. It is highly relevant in this regard that a measure of SES adds very little to the predictive accuracy of measures of performance in undergraduate, graduate, and professional schools. The better the measure of intelligence, the less does SES add. The latter appears merely to compensate a little for the inevitable error in fallible test scores. When academic grades are used as predictors, SES also adds very little to the predictive accuracy of those grades.

I have nationwide data on rate of college attendance for only two

points in time, Project Talent in 1961 (Flanagan & Cooley, 1966) and
the National Longitudinal Study in 1972 (Tabler, 1976). As a nation
we spend very little to obtain information about our human resources.
As shown in Table 3, SES has a greater effect on college attendance
among students in the highest 25% of intelligence than its predictive
accuracy warrants. If one looks only at entry to 4-year colleges, a good
deal of ground was lost between 1961 and 1972 in getting our ablest
students into higher education.[1] This was particularly true for the children of families in the second quartile of status. The growth of junior
colleges did provide an alternative for students in the lower three-
quarters of our population in status in 1972, but I have no information
concerning what happened to them thereafter. Some of our ablest
students surely settled for 2-year terminal degrees.

The 11-year postgraduation follow-up conducted on the Project Tal-

TABLE 3

*Rates of College Attendance Among the Highest 25% on Intelligence
by Socioeconomic Status (SES) Quartile*

	Quartile			
Group	1st	2d	3d	4th
	Four-year colleges			
1961				
Males	.48	.70	.73	.87
Females	.34	.67	.67	.83
1973				
Males	.38	.46	.58	.74
Females	.44	.41	.53	.76
	Junior colleges			
1961				
Males	.13	.07	.08	.05
Females	.08	.08	.08	.05
1973				
Males	.15	.24	.23	.11
Females	.22	.25	.22	.09
	Totals			
1961				
Males	.61	.77	.81	.92
Females	.42	.75	.75	.88
1973				
Males	.53	.70	.81	.85
Females	.66	.66	.75	.85

ent sample provides information concerning the award of diplomas and degrees. The data in Table 4 are for the 10th-grade cohort measured in 1960 and contacted again in 1973. It is seen that both intelligence and SES are related to progress up the educational ladder as is our new experimental measure of privilege/deprivation. Intelligence is more highly related to level achieved than to SES, and the experimental measure tends to be intermediate. In terms of the present argument, SES has a higher relationship to level attained than its merit warrants.

This conclusion is not new. Jencks (1972) concluded that a system that provided access to higher education on the basis of either test scores or high school grades would reduce the advantage of the children of middle-class parents over those of working-class parents by about one-third. I am suggesting a different way of looking at the data than in terms of democratic fairness. We could be a more productive and more competitive society if we did a better job of attracting the brightest to higher education. I also suggest that it is not rational for critics to condemn the tests as biased against working-class children while neglecting the talent among these children revealed by the supposedly biased tests.

The comparison of the sexes in Table 4 is of interest. Women were more intelligent than men at all educational levels. This is the result of disproportionate sample sizes of the sexes from one level to another with more girls at the bottom and fewer at the top. This sex comparison is timebound to the 1960s, but I doubt whether the too-high relationship between SES and educational attainment has decreased. My guess is to the contrary. The class structure has probably become more rigid since 1960.

There are interesting differences among both undergraduate and

TABLE 4

Mean Standard Scores of Intelligence, Socioeconomic Status (SES), and Privilege at Selected Educational Levels

Level	Intelligence		SES		Privilege	
	Males	Females	Males	Females	Males	Females
Doctorate	1.26	1.50	1.06	1.37	1.17	1.29
Masters	.90	1.00	.59	.78	.83	.98
Bachelors	.66	.89	.51	.69	.66	.84
High school diploma	−.41	−.05	−.49	−.30	−.41	−.09
Drop-out	−.62	−.31	−.44	−.44	−.58	−.38

graduate majors in intelligence, in the social status of their families, and in the difference in level for these two variables. Physics majors are well above all others in intelligence, but they are relatively one of the lowest in SES. Engineering majors have the same pattern, but at somewhat lower levels. Neither the choices of the physics student and his family nor the selection of the student and curricular decisions of faculties are affected positively by the social status of the student. If anything there is a small negative effect of status during the educational process.

Regression and Population Means

There are substantial numbers of very able children from families in which the parents are below the mean in intelligence, and even more from families below the mean in status. On the other hand, these same families produce more than their share of below-average children. This expectation is independent of any assumption concerning causation. Regression is an empirical phenomenon that can have diverse causes. Nevertheless, if below-average families consistently produced more children than above-average families, the mean intelligence of a population would gradually decrease in the absence of any compensatory adjustment. To deny this possibility or its consequences is, to put it bluntly, irrational.

Before I raise too many hackles by this indirect reference to eugenics, let me repeat the definition of eugenics by Sir Francis Galton in 1904 (cited by Tanner, 1966, p. 122): "the science which deals with all influences that improve the inborn qualities of a race; also with those influences that develop them [these inborn qualities] to the utmost advantage." For Galton, eugenics was a science that included *all* aspects of human development. In evaluating his definition it must be remembered that Galton was the father of research on individual differences. Both genetic and environmental determinants affect individuals. Eugenics was the science of *individual* development.

No reasonable person can object to Galton's goals. There is wide disagreement, however, concerning how those goals are to be accomplished. This disagreement has been grossly exacerbated by memories of the heinous practices of a group of evil men in Nazi Germany. Their practices, however, were antithetical to every aspect of Galton's definition. We cannot afford to allow those memories to prevent research on eugenics or discussion of possible democratic solutions if problems exist.

Half a century ago there was a good deal of concern expressed in both the popular media and in scientific journals concerning a so-called dysgenic trend in the populations of the United States and western Europe. The basic datum was the negative correlation consistently reported between family size and family socioeconomic status. A negative correlation between family size and intelligence was inferred. This concern was expressed, however, when intelligence was rising. If changes were taking place in the gene pool, they were masked by environmental factors. At midcentury, Higgins, Reed, and Reed (1962) seemingly demolished the negative effect on the gene pool by finding in a localized sample in a restricted birth cohort a sufficient number of low-scoring adults without children that the overall trend was actually slightly positive. These findings were confirmed almost immediately by others, but sampling was again limited in time and place.

Vining (1982) has published data on more recent birth cohorts showing a negative relationship between number of offspring and status of the mother. He suggested that the change from midcentury published data was a post "baby-boom" phenomenon. Now, Van Court and Bean (1985), using random samples from the total U.S. population and a range of maternal cohorts from 1894 to 1964, have confirmed the early concern, reversed the midcentury findings, and supported Vining's important effect following the midcentury high birthrates. For all of their maternal cohorts, Van Court and Bean reported small negative correlations between number of offspring and scores on a short vocabulary test used as a surrogate for an intelligence test. For mothers born through 1934, the median correlation is $-.12$. The correlation is slightly less negative for the mothers of the baby-boomers. For mothers born since 1945, however, the median correlation is $-.22$. Van Court and Bean also report correlations between mothers' vocabulary scores and the number of siblings of those mothers. In accordance with the midcentury data, the negative correlations are higher, with a median of $-.27$.

In the absence of knowledge concerning remedial measures, a correlation of around $-.20$ between mothers' intelligence and number of offspring cannot be tolerated for long in a democracy. The size of this relationship needs to be confirmed with a measure of general intelligence used in place of the vocabulary test. It is also possible that the recent negative correlations will be reduced in size when the maternal cohorts involved have completed their child-bearing years. More research is required, but social action should not be dismissed as unthinkable.

Social actions that might be taken to reverse the trend do not necessarily involve compulsory sterilization. Do our social policies encourage reproduction among those who are least able to provide for the intellectual development of their children? Can these policies be changed to reverse the trend? Are there existing policies tending to counter the trend that can be strengthened? Do we need to invent new social institutions such as public preschools? Responsible reproduction and child rearing are more important in a democracy than in a dictatorship. Any difficulties involved in agreeing on acceptable means should not deter us from analyzing the problem and being inventive concerning possible solutions.

In Summation

I have defined a phenotypic, behavioral intelligence that can be inferred from objective measurements. This is not the only possible definition of intelligence—I am quite willing to assign the equivalent of a subscript to it—but it is a definition that is useful in practice and in theory. It possesses one marked advantage in that it is closely tied to the widely used standard intelligence tests. A great deal of empirical information has been accumulated over the past 80 years concerning the correlates of these tests that this definition, in conjunction with a small number of psychological principles, describes coherently.

Among the empirical correlates of intelligence as herein defined are those concerned with three kinds of instability. One is the instability of means (and standard deviations) of populations. Another is the instability of individual differences in relative intelligence during development and decay. A third is the instability of intelligence from generation to generation. Each kind of instability has implications for policy, and I wish to emphasize particularly that these implications are independent of the unknown relationship between genotype and phenotype for intelligence.

Finally, the instability from generation to generation is not by any means complete. The degree of stability present can produce instability of population means when intelligence of parents is negatively related to the number of their offspring. We need research on individual differences that deals with all biological and cultural influences that could improve the qualities of our species, as Galton suggested 80 years ago.

NOTE

1. Since this was written, data for 1982 have become available. The proportion of high school graduates who attended 4-year colleges increased slightly from 1972 but was still below the level established in the early sixties.

REFERENCES

Anderson, J. E. (1939). The limitations of infant and preschool tests in the measurement of intelligence. *Journal of Psychology, 8*, 351–379.

Flanagan, J. C., & Cooley, W. W. (1966). *Project Talent: One-year follow-up studies*. Pittsburgh: School of Education, University of Pittsburgh.

Flanagan, J. C., Dailey, J. T., Shaycoft, M. F., Gorham, W. A., Orr, D. B., & Goldberg, I. (1962). *Design for a study of American youth*. Boston: Houghton Mifflin.

Guttman, L. (1955). A generalized simplex for factor analysis. *Psychometrika, 20*, 173–192.

Higgins, J. F., Reed, E. W., & Reed, S. C. (1962). Intelligence and family size: A paradox resolved. *Eugenics Quarterly, 9*, 84–90.

Horn, J. L., & Cattell, R. B. (1966). Refinement and test of the theory of fluid and crystallized intelligence. *Journal of Educational Psychology, 57*, 253–270.

Humphreys, L. G. (1968). The fleeting nature of the prediction of college academic success. *Journal of Educational Psychology, 59*, 375–380.

Humphreys, L. G. (1971). Theory of intelligence. In R. Cancro (Ed.), *Intelligence: Genetic and environmental influences* (pp. 31–42). New York: Grune & Stratton.

Humphreys, L. G., & Davey, T. C. (1983). *Anticipation of gains in general information: A comparison of verbal aptitude, reading comprehension, and listening* (Tech. Rep. No. 282). Urbana: University of Illinois, Center for the Study of Reading.

Humphreys, L. G., & Davey, T. C. (1988). Continuity in intellectual growth from 12 months to 9 years. *Intelligence, 12*, 183-197.

Humphreys, L. G., Park, R. D., & Parsons, C. K. (1979). Application of a simplex process model to six years of cognitive development in four demographic groups. *Applied Psychological Measurement, 3*, 51–64.

Humphreys, L. G., & Parsons, C. K. (1979). A simplex process model for describing differences between cross-lagged correlations. *Psychological Bulletin, 86*, 325–334.

Humphreys, L. G., Rich, S. A., & Davey, T. C. (1985). A Piagetian test of intelligence. *Developmental Psychology, 21*, 872-877.

Humphreys, L. G., & Taber, T. (1973). Postdiction study of the Graduate Record Examination and eight semesters of college grades. *Journal of Educational Measurement, 10*, 179–184.

Jencks, C. (1972). *Inequality: A reassessment of the effect of family and schooling in America*. New York: Basic Books.

Jones, L. V. (1984). White-black achievement differences: The narrowing gap. *American Psychologist, 39*, 1207–1213.

Kristol, I. (1978). *Two cheers for capitalism*. New York: Basic Books.

Laughlin, W. P. (1940). *Changes of intelligence scores of college students over a period of approximately four years*. Unpublished doctoral dissertation, University of Minnesota, Minneapolis.

Lerner, B. (1982). American education: How are we doing? *Public Interest, 69,* 59–82.

Lin, C., & Humphreys, L. G. (1977). Predictions of academic performance in graduate and professional school. *Applied Psychological Measurement, 1,* 249–257.

Powers, D. E. (1977). Comparing predictions of law school performance for black, Chicano, and white law students (Rep. No. 77–3). In Law School Admissions Council (Ed.), *Reports of Law School Admissions Council sponsored research: 1975–1977* (Vol. 3, pp. 721–776). Princeton, NJ: Law School Admissions Council.

Roff, M. (1941). A statistical study of the development of intelligence performance. *Journal of Psychology, 11,* 371–386.

Rosenthal, R., & Jacobsen, L. (1986). *Pygmalion in the classroom.* New York: Holt, Rinehart & Winston.

Scottish Council for Research in Education. (1949). *The trend of Scottish intelligence.* London: University of London Press.

Sternberg, R. J., Conway, B. E., Kurtin, J. L., & Bernstein, M. (1981). People's conceptions of intelligence. *Journal of Personality and Social Psychology: Attitudes and Social Cognition, 41,* 37–55.

Tabler, K. A. (1976). National longitudinal study of the high school class of 1972: Tabular summary of first follow-up questionnaire data. Washington, DC: U.S. Government Printing Office.

Tanner, J. M. (1966). Galtonian eugenics and the study of growth: The relation of body size, intelligence test score, and social circumstances in children and adults. *Eugenics Review, 58,* 122–135.

Tuddenham, R. D. (1948). Soldier intelligence in World Wars I and II. *American Psychologist, 3,* 54–56.

Tupes, E., & Shaycoft, M. (1964). Normative distributions of AQE aptitude indexes for high school age boys (Tech. Doc. Rep. PRL-TDR 64-17). Lackland Air Force Base, TX.

Van Court, M., & Bean, F. D. (1985). *Intelligence and fertility in the United States: 1912–1982).* Austin: Texas Population Research Center, University of Texas.

Vernon, P. E. (1950). *The structure of human abilities.* New York: Wiley.

Vining, D. R. (1982). On the possibility of the re-emergence of a dysgenic trend with respect to intelligence in American fertility differentials. *Intelligence, 6,* 241–264.

Wilson, R. S. (1983). The Louisville twin study: Developmental synchronies in behavior. *Child Development, 54,* 298–316.

Notes on Contributors

LEE J. CRONBACH is Vida Jacks professor of education emeritus, Stanford University. He received his PhD from the University of Chicago in 1940 and was a professor of education and of psychology at the University of Illinois at Urbana-Champaign from 1948 to 1964 before moving to Stanford. His long list of honors and awards includes the Award for Distinguished Scientific Contributions from the American Psychological Association and the Award for Distinguished Contributions to Research in Education from the American Educational Research Association. He served as president of both of these associations and vice-president of the National Academy of Education. He is a member of the National Academy of Sciences and the recipient of honorary degrees from several universities, including the University of Illinois. He is the author of numerous articles and books that have helped shape educational and psychological measurement.

ERNEST R. HILGARD is professor of psychology and education emeritus, Stanford University. He received his PhD from Yale University in 1930 and was an instructor there until 1933, at which time he joined the faculty of Stanford University where he remained until his retirement in 1969. Included among his books and numerous journal articles are *Theories of Learning* (1st ed., 1948–5th ed., 1981, with G. H. Bower), *Introduction to Psychology* (1st ed., 1953–9th ed., 1987, with R. L. Atkinson and others), and *American Psychology in Historical Perspective* (1978). He has served as president of the American Psychological Association. He is a member of the National Academy of Sciences and has received numerous awards and honors, including the Award for Distinguished Scientific Contributions from the American Psychological Association.

JOHN L. HORN is professor of psychology at the University of Southern California. He joined the faculty of the University of Denver after receiving his PhD from the University of Illinois at Urbana-Champaign in 1961, and remained as a professor of psychology at Denver until

1986. The author of over 150 journal articles and chapters in books, he is especially well known for his research dealing with multivariate methods and the measurement of personality and intelligence. He is a fellow of the American Psychological Association and of the American Association for the Advancement of Science and a recipient of the Fulbright-Hays Speaker Award and the Distinguished Publications in Multivariate Psychology Award of the Society of Multivariate Experimental Psychologists.

BARBARA LERNER is president of Lerner Associates, Princeton, NJ. She received her PhD from the University of Chicago in 1965 and her JD from the University of Chicago Law School in 1977. She has been in private practice as a clinical and consulting psychologist (1970–78) and has served as a consultant to numerous agencies including the Illinois Law Enforcement Commission. She has also been an associate professor of psychology at Ohio and Roosevelt Universities and was a senior research scientist at Educational Testing Service. Included among her honors and awards are the Joseph Henry Beale Prize in Law, member and associate editor of the *University of Chicago Law Review*, and a Certificate of Appreciation from the U.S. Department of Education. Her publications on testing, the law, and public policy have appeared in the *American Psychologist, Public Interest,* and the *Supreme Court Review.* She is the author of *Minimum Competence, Maximum Choice: Second Chance Legislation* (1980) and *Therapy in the Ghetto* (1972).

ROBERT L. LINN is professor of education, University of Colorado, Boulder. Since receiving his PhD from the University of Illinois at Urbana-Champaign in 1965, he has been a senior research psychologist at Educational Testing Service and a professor of educational psychology and of psychology at the University of Illinois at Urbana-Champaign (1973–87). He has served as president of the National Council on Measurement in Education and vice-president of the American Educational Research Association. His awards and honors include an Award for Distinguished Contribution to the Theory and Practice of Psychological Measurement and Assessment from the American Psychological Association. He is the editor of the third edition of *Educational Measurement* and the author of numerous journal articles and book chapters on educational and psychological measurement.

SANDRA WOOD SCARR is Commonwealth Professor of psychology, University of Virginia. She received her PhD from Harvard University in 1965. Prior to joining the University of Virginia in 1983, she was professor of psychology, Yale University (1977–83), and was on the faculties of the University of Minnesota (1971–77), the University of Pennsylvania (1966–71), and the University of Maryland (1965–66). She has served as president of the Division of Developmental Psychology and as a member of the Council of Editors, the Council of Representatives, and the Board of Scientific Affairs of the American Psychological Association. She is a former president of the Behavior Genetics Association. She has been editor of *Developmental Psychology* and associate editor of *American Psychologist*. Her approximately 150 publications have appeared in such journals as the *American Psychologist, Intelligence, Human Genetics,* and *American Sociological Review.* She is the author of *Race, Social Class and Individual Differences in IQ: New Studies of Old Issues* (1981) and *Mother Care/Other Care* (1984).

ROBERT J. STERNBERG is professor of psychology, Yale University, where he has been on the faculty since he received his PhD in psychology from Stanford University in 1975. Included among the numerous awards and honors that he has received are the Distinguished Scientific Award for an Early Career Contribution to Psychology from the American Psychological Association, the Boyd R. McCandless Young Scientist Award of the Division of Developmental Psychology from the American Psychological Association, and the Cattell Award of the Society of Multivariate Experimental Psychology. He is the editor or co-editor of several books, including *How and How Much Can Intelligence Be Increased?* (1982) and the first three volumes of *Advances in the Psychology of Human Intelligence* (1982, 1984, 1986). He is the author of *Human Intelligence: Perspectives on Its Theory and Measurement* (with D. K. Detterman, 1979), and *Beyond IQ: A Triarchic Theory of Human Intelligence* (1985) as well as over 150 articles.

LLOYD G. HUMPHREYS was born in Lorane, Oregon, on December 12, 1913. He did his undergraduate work at the University of Oregon where he received the degree of Bachelor of Science in 1935. The following year he received a Master of Arts degree from Indiana University, and two years later (1938) he earned the degree of Doctor of Philosophy from Stanford University.

While a graduate student at Stanford, Humphreys met Dorothy Jane Windes, a fellow student, whom he married in 1937. They are the parents of four children: John D., Michael S., Margaret A., and Susan J.

His doctoral dissertation, *Effects of Random Alternation of Reinforcement on the Acquisition and Extinction of Conditioned Eyelid Responses,* was directed by Professor Ernest R. Hilgard. This work, a version of which was subsequently published in the *Journal of Experimental Psychology* (1939, 25, 141–158), and several related studies made a major contribution to the understanding of the effects of partial reinforcement and has been widely cited during the 50 years since it was completed.

After receiving his PhD, he spent a year (1938–39) as a National Research Council Fellow at Yale University before becoming an instructor in psychology at Northwestern University, a position he held from 1938 to 1945. However, because of a Carnegie Fellowship in Anthropology, which he spent at Columbia University (1941–42), and the Second World War, he was on leave from Northwestern for all but the first two years and the last four months of that time.

During the Second World War, Humphreys served in the Army Air Force, Aviation Psychology Program. It was during that period that he developed further an interest in the psychology of individual differences, an interest that received its initial impetus when he was an undergraduate working under Robert H. Seashore and Howard R. Taylor. This revived interest in individual differences led to a shift in his research program from the experimental psychology of learning that he had pursued before the war. Intelligence, the organization of human abilities, and the uses of correlational techniques became the foci of his research.

Following the Second World War, Humphreys returned to Northwestern University as an assistant professor of psychology for a few months before accepting an appointment as an associate professor of psychology and director of the Testing and Guidance Division at the University of Washington, a position he held until 1948. In 1948 he returned to his alma mater, Stanford University, as an associate professor of education and psychology. He left Stanford in 1951 to assume the position of research director, Personnel Laboratory, Air Force Personnel and Training Research Center, Lackland Air Force Base, where he remained until 1957 when he became a professor of psychology at the University of Illinois at Urbana-Champaign.

From 1957 until his retirement and appointment as professor emeritus in 1984, Humphreys played a leading role in the shaping of the department of psychology, which he served as head from 1959 to 1969. In 1970–71 he took a leave of absence from the University of Illinois to accept a presidential apppointment as assistant director for education of the National Science Foundation. Professor of education was added to his title of professor of psychology upon his return to the University in 1971. In 1979–80 he served as acting dean of the College of Liberal Arts and Sciences of the University of Illinois at Urbana-Champaign.

Humphreys has held a variety of offices in professional associations. He is a former president of the Psychometric Society (1959–60), and of two of the divisions of the American Psychological Association (Division of Military Psychology, 1957–58; and the Division of Evaluation and Measurement, 1960–61). He has served as vice-president of the American Association for the Advancement of Science and chairman of two of its divisions (I in 1963 and J in 1980). He has served as a member of the Board of Directors of the American Psychological Association, of the Board on Human Resources Data and Analysis, and of the Commission on Human Resources of the National Academy of Sciences. He was editor of the *Psychological Bulletin* from 1964 to 1969 and editor of the *American Journal of Psychology* from 1968 to 1979.

His research has contributed to the understanding of the organization of human abilities and to the theoretical and practical implications of individual differences. Never having been reluctant to express his views or to take a position on a controversial issue, Humphreys consistently makes his own ideas, as well as those of others, withstand the challenge of the best existing data, the most searching analyses, and relevant scientific understandings. To his students he gave a healthy respect for data, an understanding of the importance of appropriate analytical techniques, and a love of research.

A complete listing of Humphreys's many publications follows.

Publications of Lloyd G. Humphreys

Except where noted, Lloyd G. Humphreys is the sole author of the publication listed.

1935

Buxton, C. E., & Humphreys, L. G. The effect of practice upon intercorrelations of motor skills. *Science, 81,* 441–482.

1937

———. The factor of time in pursuit rotor learning. *Journal of Psychology, 3,* 429–436.

1938

Buxton, C. E., Humphreys, L. G., & Taylor, H. R. Steadiness and rifle marksmanship. *Journal of Applied Psychology, 50,* 680–688.

Hilgard, E. R., & Humphreys, L. G. The effect of supporting and antagonistic voluntary instructions on conditioned discrimination in man. *Journal of Experimental Psychology, 22,* 291–304.

Hilgard, E. R., & Humphreys, L. G. The retention of conditioned discrimination in man. *Journal of General Psychology, 19,* 111–125.

1939

———. Acquisition and extinction of verbal expectations in a situation analogous to conditioning. *Journal of Experimental Psychology, 25,* 294–301.

———.The effect of random alternation of reinforcement on the acquisition and extinction of conditioned eyelid reactions. *Journal of Experimental Psychology, 25,* 141–158.

———. Generalization as a function of method of reinforcement. *Journal of Experimental Psychology, 26,* 361–372.

———. The stability in pattern of factor loadings: A comment on Dr. Smart's conclusions. *Journal of Educational Psychology, 30,* 231–237.

1940

———. Distributed practice in the development of conditioned eyelid reactions. *Journal of General Psychology, 22,* 379–383.

———. Extinction of conditioned psychogalvanic responses following two conditions of reinforcement. *Journal of Experimental Psychology, 27,* 71–75.

————. The variability of extinction scores in "Skinner-box" experiments. *Journal of Experimental Psychology, 26,* 614–617.

Humphreys, L. G., Miller, J., & Ellson, D. C. The effect of the inter-trial interval on the acquisition, extinction and recovery of verbal expectations. *Journal of Experimental Psychology, 27,* 198–292.

1941

Ferguson, L. W., Humphreys, L. G., & Strong, F. W. A factorial study of interests and values. *Journal of Educational Psychology, 32,* 197–204.

1943

————. Measures of strength of conditioned eyelid responses. *Journal of General Psychology, 29,* 101–111.

————. The strength of a Thorndikian response as a function of the number of practice trials. *Journal of Comparative Psychology, 35,* 101–110.

1947

————. The program of printed test development; Some commonly used statistical techniques; Introduction to intellectual and information tests. In J. P. Guilford & J. I. Lacey (Eds.), *Research with printed tests* (Chaps. 2, 3, 4). [Includes about 12 factor analyses for which Humphreys had major responsibility.] Washington, DC: U.S. Government Printing Office.

1949

Humphreys, L. G., & Jones, L. V. [Review of *Quantitative methods in psychology* by Don Lewis.] *Psychometrika, 14,* 163–165.

1950

————. Intelligence and intelligence tests. In W. S. Monroe (Ed.), *Encyclopedia of educational research* (rev. ed., pp. 600–612). New York: Macmillan.

1951

————. Transfer of training in general education. *Journal of General Education, 5,* 210–216.

1952

————. Individual differences. In C. P. Stone & D. Taylor (Eds.), *Annual review of psychology* (Vol. 3, pp. 131–147). Palo Alto, CA: Annual Reviews.

1954

APA Committee on Test Standards. Technical recommendations for psychological tests and diagnostic techniques. *Psychological Bulletin, 51,* (Suppl.), 38 pp.

1955

————. Clinical vs. actuarial prediction. *Proceedings of the 1955 Invitational*

Conference on Testing Problems (pp. 129-135). Princeton, NJ: Educational Testing Service.

———. The importance of aptitude: A reply to Kubie's "Problems of the scientific career." *American Scientist, 43,* 100–105.

1956

———. The normal curve and the attenuation paradox in test theory. *Psychological Bulletin, 53,* 472–476.

———. Note on "Wishing with Dice." *Journal of Experimental Psychology, 51,* 290–292.

1957

———. Types vs. traits: A comment on Sheldon's methodology. *Psychological Bulletin, 54,* 218–228.

1960

———. Investigations of the simplex. *Psychometrika, 25,* 475–483.

———. Note on the multitrait-multimethod matrix. *Psychological Bulletin, 57,* 86–88.

1962

———. The nature and organization of human abilities. *19th yearbook of the National Council on Measurement in Education* (pp. 39–45). Ames, IA: National Council on Measurement in Education.

———. The organization of human abilities. *American Psychologist, 17,* 475–483.

Paul, G. L., Eriksen, C. W., & Humphreys, L. G. Use of the temperature stress with cool air reinforcement for human operant conditioning. *Journal of Experimental Psychology, 64,* 329–335.

1964

———. Number of cases and number of factors: An example where N is very large. *Educational and Psychological Measurement, 24,* 457–466.

1967

———. Critique of Cattell's "Theory of fluid and crystallized intelligence: A critical experiment." *Journal of Educational Psychology, 58,* 129–136.

———. Problems in personnel research. In A. L. Fortuna (Ed.), *Proceedings: 25th Anniversary Symposium, Personnel Research and Systems Advancement* (pp. 67–75). Lackland Air Force Base, TX.

1968

———. The fleeting nature of the prediction of college academic success. *Journal of Educational Psychology, 59,* 375–380.

———. The Miller analogies test; The measurement of skill. In O. K. Buros (Ed.). *The sixth mental measurements yearbook* (pp. 472, 775). Highland Park, NJ: Gryphon Press.

———. Psychological interpretations of factors. In D. L. Sills (Ed.), *Encyclopedia of the social sciences* (pp. 281–287). New York: Free Press.

1969

Humphreys, L. G., & Dachler, P. Jensen's theory of intelligence. *Journal of Educational Psychology, 60,* 419–426; a rebuttal, 432–433.

Humphreys, L. G., & Ilgen, D. Note on a criterion for the number of common factors. *Educational and Psychological Measurement, 29,* 571–578.

Humphreys, L. G., Ilgen, D., McGrath, D., & Montanelli, R. Capitalization on chance in rotation of factors. *Educational and Psychological Measurement, 29,* 259–272.

1970

———. Analytical approach to the correlation between related pairs of subjects on psychological tests. *Psychological Bulletin, 74,* 149–152.

———. Footnote to the Scottish survey of intelligence. *British Journal of Educational Psychology, 40,* 72–74.

———. New directions of the National Science Foundation: High technology manpower education. In *Proceedings on manpower for industry in the seventies* (pp. 47–52). Athens: University of Georgia Press.

———. A skeptical look at the factor pure test. In C. E. Lunneborg (Ed.), *Current problems and techniques in multivariate psychology: Proceedings of a conference honoring Professor Paul Horst* (pp. 23–32). Seattle: University of Washington Press.

Humphreys, L. G., Tucker, L. R., & Dachler, P. Evaluating the importance of factors in any given order of factoring. *Multivariate Behavioral Research, 5,* 209–215.

1971

———. The curriculum never changes—only the reasons for offering it change. *Journal of College Science Teaching,* October, *1,* 40–43.

———. Education in science for nonscientists. *Journal of Chemical Education, 48,* 216–217.

———. The humanist movement in psychology and education. *Science Teacher,* September, *38,* 29–31.

———. Theory of intelligence. In R. Cancro (Ed.), *Intelligence: Genetic and environmental influences* (pp. 31–42).New York: Grune & Stratton.

1973

———. Implications of group differences for test interpretation. *Proceedings of the 1972 Invitational Conference on Testing Problems: Assessment in a Pluralistic Society* (pp. 56–71). Princeton, NJ: Educational Testing Service.

———. Statistical definitions of test validity in a minority group. *Journal of Applied Psychology, 58,* 1–4.

Humphreys, L. G., Levy, J., & Taber, T. Predictability of academic grades for students of high and low academic promise. *Educational and Psychological Measurement, 33,* 385–392.

Humphreys, L. G., & Taber, T. Ability factors as a function of advantaged and disadvantaged groups. *Journal of Educational Measurement, 10,* 107–115.

Humphreys, L. G., & Taber, T. A comparison of squared multiples and iterated diagonals as communality estimates. *Educational and Psychological Measurement, 33,* 225–229.

Humphreys, L. G., & Taber, T. Postdiction study of the Graduate Record Examination and eight semesters of college grades. *Journal of Educational Measurement, 10,* 179–184.

1974

————. The misleading distinction between aptitude and achievement tests. In D. R. Green (Ed.), *The aptitude-achievement distinction* (pp. 262–274). Monterey, CA: McGraw-Hill.

————. Statistical substitutes for experimental control. *Psychological Reports, 35,* 336–338.

Humphreys, L. G., & Fleishman, A. Pseudo-orthogonal and other analysis of variance designs involving individual differences variables. *Journal of Educational Psychology, 66,* 464–472.

1975

Cleary, T. A., Humphreys, L. G., Kendrick, S. A., & Wesman, A. Educational uses of tests with disadvantaged students. *American Psychologist, 30,* 15–41.

————. Research practice is a fallible guide [Review of *Behavioral research: Theory, procedure, and design* by L. S. Meyers & N. E. Grossen]. *Contemporary Psychology, 20,* 325–326.

Humphreys, L. G., & Montanelli, R. An investigation of the parallel analysis criterion for determining the number of common factors. *Multivariate Behavioral Research, 10,* 183–206.

Humphreys, L. G., Tucker, L. R., Pins, C., & Long, J. Factors in the allocation of votes to divisions and state associations by members of the American Psychological Association. *American Psychologist, 30,* 593–597.

1976

————. The analysis of data from pre- and posttest designs: A comment. *Psychological Reports, 38,* 639–642.

————. A factor model for research on intelligence and problem solving. In L. Resnick (Ed.), *Proceedings: The nature of intelligence* (pp. 329–340). New York: Wiley.

————. The phenomena are ubiquitous—but the investigator must look. *Journal of Educational Psychology, 68,* 521.

————. Prediction of grades *is* fleeting: A comment. *Journal of Educational Psychology, 68,* 518–519.

————. Race and sex differences and their implications for educational and occupational equality. In M. L. Maehr & W. M. Stallings (Eds.), *Culture, child, and school* (pp. 124–141). Monterey, CA: Brooks/Cole. Also, *Educational Theory, 26,* 135–146.

————. Strategy training has no significant effect on race differences in nonverbal reasoning. *Journal of Educational Psychology, 68,* 128–129.

Humphreys, L. G., Lin, P., & Fleishman, A. The sex by race interaction in cognitive measures. *Journal of Research in Personality, 10,* 42–58.

Montanelli, R., & Humphreys, L. G. Latent roots of random data correlation matrices with squared multiple correlations on the diagonal: A Monte Carlo study. *Psychometrika, 41,* 341–348.

1977

Atkin, R., Bray, R., Davison, M., Herzberger, S., Humphreys, L., & Selzer, U. Ability factor differentiation, grades 5 through 11. *Applied Psychological Measurement, 1,* 65–76.

Atkin, R., Bray, R., Davison, M., Herzberger, S., Humphreys, L., & Selzer, U. Cross-lagged panel analysis of 16 cognitive measures at four grade levels. *Journal for Research in Child Development 48,* 944–952.

————. Predictability of employee theft: The importance of the base rate. *Journal of Applied Psychology, 62,* 514–516.

————. Theory of intelligence and the management of classroom learning. *Interchange, 7,* 45–50.

Humphreys, L. G., Fleishman, A., & Lin, P. Causes of racial and socioeconomic differences in cognitive tests. *Journal of Research in Personality, 11,* 191–208.

Humphreys, L. G., & Parsons, C. K. Partialling out intelligence: A methodological and substantive contribution. *Journal of Educational Psychology, 69,* 212–216.

Humphreys, L. G., & Stubbs, J. A longitudinal analysis of teacher expectation, student expectation, and student achievement. *Journal of Educational Measurement, 14,* 261–270.

Lin, P., & Humphreys, L. G. Predictions of academic performance in graduate and professional school. *Applied Psychological Measurement, 1,* 249–257.

1978

————. Differences between correlations in a single sample: A correction and amplification. *Psychological Reports, 43,* 657–658.

————. Doing research the hard way: Substituting ANOVA for a problem in correlational analysis. *Journal of Educational Psychology, 70,* 873–876.

————. Relevance of genotype and its environmental counterpart to the theory, interpretation, and nomenclature of ability measures. *Intelligence, 2,* 181–193.

————. Research on individual differences requires correlational analysis, not ANOVA. *Intelligence, 2,* 1–5.

————. To understand regression from parents to offspring, think statistically. *Psychological Bulletin, 85,* 1317–1322.

Humphreys, L. G., & Parsons, C. K. Search for a common factor model to describe a cross-lagged correlation difference. *Applied Psychological Measurement, 2*, 257–267.

1979

————. The construct of general intelligence. *Intelligence, 3*, 105–120.

————. Rejoinder to Baucom and Welsh. *Intelligence, 3*, 165–166.

————. [Review of *Heredity and environment* by A. H. Halsey.] *Educational Researcher, 8*, 19–20.

Humphreys, L. G., Park, R. K., & Parsons, C. K. Application of a simplex process model to six years of cognitive development in four demographic groups. *Applied Psychological Measurement, 3*, 51–64.

Humphreys, L. G., & Parsons, C. K. Piagetian tasks measure intelligence and intelligence tests assess cognitive development. *Intelligence, 3*, 369–382.

Humphreys, L. G., & Parsons, C. K. A simplex process model for describing differences between cross-lagged correlations. *Psychological Bulletin, 86*, 325–334.

Humphreys, L. G., Parsons, C. K., & Park, R. K. Dimensions involved in differences among school means of cognitive measures. *Journal of Educational Measurement, 16*, 63–76.

1980

————. The importance of a difference should be evaluated independently of its causes [Comment on *Bias in mental tests* by A. R. Jensen]. *Behavioral and Brain Sciences, 3*, 347–348.

————. Me thinks they do protest too much. *Intelligence, 4*, 179–183.

————. Race and intelligence reexamined. *The Humanist*, July–August, 52–55.

————. The statistics of failure to replicate: A comment on Buriel's conclusions. *Journal of Educational Psychology, 72*, 71–75.

Hulin, C. L., & Humphreys, L. G. Foundations of test theory. In *Construct validity in psychological measurement* (pp. 5–10). Proceedings of a colloquia on theory and application in education and employment. Princeton, NJ: U.S. Office of Personnel Management and Educational Testing Service.

1981

————. The primary mental ability. In M. P. Friedman, J. P. Das, & N. O'Connor (Eds.), *Intelligence and learning* (pp. 87–102). New York: Plenum Press.

————. Race differences in tested intelligence: Important socially, obscure casually [Review of *Bias in mental tests* by A. R. Jensen]. *Proceedings of the National Academy of Education, 7*, 1–41.

————. [Review of *The intelligence controversy* by H. J. Eysenck & L. Kamin.] *Applied Psychological Measurement, 6*, 237–244.

Humphreys, L. G., & Park, R. K. Analysis of variances and covariances is misleading as a guide to a common factor model. *Intelligence, 2*, 157–163.

1982

————. The hierarchical factor model and general intelligence. In N. Hirschberg

& L. G. Humphreys (Eds.), *Multivariate applications in the social sciences* (pp. 223–240). Hillsdale, NJ: Erlbaum.

————. Inadequate data in, attractive theory out. *Journal of Educational Psychology, 74,* 424–426.

1983

————. [Review of *Ability testing* by A. K. Wigdor & W. R. Garner.] *American Scientist,* May-June, 302–303.

————. [Review of *The mismeasure of man* by S. J. Gould.] *American Journal of Psychology, 96,* 407–416.

Humphreys, L. G., & Davey, T. C. (1983). *Anticipation of gains in general information: A comparison of verbal aptitude, reading comprehension, and listening* (Tech. Rep. No. 282). Urbana: University of Illinois, Center for the Study of Reading.

1984

————. General intelligence. In C. R. Reynolds & R. T. Brown (Eds.), *Perspectives on bias in mental testing* (pp. 221–247). New York: Plenum Press.

————. A rose is not a rose: A rival view of intelligence. *Behavioral and Brain Sciences, 7,* 292–293.

————. Women with doctorates in science and engineering. *Advances in Motivation and Achievement, 2,* 197–216.

Green, B. F., Bock, R. D., Humphreys, L. G., Linn, R. L., Reckase, M. D. Technical guidelines for assessing computerized adaptive tests. *Journal of Educational Measurement, 21,* 347–360.

1985

————. Attenuated hypothesis or attenuated test of hypothesis? *Intelligence, 9,* 291–295.

————. A conceptualization of intellectual giftedness. In F. D. Horowitz & M. O'Brien (Eds.), *The gifted and the talented: A developmental perspective* (pp. 331–360). Washington, DC: American Psychological Association.

————. Correlations in psychological research. In D. K. Detterman (Ed.), *Current topics in human intelligence: Vol. 1. Research methodology* (pp. 1–24). Norwood, NJ: Ablex.

————. General intelligence: An integration of factor, test, and simplex theory. In B. B. Wolman (Ed.), *Handbook of intelligence: Theories, measurement, and applications* (pp. 201–224). New York: Wiley.

————. Race differences and the Spearman hypothesis. *Intelligence, 9,* 275–283.

Humphreys, L. G., Davey, T. C., & Park, R. K. Longitudinal correlation analysis of standing height and intelligence. *Child Development, 56,* 1465–1478.

Humphreys, L. G., Rich, S. A., & Davey, T. C. A Piagetian test of intelligence. *Developmental Psychology, 21,* 872–877.

1986

——. An analysis and evaluation of test and item bias in the prediction context. *Journal of Applied Psychology, 71,* 327–333.

——. Commentary. *Journal of Vocational Behavior, 29,* 421–437.

——. Describing the elephant. In R. J. Sternberg & D. K. Detterman (Eds.), *What is intelligence?* (pp. 97–100). Norwood, NJ: Ablex.

Humphreys, L. G., Davey, T. C., & Kashima, E. Experimental measures of cognitive privilege/deprivation and some of their correlates. *Intelligence, 10,* 355–376.

1987

——. Quantitative methodology: Then, now, and the future. In J. A. Glover & R. R. Ronning (Eds.), *Historical foundations of educational psychology* (pp. 403–414). New York: Plenum Press.

1988

Humphreys, L. G., & Davey, T. C. Continuity in intellectual growth from 12 months to 9 years. *Intelligence, 12,* 183–197.

In press

——. Trends in levels of academic achievement of blacks and other minorities. *Intelligence.*